Y0-BVN-646

The QUALITY-EMPOWERED BUSINESS

Robert H. Wilkins

PRENTICE HALL
Englewood Cliffs, New Jersey 07632

Prentice Hall International (UK) Limited, *London*
Prentice Hall of Australia Pty. Limited, *Sydney*
Prentice Hall Canada, Inc., *Toronto*
Prentice Hall Hispanoamericana, *S.A., Mexico*
Prentice Hall of India Private Limited, *New Dehli*
Prentice Hall of Japan, Inc., *Tokyo*
Simon & Schuster Asia Pte. Ltd., *Singapore*
Editora Prentice Hall do Brasil, Ltda., *Rio de Janeiro*

10 9 8 7 6 5 4 3 2 1

Library of Congress Cataloging-in-Publication Data

Wilkins, Robert H. (Robert Harvey)
    The quality-empowered business : creating a Circle-4 quality system for
success / Robert H. Wilkins.
    p. cm.
    Includes bibliographical references and index.
    ISBN 0-13-104647-0
    1. Total quality management. I. Title.
HD62.15.W54 1994
658.5'62—dc20   93-40392
                                                     CIP

ISBN 0-13-104647-0

Prentice Hall
Career & Personal Development
Englewood Cliffs, NJ 07632
Simon & Schuster, A Paramount Communications Company

Printed in the United States of America

To my colleagues who understand

life is learning
learning is change
change is success
success is profit
profit is satisfaction
satisfaction is life

TABLE OF CONTENTS

LIST OF ILLUSTRATIONS

INTRODUCTION

The philosophy of total quality management has suffused and enveloped the business community for almost a decade. Why then have we seen so little impact from TQM on the real success of our businesses? Why does employee empowerrment inevitably surrender to bottom-line profitability? Why are so few companies able to extend their commitment to continuous improvement beyond the first year? Why have past Malcolm Baldridge Award winners turned out to be average companies at best, and floundering enterprises at worst? Why are there only a relatively small number of companies that have acquired a reputation for complete and consistent customer satisfaction? Let's face the facts, the principles of total quality have made only a very small ripple on the big pond of American business.

The concepts promoted by TQM philosophy are not at fault. The ideas of customer satisfaction, employee empowerment and continuous improvement are based on solid principles that can, if properly applied, improve the current and future success of any business operation.

The fault lies in the application of TQM principles to our businesses, or more accurately, the misapplication of TQM. The failure to achieve significant business improvement through total quality management rests squarely on the shoulders of senior managers. As a senior manufacturing executive, I've spent the past 15 years manufacturing electronic products, so I understand the realities of the business world. The fact that most of us have struggled mightily to improve our businesses, and failed, should not be taken as a personal affront. Most senior and middle managers work harder and longer each week than the factory workers. We have a genuine desire and motivation to succeed and to see our operation succeed.

Our failure can be characterized using the basic difference between perspective and paradigm. Our perspective of the business world is how we view the relationships of the major players. Our paradigm of the business world is how we view our role within those relationships. Traditional business perspective is that there exist suppliers, producers and customers. Our traditional business paradigm is that we're either a supplier , a producer, or a customer, at any given time. If we're a supplier, we must satisfy our producer. If we're a producer, we must satisfy our customer. What we've tried to do in the past is apply the principles of total quality management to this existing business paradigm.

What I hope to accomplish with *The Quality-Empowered Business* is to show you how to apply the concepts of total quality to a new paradigm of the business. I want you to see yourself in a completely different role when you finish reading this book. Your perspective will be the same, there will still be suppliers, producers and customers within the business world. How you see your role within that world, however, will be very different.

Our new business paradigm will include many new terms, which we'll define carefully and completely. We'll talk about who our customers really are, and we'll explore the evolution of quality until we arrive at a definition for Circle-4 Quality. Circle-4 Quality is the result of satisfying the prioritized requirements of the Circle-4 Customer. Circle-4 Quality is the consideration of the Circle-4 Customer in all business activities and decisions. Circle-4 Quality is the commitment to work in cooperation with the Circle-4 Customer in the pursuit of a profitable business. We will accept that our Circle-4 Customer is comprised of the four major groups which will influence our success; the Shareholder, the End-user, the Employee, and the Supplier. Once we've solidified our new business paradigm, we'll define a Quality System which will make total quality a reality. We'll identify the necessary elements of our Quality System; Quality Organization, the Quality Information System, and the Quality Delivery System. In the final section of the book, we'll explore in systematic detail, the interrelated actions required to examine the current state of our operation, establish a solid foundation for customer satisfaction, and ultimately arrive at a responsive, evolving, and profitable Quality System.

In a world where we're required to juggle dozens of priorities and issues, our commitment to a worthwhile project often consists of attaching our name and position to the project during its introduction, followed by delegating definition and implementation to our qualified subordinates. The conversion of your business paradigm and the evolution of your operations into a Quality System is so vitally important to your own interests and your own success, that it cannot be delegated. You can only create a successful Quality System if you roll up your sleeves and commit yourselves to the understanding and improvement of your operations in detail. You must accept personal responsibility for establishing the interrelationships between the functional components of your operation and for ensuring that all your employees fully understand and accept their roles within our new definitions. Within these pages, you won't find a list of ten or twenty simple steps that will assure success. The process of creating a quality operation is complex, requiring interrelated systems, a comprehensive blueprint for change, and daily nurturing throughout the life of the business. *The Quality-Empowered Business* will provide the building blocks to create a comprehensive picture of a functioning total quality operation. Bringing that vision to life will be your goal, and your basis for future success and profitability.

As we begin *The Quality-Empowered Business*, our initial frame of reference will consider that all of us have some level of education and experience in the business of management. Basic business management, business organization and operation, and the fundamentals of total quality management will only be described with the detail applicable to the development of our Quality System.

Finally, let me comment briefly about the structure of the chapters within *The Quality-Empowered Business*. My intent is for this book to be a useful tool for the business management team, the group of senior and middle managers who run the business unit. To that end, I have incorporated several features which will permit rapid application of the discussed concepts, and hence, a faster improvement of your business. First, at the end of each chapter, a Chapter Summary will be presented which enumerates the major concepts within the chapter. Second, in appropriate chapters, following the Chapter Summary will be a list of Quality Application items; tasks to be undertaken by your management team in order to apply the chapter concepts to your business operation. Finally, where Quality Applications have been defined, they'll be followed by a list of Quality Benefits, which will enumerate the qualitative benefits of pursuing the recommended action. Taken together, the Chapter Summary, Quality Application and Quality Benefit features will provide busy executives with easily accessible "pressure points", promoting easy review, directed reading, and a structured template for pursuing development of a Quality System.

PART 1

DESIGNING A QUALITY PHILOSOPHY

1

THE CURRENT VIEW
OF QUALITY

Everyone has a definition of quality. The definitions range from attaching qualifying parameters, such as "quality of design" or "quality of assembly" through trying to describe the result of quality, such as "zero defects," "meeting the requirements," or "customer satisfaction." My favorite definition for quality comes from the International Standards Organizations, ISO 8402 Glossary of Terms, which says quality is "the totality of features and characteristics of a product or service that bear on its ability to satisfy a given need." Some practitioners have concluded that in today's environment, quality means total quality. We can create a rather lengthy list of definitions for quality if we search back through history to the first use of the word. All of the various definitions and descriptions can be reasonably justified, and all seem correct within their context and frame of reference. If they are all correct, why do they seem so diverse, and often incompatible? Why isn't there a comprehensive definition for quality that covers all possible nuances and circumstances? Quality of design and quality of assembly are important characteristics of the production process, but they're not necessarily applicable to the quality of our sales and marketing effort. Zero defects can be a worthwhile goal if we thoroughly understand and measure against specific requirements, but it may not apply for a prototype manufacturing shop. Within the context and intended universe of each specific definition, our business would do well to consider *all* the definitions and perspectives of quality as we look at creating a total quality operation. Is it possible for us to create a common definition of *total quality* that encompasses all the various definitions of quality and supports the intent of our business?

HOW THE QUALITY MINDSET EVOLVED

My first exposure to quality was in the early seventies, working with defense contractors while I was in the U.S. Navy. It seems that the overriding motivation in those days was to meet the requirements of the standard. MIL9858, for example, stated that the computers used for our command and control systems had to function flawlessly for at least one hour completely submerged in salt water. I always wondered if the computer operators were supposed to hold their breath for that long! Requirements defined by the standards didn't always reflect the real world. As I moved into commercial manufacturing, we were still inspecting to a standard, often times much more lenient than the military variety, though just as unrealistic. When asked for the basis of our product quality, "standard commercial practices" was often the stock answer. I think that's another way of saying, "whatever we can get the customer to buy." As we began to realize the importance of quality, we moved away from a separate quality function and made the workforce responsible for the quality of the products they produced. "Zero defects" flared up for a while, then we started looking for "quality at the source," focusing on design for manufacturing, design of experiments, supplier quality, and the like. During the last three or four years, we've turned our attention to the "customer," striving for "total customer satisfaction" and in the process creating a bewildering plethora of "customer-supplier" relationships throughout our universe. While my own experience, and probably yours, may not precisely follow the industry evolution with its corresponding new definitions of quality, I'm sure we're reasonably close.

As I reflect on the evolution of the quality mindset, I'm struck by several common threads that have woven their way through history. First, the evolving quality thinking has served, in all cases, to catalyze business improvements. We've all had the opportunity to apply quality thinking—some to a greater degree than others—toward improving our products and our profitability. Second, despite its positive influence, our businesses have seen no revolutionary restructuring or "re-engineering" as a result of quality thinking. By that, I mean that our basic business structure, the sequence of events for converting raw materials to finished products, has changed little in its framework and flow as a result of evolving quality concepts. Certainly we have benefited from improved technology, more sophisticated software support, and other high-tech aids. However, the required functional blocks that together depict our total business operation are essentially the same today as they were forty or fifty years ago. Although the evolution in quality thought has provided us with invaluable insight and assistance, it has not resulted in any fundamental change in the business process. This realization leads to my conclusion that the evolution of quality thinking can be viewed as a periodic shift in focus to different aspects of our business system. That is, if we're serious about quality, we cannot focus only on the "quality theory of the month." Instead, we have to consider all that has gone before. It is important to meet a standard, the right standard. It is important to meet the requirements, the accurate requirements. It is important to satisfy the customer, once we understand our customer. More than an evolution, quality thinking has built upon itself, creating an ever-increasing body of truths, maxims, and practices that, if put to use, will most certainly make a positive contribution to our success. While this may seem to confuse the definition of quality, consider instead that we've pulled back our perspective; now we're looking at quality as it applies to the total business.

Handling the Concept of Customer Satisfaction

Looking at the total business focuses our attention on the idea of total quality. I would guess that many of you are now working on, or operating with, total quality management. If you are, I give you a standing ovation. If you're not, get busy. Unless you consider the quality aspects of every area of your business, you will never achieve real customer satisfaction. TQM is the current culmination of all that has passed before; it is the philosophy of considering quality synonymous with business; it is extremely difficult and time-consuming to create. You already know this, however, or you wouldn't have read this far. Creating a total quality environment is about as easy as changing a flat tire—while you're moving down the freeway at 55 miles per hour! Keep in mind that the greatest rewards in life are preceded by the greatest effort.

One of the cornerstones of total quality is the concept of customer satisfaction. It makes common sense to realize that we've succeeded in creating quality if we've satisfied our customers. We know all too well the consequences of creating a dissatisfied customer. Nothing travels faster than bad news. Our disgruntled customers often tell twenty of their friends before they get around to telling us about the problem. Calculate the necessary advertising budget to overcome that. (We could all think of better ways to spend that money!)

IDENTIFYING YOUR CUSTOMERS

In an effort to quantify the concept, total quality management has subdivided the customer into the smallest identifiable units. First we have internal and external customers. Looking for a moment at only the internal customers, we find innumerable *customer-supplier relationships*. Everyone in the company is a customer for someone in the business process. Everyone in the company is also a supplier for someone in the business process. If we subdivide things a little further and look at the nature of business transactions, we'll see that in any given successful transaction, each involved individual must act both as a customer and as a supplier. At some point in any relationship, each party must play the role of customer in order to communicate and receive some benefit from the relationship. If this doesn't happen, one of the two parties will not be satisfied, thus damaging the customer-supplier bond. A customer-supplier relationship where each party understands and is committed to benefit the other, is called a *win/win relationship*. The concept of creating win/win relationships is a vital ingredient in achieving total quality and in creating a total quality operation. Proactively seeking win/win is a cornerstone of the self-management paradigm developed by Dr. Stephen R. Covey in *The Seven Habits of Highly Effective People*. In considering successful business relationships, Dr. Covey maintains, "Anything less than Win/Win in an interdependent reality is a poor second best that will have impact in the long term relationship. The cost of that impact needs to be carefully considered."[1]

External Customers

Let's look at an example within the traditional view of external customers. I manufacture and sell large mainframe computers. I have just closed a deal with you, my customer, for a $1M MegaTurbo mainframe, which we both agree will provide the ideal solution to your mushrooming networking and data-management requirements. Let's look at the general sequence of events in our relationship, identifying the instances where we either assume the role of customer (C) or supplier (S):

Transaction	You	Me
1. Offer of product and terms.	C	S
2. Accept offer and agree to pay.	S	C
3. Offer to install and train.	C	S
4. Agree to regular feedback on computer performance.	S	C

[1] Covey, Steven R., *The Seven Habits of Highly Effective People* (New York: Simon & Schuster, 1989), p. 214.

In this simple example, you will be a satisfied customer if I successfully supply the product you expect, and if I deliver the expected installation and training. From my perspective, I will be satisfied if you pay the agreed price and if I receive the kind of feedback that will allow me to improve my products and services. If any of these elements fall short of expectations, one of us will become dissatisfied—with the predictable result. If we both perform as we agreed, we're both satisfied, and we both win. That's the essence of win/win. Of course, in the real world our relationship will be much more complex; we'll need to make sure our mutual expectations are thoroughly defined and well understood by both of us. There is no room for assumptions in the creation of win/win relationships.

Internal Customers

Let's look at another example, using internal customers this time. As part of the manufacturing process, the Storeroom issues kits of parts as work orders to the Assembly department for conversion into products. A simplified view of this relationship might look like this:

Transaction	Storeroom	Assembly
1. Release work order 24 hours before kit issue.	C	S
2. Kit work order and issue parts "fit for use."	S	C
3. Advise on kit errors.	C	S
4. Immediately correct errors.	S	C

As in the previous example, the real world will require specifically defined procedures and interactions. If the agreed-upon requirements are met and the procedures are followed, both Storeroom and Assembly will be satisfied, and we will have a win/win relationship. Far too often we see the scenario where, for example, the Storeroom will say, "Our schedule will only allow us to kit factory work orders on Tuesdays and Thursdays, so Assembly will have to adjust its work schedule accordingly." The result is frustration and conflict between the two operations, culminating in wasted time and added cost because the defined output from the Storeroom doesn't satisfy the input needs of Assembly. This is a classic *win/lose relationship*; the Storeroom is of course sticking to its schedule, at the expense of Assembly. The importance of subdividing the organization into customer-supplier relationships and further realizing the *dual* role of each player, drives home the necessity for the customer to be responsible for defining the requirement. This includes the definition of your expectations, as well as understanding the expectations of your customers in all external customer-supplier relationships. This same duality must also be considered for internal and micro customer-supplier relationships.

DEFINING YOUR MANAGEMENT TEAM AS THE COMPANY

So far we have established that a definition of quality must encompass all of the known aspects of the philosophy—total quality. We also know that creating a total quality operation depends upon:

1. customer satisfaction,
2. win/win customer-supplier relationships, and
3. customer-defined requirements.

Keeping in mind that we want to approach the issue of creating a total quality operation from our senior management perspective, our job will be easier if we create and define unique terminology to simplify communicating. When considering ourselves, we may define senior management as the management team responsible for the performance of a defined business unit. This business unit may be a complete company, large or small, encompassing operations from sales through manufacturing and customer support. Or, the business unit may be a relatively autonomous component of a large corporation, such as a manufacturing division. The management team consists of the general manager, that person who is organizationally in charge of the business unit, and his or her direct reports. Let's agree that the managers reporting directly to the GM represent all the critical functions of the business unit. Throughout *The Quality-Empowered Business,* I will refer to this management team as the *Company.*

I've chosen this label for a specific reason. From your employees' point of view, you are the leaders of the business. Whether or not any additional corporate structure exists, your workforce sees you as the group establishing the direction and managing the operation toward expected results. Whomever you report to, stockholders, board of directors, or corporate management, you're viewed as the group responsible for the results and performance of your business unit. The entities you deal with externally also view you as having the authority and responsibility to represent your business unit. You are, in fact, the Company.

In creating a total quality operation, your goal is complete customer satisfaction. As we have seen, it is possible and necessary to subdivide customer-supplier relationships down to specific operations or processes. Internally, within your business unit, there may be hundreds of customer-supplier relationships. If you begin to look externally, the total number may increase exponentially. Should the Company focus on all of these relationships? Realizing the impracticality of the question, how can we group these customer-supplier relationships into larger entities which have identifiable characteristics and influence on your business process? We cannot progress in creating a Company definition for quality, and we cannot begin to create total quality and customer satisfaction—until we clearly identify your customers. In Chapter 2, we'll define the Customer from the point of view of the Company.

SUMMARY

1. All definitions for quality are applicable within their intended universe.
2. Quality thinking has catalyzed business improvement but has not caused basic restructuring of the business.
3. Customer satisfaction is the cornerstone of total quality.
4. Successful customer-supplier relationships are based on win/win.
5. Total quality, and customer satisfaction, must be approached from the perspective of the business unit management team, which we will call the Company.

2

FOCUSING ON
THE CUSTOMER

As we discussed in Chapter 1, a fundamental element in creating a total quality operation is achieving customer satisfaction. We demonstrated the validity and duality of the customer-supplier relationship and we talked about the need to create win/win relationships throughout the business process. We have also defined the Company as the management team responsible for directing the business, and the entity accountable for the results. In order to carry out that responsibility, you have a defined organization, with defined objectives and responsibilities. At the micro level, out on the shop floor, it is a fairly straightforward process to identify and agree to the various customer-supplier relationships that need to exist. Most of the current total quality philosophies, however, inadequately define customer-supplier relationships that must exist at the Company level.

I think we can readily agree that you cannot, and should not be involved with all those micro customer-supplier relationships just described. You don't have enough time in the day to direct and nurture the hundreds of such relationships that exist within your company. Even more to the point, the reason you created an organization and staffed it with competent management is precisely to manage the micro. Should you then manage the relationships between your major departments? A great many senior management teams today do spend a lot of time doing just that; managing the *conflicts* between their major functional departments. Later on, when we talk about the *quality organization* and later still, when we discuss driving objectives down the organization, I will try to convince you that having to manage the relationships between your major departments is not necessary and, in fact, is a cost-added management activity.

DEFINING THE INTEGRATED BUSINESS SYSTEM

Let's set our sights just a little higher and look at the entire business process, the integrated business system (IBS). The IBS represents the totality of your control, the medium through which you can create customer satisfaction, and the operation through which you desire to diffuse total quality thinking. Looking at this broad view, what are the major influences on your ability to achieve these goals? In examining this question, I've arrived at four major groups which, taken as a whole, cover the entire IBS. These groups are the real customer or End-user, the Shareholder, the Employee, and the Supplier. Figure 2.1 illustrates how these four groups surround and influence the entire business operation. The Shareholder's main influence is through the Company, the management team. The Supplier is most prevalent across that portion of your business involved with the development, purchasing and production of your product. The End-user exerts influence at each end of the IBS, first in marketing, research, and development, and again in selling, distribution, and service. In terms of affecting your ability as the Company to perform, I cannot think of any other internal or external influences that do not fit into one of these four categories. Given the four, should you consider each to be your customer as you seek to define the customer-supplier relationships for your Company? Let's have a look at each group, and see what we learn.

HOW END-USERS INFLUENCE YOUR BUSINESS

There's little argument or disagreement that the end-users or the "real" customers, create the most influential impact on your busi-

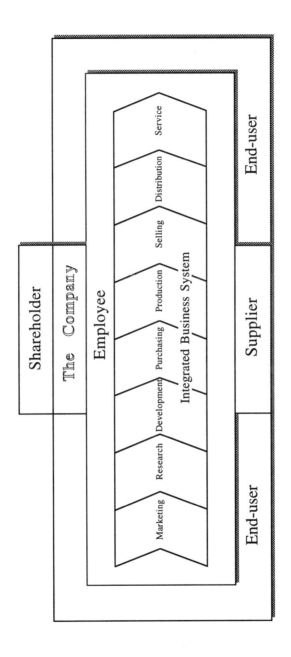

Figure 2.1 The four major influences on the Integrated Business System

ness. Their demand is your very existence, their numbers are your biggest growth variable, and their input is the only true voice to steer your product evolution. There's no disputing that they are your customers. In considering a customer-supplier relationship with the end-user, it is important to keep in mind that there are instances wherein they are the supplier and you are the customer; again the duality of the relationship and the essence of win/win. As demonstrated by the simple example in Chapter 1, the relationship must be based on mutually understanding and then satisfying requirements. For example, if you assume the role of *defining* a new product and then expect your end-user to buy it, you may end up with win/lose, which rapidly degrades into lose/lose as customer dissatisfaction grows. Because your End-users are seeking solutions to *their* problems, their involvement in defining product solutions is mandatory. Conversely, if the end-users don't control the evolution of their requirements and force you to create solutions outside the bounds of reality, lose/win may be the result. A widespread example is the often unreasonable pressure to reduce selling price. End-users may become so single-minded in their pursuit of low prices that it takes the inevitable sharp decrease in product performance to bring them back to reality. If the situation is not rectified and returned to win/win, then lose/lose is always the ultimate result.

Crucial close relationships with your end-users are possible only through clearly communicated and understood expectations. The end-users must communicate their problems, expectations, and requirements. Equally important is your full disclosure of your capabilities, limitations, and expectations. Mutual understanding will enable a lasting, successful relationship.

How Shareholders Affect Your Business

Nearly as important as the bill-paying "real" customers, the shareholders pay the bills from a different perspective. They establish the vision, the mission, and the general direction for the company. Your survival as a management team depends upon satisfying the demands of this group, within the constraints established by the end-users. Most shareholders recognize this secondary position, but when they don't, situations often arise where the end-user is short-changed in order to satisfy shareholder directives. You have a real obligation to not only satisfy shareholder objectives, but to also act as their bridge to your marketplace, so that they understand the constraints imposed by your real customers *before* those constraints lead to conflict. The need to create this bridge with your market-place points to the need to have a real relationship with the Shareholder. A simple example of such a relationship, again identi-fying the dual customer (C) and supplier (S) roles, might look like this:

	Transaction	Company	Shareholder
1.	20 percent annual profit increase	S	C
2.	Sufficient operating capital	C	S
3.	Evidence of future stability and growth	S	C
4.	Market expectations	S	C
5.	Long-range business mission	C	S

It's easy to predict the outcome if you allow win/win to get out of balance in this relationship. The ultimate consequence is your replacement as the Company--certainly not one of your desired expectations. Shareholders are indeed customers, and it is in your best interest to nurture a satisfying customer-supplier relationship with them.

CONSIDERING EMPLOYEES AS CUSTOMERS

It's difficult to look at employees as customers, especially for those of us who have been exposed to hierarchal, compartmental-ized organizations. It's also a "buyer's market" as far as "employees" are concerned: If Joe doesn't fall in line and follow orders, there are plenty of other people looking for work. Don't talk to us about employ-ee satisfaction. We can't pay for the benefits they're getting today, how can we afford to find out what else our employees need to be "satisfied customers"? Can we really accept employees as a customer group?

I hope some of you are ready to refute these arguments. As managers, *you should treat your employees in the same manner as you expect them to treat your best customers*. For supplying and satisfying end-users and shareholders, the single most valuable producing resource you have is your human resource. We can all name the stars in our organization, the most brilliant engineer, the most tenacious buyer, not to mention the magician who runs production. Why, he's so good we don't even need to consider leadtimes anymore! He always gets the job done! Certainly these people are worthy of a win/win relationship with the company. What about the supporting cast? The brilliant engineer is so prolific because she has a dedicated CAD layout team, because Manufacturing Engineering matches her design pace with work instructions, test procedures and prototype manufacturing, and because her assigned buyer makes parts appear overnight, slashing prototype cycle times in half. That tenacious buyer has a components engineer continually feeding him part substitutes, upgrades, and improvements. And the production manager? Direct labor departments are the court of last resort. They absorb all the mistakes and inefficiencies in the system, yet somehow find the means to deliver the product on time, at least most of the time. Provided that you have proficient managers and that you have created a living organization (discussed in Chapter 7), your supporting staff is equally worthy of a win/win relationship with you, the Company. Employees as a whole should also be considered sometime supplier and sometime customer, as shown in the following example:

	Transaction	*Company*	*Employee*
1.	Clear understanding of job responsibilities and expectations	S	C
2.	Continuously improving performance	C	S
3.	Reward/recognition for performance	S	C
4.	Responsible control and decision making	C	S

If you fail to empower your employees with the responsibility for being involved participants in the business, and if you fail to demonstrate the behavior and values you expect them to use in creating customer satisfaction, you have no hope of achieving a total quality operation. The potential and the influence of the Employee must be chanelled productively through win/win customer-supplier relationships.

Considering Suppliers as Customers

Have you solved the apparent dichotomy of a supplier also being a customer? Let's examine suppliers from a win/win perspective. Suppliers constitute the front end of the quality delivery system. In Part 3, we'll build a quality delivery system from the ground up. In refining and improving your ability to supply quality products and services to your End-user, the performance of your suppliers has a direct and profound impact on the entire business process. If on-time delivery of raw material is 90 percent, your scheduling and execution systems must function to perfection if there is any hope of achieving 90% on-time delivery of finished products. If your suppliers' quality acceptance percentage is less than 100 percent, there will be an additional high risk to achieving even 90 percent delivery performance. Sure, you can compensate in the short term with Average order quantities, yield percentages, shrink factors, and other aliases for excess inventory, but time will prove that such a course is unprofitable. The impact of Supplier performance on your business can be a classic, living example of a "garbage in—garbage out" system. If we satisfy the goals and requirements of our suppliers and create true supplier partnerships, we'll certainly make our internal management tasks much easier. Because they can easily become the tail wagging the dog, the Supplier group is absolutely worthy of being one of your customers. The following example illustrates that in certain transactions, suppliers are, in fact, customers:

Transaction	Company	Shareholder
1. Clear definition of requirements	S	C
2. Performance to contract	C	S
3. Payment and fair profit	S	C
4. Market evolution and trends	C	S

When viewed as your customer, the Supplier will expect, in general terms, a clear definition of your requirements, prompt payment for delivered material, and the ability to make a fair profit for their business. From your supplier you will expect performance to contract, participation in new product design and communication of market evolution and trends within their purview. Nothing but good can come from creating a solid partnership with the Supplier. A real synergy is possible because your goals are precisely complementary. A partnership allows mutual reduction of operating expenses. The Supplier would require less of a sales resource, which could free up people for market expansion, or toward improving conformance to requirements. The Company would see a reduction in the need for traditional "buying" activity, which may allow buyers to focus on contract management. The dovetailing effect continues with other remaining goals, as well. Since you have a desire for 100 percent on-time delivery of 100 percent high quality "fit-for-use" components, and since your Supplier is seriously concerned with your satisfaction, you're working consistently toward the same result. Your Supplier would like to make a fair profit to fuel business growth, and you now consider raw material cost as a long-term, third priority, after raw material quality and on-time delivery. This sets the stage for a working relationship that reaches decisions based on the partnership, and decisions that are mutually beneficial—again, decisions which are win/win.

IDENTIFYING THE CIRCLE-4 CUSTOMER

What we've really shown for these four groups that exert the most influence over any business is that we must create a partnership with each group. That's what win/win is all about. So that we keep our focus on customer satisfaction, let's combine these four groups into one unit called the Circle-4 Customer (also referred to as the Customer), since we've shown that as a group they completely encircle our business. Figure 2.2 illustrates the relationship between each influence group of the Circle-4 Customer and the Company. The communications interface that exists is only between each group and the Company. We have a responsibility to create a flow of information that supports and sustains the relationship created with each major group. In other words, each time you seek to establish or strengthen a partnership with one of your customer groups, you must be prepared to represent, consider and communicate the goals and requirements of the other three groups. Accepting this responsibility represents the beginning of a new Circle-4 Quality paradigm. We no longer view our customer satisfaction role as one which is focused on the ultimate purchasers of our commodities. The new paradigm demands our involvement in the satisfaction of all groups which can influence our success, our Circle-4 Customer. In the next chapter we'll establish the requirement base for each of our customer groups. Now that we've identified the Circle-4

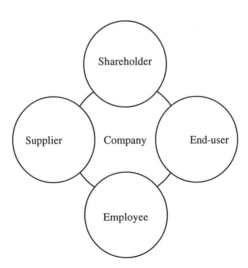

Figure 2.2 Relationship between the Circle-4 Customer and the Company.

Customer, how can we be sure we're focused on customer goals and requirements? Answering this question is the next step in defining quality and in creating a quality system.

SUMMARY

1. The Integrated Business System (IBS) represents the totality of our control, the medium through which we can create customer satisfaction, and the operation through which we desire to diffuse total quality thinking.
2. The four major groups which influence our ability to realize our business objectives are the End-user, Shareholder, Employee and Supplier.
3. Taken together, these four influence groups constitute our Circle-4 Customer.
4. To be successful, we have a responsibility to create a *win/win* relationship with each of the four influence groups.
5. As we strive for Circle-4 Customer satisfaction, we have an obligation to act as a communication link between the four groups. Our concerted efforts must represent, consider, and communicate the goals and requirements of the Customer.

QUALITY APPLICATIONS

1. Discuss the ownership of your company. What do you perceive to be your requirements to satisfy your Shareholders?
2. Identify the markets or market segments served by your products and services. Discuss the unique End-user requirements for each market or market segment.
3. Discuss the demographics of your Employees. What specific Employee requirements are being addressed, or need to be addressed, in order to realize optimum productivity of your operations?
4. Using the 80/20 rule, list the vendors with which you do the most business. Are you satisfied with the current performance of your Suppliers? Why or why not?

QUALITY BENEFITS

1. The discussions indicated will allow the management team (the Company) to begin to see the impact and importance of each of the four influence groups of the Circle-4 Customer on your business. When I was General Manager for an electronics manufacturing company, for years I spent most of my time making sure the End-users, Shareholders, and my Employees were satisfied. I rarely dealt with Suppliers, incorrectly delegating that job to the purchasing department. When I did get involved, it was usually to resolve a crisis; unavailable components, single sources no longer manufactured, and doubling or tripling of leadtimes are typical examples. My management team and I committed ourselves to *actively* understanding our Suppliers and to participating in a supplier certification program when we realized that in one year alone, the types of crises just mentioned cost us well over $200K in additional expense and inventory. You might say I found 200,000 reasons for building relationships with my Suppliers. After a full year of seriously communicating with our Suppliers, even though we were learning about TQM in the process, our additional expense and inventory as a result of Supplier "surprises" was less than $100K.

2. The Company will realize that they provide the bridge which links the success and performance of the four groups, thus enabling their own success.

3. The initial perceptions documented by the Company concerning Customer requirements will either be validated or improved as Customer relationships are nurtured.

3

UNDERSTANDING THE MOTIVATION, GOALS, AND REQUIREMENTS OF THE CIRCLE-4 CUSTOMER

In order to develop a thorough understanding of our Circle-4 Customer we need to understand its motivation, goals and requirements. As shown below in Figure 3.1, there is a definite progression from motivation to requirements and hence a defined relationship between motivation, goals, and requirements. Motivation will give rise to long-range vision and goals. Requirements, or necessary short-term results, are derived from goals.

Let's take a moment to clarify terminology. Much is lost in communicating without a common understanding of terms. I worked for a multinational corporation for years, and surprisingly enough, language was not nearly as big a communication problem as was a poor understanding of one another's terms. For example, we spent several years hearing complaints from our business unit in Germany that we didn't adequately test our products and that they never received test results, when we knew all along that the products were well tested and that the test results were taped to the back of each product. Finally, after listening again to the same complaints during one of my many visits to Germany, I made a spur-of-the-moment request: "Show me what a well-documented

25

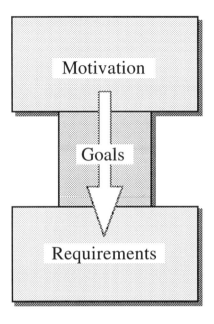

Figure 3.1 The progression from motivation to requirements.

and well-tested product looks like." After spending an hour in their factory and looking at their examples, I concluded that we had indeed been sending them "undocumented, untested" product for years! Because, you see, by their definition, adequate testing was done with a tightly monitored, computer-controlled test fixture, and by their definition, valid test results were clean and accurate computer printouts! Manual testing and handwritten test results were not acceptable. Since they were my customers for this particular product, I had to conclude that they were absolutely correct. How much wasted time and aggravation could we have saved as a company had we asked the right question when the issue was first raised? As you create partnerships with your Circle-4 Customer make sure there's agreement on terminology and what it means.

DEFINING OUR TERMS

Motivation is the drive or incentive required to precipitate action. A *goal* is the defined desired outcome. A goal must allow score-keeping so we can measure attainment. Therefore, a goal can be motivation expressed as a defined result. An athlete's motivation might be a desire to "be the world's fastest sprinter." Expressed as a goal, the athlete might be committed to "run the 100 meters in 9.0 seconds, or under, by the 1996 Summer Olympics." It's possible to derive a *probable* motivation by analyzing a goal statement. In this example, we know the result implies a desire to compete for a gold medal in the summer Olympic games; we can therefore propose that our athlete wants to run faster than anyone else. However, we cannot derive a goal just by hearing the motivation. There are too many chances of being wrong. Faced with our original statement of motivation, to "be the world's fastest sprinter," we don't know whether our athlete will run in the 50 meters, 100 meters, 200 meters, or whether she'll choose the hurdles as the best expression of her capabilities. Goals should be motivational. Understanding a customer's goals allows insight into their motivation; understanding only their motivation is worthless.

Requirements are the necessary conditions for reaching our goals. You notice I said *necessary conditions* instead of *conditions necessary* for reaching our goals. *Conditions necessary* implies that we can define and control the conditions. *Necessary conditions* implies living within externally established constraints. For our athlete, requirements will include the training schedule, preliminary event schedule, promotional appearances, and a variety of other activities that are beyond her control. The reason you need to understand the goals of your Circle-4 Customer is because you must live with the "necessary conditions" they've established for your business environment. If you understand their goals, you have an opportunity to influence their requirements. If all you understand are their requirements, all you can do is strive for compliance and prepare your business to change when requirements change—usually with no warning! Being aware of motivation allows you to validate a customer's goals as a set: Is there a common motivation, several motivations, or conflicting motivations? Understanding motivation, goals, and requirements together is the key to creating a successful partnership with the Customer. If any one of the three is missing, you risk incorrect decisions, because you can't see the complete picture.

IDENTIFYING THE PRIMARY MOTIVATION OF THE CIRCLE-4 CUSTOMER

Let's explore the motivation of our Circle-4 Customer. Do they share a common motivation? Evidence of a common motivation will allow us to create a collective process for identifying goals and requirements, after which we can validate (or invalidate) the motivation for each customer group. That validation process will permit us to improve our communications as we continue to interact with them.

Within the four influence groups of our Circle-4 Customer, two can be characterized as businesses, or being within a business framework. The Shareholder and the Supplier are both distinctly businesses. The end-user may or may not be a business. The employee, by definition, is not a business, but is part of the business operation. In his book, *The Haystack Syndrome*, Dr. E. M. Goldratt creates an eloquent argument which concludes that the primary motivation for any business is "to make more money now and in the future."[2] I should note that Dr. Goldratt uses the word "goal" in a more general context than I do. For him, goals encompass both motivation and goal, per my definition. I believe my distinction is valid, as I will continue to demonstrate. The simple statement, "make more money now and in the future," encompasses the intent as well as the vision in expressing a general motivation for a business. We want to "make more money," meaning we seek growth and increasing reward for our efforts. "Now and in the future" shows a concern for both short- and long-term results; we're inter-

---

[2] Goldratt, Eliyahu M., *The Haystack Syndrome*, North River Press, Inc., 1990, pg. 14.

ested in establishing a trend for improving financial success. I doubt that any of us will question the general validity of stating that most businesses are motivated by the desire to make more money now and in the future. If this is a valid motivation for the Shareholder and the Supplier, does it apply as clearly to the Employee and the End-user?

Evaluating the Employee's Motivation

Let's look at the Employee first. Several years ago, I conducted a survey of my employees to determine their expectations for total quality reward/recognition programs. The survey covered a variety of topics, including Employee of the Month, production incentive programs, promotions, and annual pay increases. From the survey results, I reached a number of conclusions, two of which apply to this discussion:

1. People want to be recognized and appreciated for their efforts.
2. Any recognition for good performance must be validated, now or later, with a reward.

Let's look at a couple of examples. Sally Jurgensen was selected as Employee of the Month for April by a selection committee of her peers. The recognition entailed her picture on a plaque in the lunchroom and a letter for her personnel file. She was also rewarded with a $100.00 savings bond. Sally felt immediate closure for her efforts; she had been recognized *and* rewarded for her commitment and quality work.

Joe Bernard received a letter of commendation from his supervisor for the excellent work he did in configuring a particularly complex customer order. A copy of the letter was presented to him during a department quality meeting and another copy placed in his personnel file. It was close to year-end, so Joe figured the commendation was worth at least 0.5 percent in the upcoming annual "merit" raise, since no specific reward accompanied his recognition. When he received the company average raise of 4 percent, his earlier recognition was invalidated, because the reward did not meet his expectation. Even though there was no expressed or implied promise of a reward, Joe felt that his commendation demonstrated an increased worth to the company. An important behavioral relationship is worth mentioning here. It may be interesting for us to examine, on our own, the hypothesis that "the closer the reward is to the recognition, the greater the employee satisfaction, with the least cost to the company." Briefly, a less costly reward given immediately upon recognition will have a greater positive impact on employee satisfaction than if that same reward were offered weeks after the recognition.

When recognition is given to an employee for any reason, there is always the expectation of a reward. If the reward accompanies the recognition, as is usually the case with say, a promotion, the recognition is immediately validated for the employee, provided the magnitude of the reward falls within the employee's expectation. If the reward does not accompany the recognition, it will be expected later, whether or not it is explicitly promised. If not rewarded, the recognition will become invalidated either by time or by the passage of some milestone in the mind of the employee. As we saw in Joe's case, his expectation to be rewarded for his commendation was not satisfied by the annual merit increase, which was his established milestone. As a result, the commendation was greatly devalued in Joe's eyes. Any future commendations will likely be met with either indifference or scorn.

Employees work in order to create their chosen lifestyle. No one that I know has chosen a lifestyle that says, "I will be poorer next year than I am this year." In fact, considering inflation, most employees will conclude that staying on an even keel financially from one year to the next is becoming poorer. We've all been conditioned to pursue the American dream, though it may manifest itself differently for each of us. This basic incentive leads to the conclusion that most employees are motivated to "make more money now and in the future." We all want to be recognized and rewarded for extra effort and quality performance.

Evaluating the End-User's Motivation

What about the End-user? This customer group is perhaps the most difficult to characterize in any general manner. For some of us, end-users are consumers, for others they're commercial companies, for still others they're GSA or defense contracts, and so on. It's safe to say that end-users within traditional businesses are motivated by the desire to make more money now and in the future. What about consumers? If we're selling a product directly to a consumer, the most real of all end-users, they're motivated to purchase the most product for the lowest investment. Is there anything driving this motivation? Consider this example. One of my hobbies is wood-working, and I have a weakness for the latest and highest quality hand and power tools. When digitally controlled plunge-cut routers were introduced a few years ago, I had to have one. When I brought my purchase home, I had a ready explanation—well used I might add. "Dear, remember that router I've been telling you about? Take a look at this beauty! And it was on sale, so I saved $50.00!" Boy, was I proud of myself! In reality, I hadn't saved any-thing. All I had done was spend an unplanned $100.00 from the family budget, instead of $150.00. Why do many of us use a simi-lar rationale from time to time? We're creating the illusion for our-selves that our buying power has increased and we're giving strokes to that little motivator, "make more money now and in the future." Didn't I just create $50.00? Of course I did, if only for my own ego. By recognizing that I got a satisfactory return for the least money, I reasoned that I now had $150.00 worth of assets for investing $100.00, therefore my net worth increased by $50.00. Go from there directly to "make more money now and in the future," and then on to the American dream, and you'll see that the consumer fits the same profile as all end-users.

We've established that there's a common, primary motivation dri-ving our Circle-4 Customer. The primary motivation is profit, the desire to "make more money now and in the future." Understanding this, we've created the correct mindset to begin examining their goals and requirements.

How to Determine the Goals
of the Circle-4 Customer

Let's stand back for a moment and look again at the big picture. In *The Haystack Syndrome*, Dr. Goldratt argues convincingly that goals can only be established by the shareholder, or owner, of the business. "The goal of the organization must be determined solely by the owners of that organization. Any other answer will force us to redefine the meaning of the word 'ownership.'"[3] This argument is right on the mark, and it holds two implications for us. First, we cannot determine our Customer's goals by creating logical arguments within this or any other book. There is no substitute for communicating directly with them and listening to their defined goals. Second, in the course of that communication, we must be very careful *not* to express our opinion or otherwise try to influence the goals expressed. As I mentioned previously, a thorough understanding of the Customer's goals will allow us to influence the requirements, but not the goals themselves. If we can demonstrate, and reach agreement on, an improved method for satisfying the requirements, the Customer *may* choose to modify the requirements, the goals, or both. However, we must always take the position of understanding and supporting the goals as they're communicated, provided we wish to continue our business relationship.

Let's turn our attention to defining a process through which we may come to understand the goals and requirements of the Circle-4 Customer. The basic process is communication, and the Company must be involved; this process cannot be delegated. Beginning with identifying a focus group for each of our Circle-4 Customers, we progress toward a structured dialogue, followed by an analysis. The results of the analysis will provide critical data for establishing the objectives of the Company, keeping in mind that our goals are set by the shareholder. We will explore how this process allows us to establish real objectives in the next chapter. The entire process must be repeated at regular intervals once we create the quality information system, which will be introduced in Chapter 6. The initial execution of the process will create a climate of open communication, which can be exploited by our complete business. It will permit

---

[3] *Ibid.*, p. 10.

meaningful discussions on product evolution, it will allow participation by vendors in product design, it will catalyze employee involvement and empowerment, and it will create a climate of trust with our shareholder.

Selecting Sample Groups from Your Circle-4 Customer

Within each of the four influence groups of the Circle-4 Customer, you first need to identify a sample size which you feel fairly represents the majority of that group. Your Shareholder is likely to be a familiar individual or group, such as a board of directors. For the Supplier, you may want to use the 80-20 rule and select as a sample the 20 percent of vendors with which you do 80 percent of your business. For the End-user, you may want to use geographic representation, product family segmentation, or you may include all end-users in your sample. Likewise for the Employee, you may want to include all employees initially, and move to a smaller sample size after collecting your initial data.

Once you're comfortable with your selected sample, it's time to plan and conduct structured communication. Face-to-face meetings are preferable, though not always realistic. Telephone interviews are a good second choice, and I would recommend using written surveys or questionnaires as a last resort. They tend to depersonalize the process and they don't allow for any interchange to clarify or amplify discussion points.

The first step in planning to communicate is identifying the specific players you want to talk to within your selected samples. The players involved in the Shareholder and Employee groups should be clear at this point. Within the End-user and Supplier selected samples, your goal should be to meet with at least your counterparts; their equivalent of your management team. If it's possible to meet with Shareholders within these groups, so much the better. Meeting at least with their Company will give you direct insight into the goals and requirements of their business. Their management teams will, after all, communicate the goals and establish the requirements for their operations.

How to Hold Effective Meetings to Clarify Goals

You need to focus on a purpose for your meetings; you want to get to know your Circle-4 Customer. To create and maintain this mindset, you might want to do a little self-coaching before each meeting along the following lines:

1. I'm here only to *listen.*
2. I will ask questions only to *clarify* my understanding.
3. I want to clearly understand the *goals* of my Customer.
4. I want to clearly understand what this Customer has defined as *requirements* necessary to reach those goals, and I want to understand our potential role in satisfying those requirements.
5. *(Optional)* I'm here to see if there is an *immediate issue* in our relationship that I can take action to resolve.

The fifth purpose of the meeting is optional and should be employed only if you're committed to resolving whatever problem might be put on the table. The Customers might expect this to be included in the meeting. If so, it's better to deal with immediate problems first, so the Customer can express them and thus be mentally ready to discuss goals and requirements in a more general sense.

All formal meetings or communications should follow an agenda, and the Customer should have final approval of that agenda. We won't talk about the format or detailed preparation for the agenda. Let me just recommend that you structure the flow of the meeting so that you account for your current knowledge of the customer and you satisfy your objectives for the meeting. An example of a typical meeting process, structured in the form of questions, might be:

1. What are the problems and issues affecting your business today?
2. Are there specific areas of our current relationship that we need to address for you?
3. Where do you see your company (yourself) in 5 years? in 10 years? in 20 years?

4. What are your overall expectations for your (suppliers, customers, division, management, etc.)? (Fill in your role with respect to this Customer.)

5. May we establish additional (or improve existing) communications links between us so that the details of your requirements will be fully understood by our employees? (This question also needs to be tailored to the specific type of customer you're meeting with. Shareholders and Employees would be asked something slightly different.)

Given that we're all professional managers, we should understand the dynamics of conducting effective meetings. Therefore, we'll focus on the fact that you've collected customer information from your meetings and you've laid the groundwork for further communication. It's now time to collate and analyze the information you've received.

How to Define Your Customer's Requirements

Customer information should be grouped into the general categories of goals and requirements for each major customer group. The defined requirements should be subdivided into those you will be involved in satisfying and those where your business will have no involvement. Even if you're not involved in satisfying a particular requirement, for example the expected delivery performance of suppliers to your Supplier, you need to retain visibility for that requirement. Such downstream or upstream requirements will establish the *limits* on your direct requirements. In this example, if your supplier requires an average of 90-percent on-time delivery from its suppliers, what is the potential impact if you require 95-percent on-time delivery from your supplier? Your supplier will need to change the requirement from their suppliers, or invest in additional inventory, or create a leadtime buffer, or they'll fail to meet your requirement. So you see, it's important to have enough visibility to ask, "What evidence do we have that gives us confidence that requirements can be met?" The same visibility is required for all groups within the Circle-4 Customer, including the End-user. You need to understand how your end-users satisfy their customers, so that you'll have confidence that your products and services will contribute to their efforts. Requirements should also always be expressed quantitatively if any useful analysis is expected.

Once you've collated and grouped the requirements of your Circle-4 Customer, you should logically evaluate the expressed goals and the defined requirements against the following tests for each of the four influence groups:

1. Can the expressed goals be achieved if the defined requirements are satisfied?
2. Are the goals complementary? That is, will the achievement of a goal strengthen or weaken the other goals?
3. Do the goals appear to arise from a similar motivation?
4. If multiple motivations are evident, are they complementary?

When exceptions are noted during the above tests, further clarification with the customer sample is justified. First re-examine the customers responsible for the conflicting goals to ensure that you understood them correctly. If no corrections occur here, consider expanding your examination to clarify the goal across the entire customer sample. If they validate the conflicting goal, you must consider the goal valid, and re-examine all other goals against it. If you cannot validate the conflicting goals across the sample, move it to the bottom of your goals list, under the heading of "Conflicting Goals." These goals should be periodically re-examined against current goals. Once all goals have either been found to be complementary, or segregated as conflicting, tests 3 and 4 above should be rerun. If the goals are truly complementary, the motivations will be complementary.

Now you've created an information file for your Circle-4 Customer. You've validated the evident motivations. You've been given goals and specific expectations in the form of requirements. Any surprises? Maybe or maybe not. In any case, you're well on your way to understanding your customers, and you've established the foundation for defining quality in terms of customer satisfaction. We will arrive at a definition for Circle-4 Quality in the next chap-

ter as we talk about using the Customer information we've collected to create realistic business unit objectives for the Company.

SUMMARY

1. *Motivation* is the drive or incentive required to precipitate
   action.
2. *Goals* are the defined and desired outcome.
3. *Requirements* are the necessary conditions for reaching goals.
4. We must understand the motivation, goals, and requirements
   of the Circle-4 Customer.
5. If we understand the motivation and goals of the Customer, we
   have given ourselves the capability of influencing their
   requirements.
6. The common, primary customer motivation is the desire for
   profit.
7. Direct, structured communication with the Customer is
   required in order to understand their goals and requirements.
8. Within each of the Circle-4 Customer influence groups, goals
   should be complementary, achieving defined requirements
   should satisfy the expressed goals, and goals should arise from
   a common motivation or from complementary motivations.

Quality Applications

1. Using a forum applicable to your company, meet with the
   Shareholder and document their goals and requirements. How
   do the results compare with the perceptions you discussed following Chapter 2?
2. Through your sales organization, arrange to visit a number of
   key end-users. Be prepared to resolve any current issues that
   may be raised. Collect the following information for each
   account visited:
   a. Who is their Customer (Shareholder, End-user, Employee,
      Supplier)?

    b. What products or services do they provide?

    c. What are their overall business goals and requirements? Long-term goals?

    d. What is their current perception of you as their supplier in terms of size, quality, responsiveness, and performance?

3. Disregarding organizational boundaries, meet with randomly selected small groups of employees. Encourage a free and open discussion (let the employees know you're trying to better understand their needs and their expectations) and collect information in the following general categories:

    a. Positive/negative feelings about the current workplace

    b. Perceived problems with the current operation

    c. General ideas to improve morale, productivity, and efficiency

    d. Personal and/or career goals and expectations

4. Through your purchasing organization, arrange to visit the key suppliers you identified at the end of Chapter 2. If you have an unresolved issue with a particular supplier, take it with you in order to personally observe their response. Collect information about the following aspects of each business you visit:

    a. Who is their Customer? What are their business goals and objectives? Long-term goals?

    b. What portion of their business do you account for?

    c. Who are their other customers, markets?

    d. What systems are in place to help them meet their business goals?

    e. Do they utilize any special or unique processes to satisfy your requirements or the requirements of any other customers? How do those unique processes affect their ability to meet your requirements?

    f. What requirements do they place on their suppliers?

    g. How do they perceive your current relationship?

5. Based on the information collected in actions 1 through 4, create a profile for each of the four influence groups in terms of motivation, goals and requirements. Segment each group, as necessary, to create accurate profiles.

6. Prepare and supply feedback to the businesses and groups you met with in actions 1 through 4. The intent of your feedback is to confirm your findings. You may indicate that the information will be used to improve your business; however, don't make any promises unless you know you can follow through.

7. As a group, discuss your customer profiles. Highlight those goals and requirements that apply to your business. Discuss whether the goals and requirements are complementary, both within an influence group and for the entire Customer. Make an initial assessment of your performance in meeting the requirements of the Customer.

Quality Benefits

1. Through direct communication, you have achieved a clearer understanding of the goals and requirements of your Circle-4 Customer.

2. You have started or sustained the communication and feedback process between yourselves (the Company) and the Shareholder, End-user, Employee, and Supplier.

3. Perhaps for the first time, you have considered the collective requirements of the Circle-4 Customer as the necessary conditions for running your business. You may sometimes be surprised with the results. At my previous company, the entire corporation, including its parent company, began a multimillion-dollar development program for high-definition television (HDTV) products. HDTV involves relatively new technology, so the first products are very expensive. Since our responsibility was for professional studio products, about a year into the development program we began to validate our progress with our end-users. To the surprise of some corporate managers, we perceived a very indifferent and noncommittal attitude toward the new technology. In fact, one of the major networks

told us they had no intention of converting their studio to HDTV operation until 70 percent of the households in the U.S. had HDTV receivers. Needless to say, the pervasiveness of similar views among all end-users caused the entire corporation to scale back its HDTV investment and lengthen its timeline for market entry of new HDTV products. To have continued blindly forward with the new technology, without listening to the Customer, would have been devastating for the Company.

4

DEFINING CIRCLE-4 QUALITY

Our overall quality objective is complete customer satisfaction. We have defined our Circle-4 Customer, from the point of view of the Company, as the combined influence groups: the End-user, the Shareholder, the Employee, the Supplier. We understand the motivation, goals, and requirements of our Circle-4 Customer. We have documented and analyzed these characteristics, and we understand our expected role as a defined subset of their total requirements. What do we have to do now, as the Company, to turn these expectations into customer satisfaction?

ESTABLISHING PRIORITIES FOR CUSTOMER SATISFACTION

Let's prioritize our responsibilities. We have identified four major influence groups that we call the Circle-4 Customer, and we'd like to keep them all happy and working toward the same vision, "make more money now and in the future." However, we have to approach the task of customer satisfaction with total clarity for the priorities. Our primary responsibility is to support the goals of the Shareholder by satisfying their defined business objectives. In order to satisfy the Shareholder, we will provide, at a profit, products or services as defined by the End-user. We will empower and reward the Employee in order to satisfy the End-user. To support and sustain the Employee, we will require quality performance from the Supplier. In order to make the Supplier an involved partner, we will support reasonable profit and expanded participation in our operation. Our customer satisfaction priorities are:

1. The Shareholder
2. The End-user
3. The Employee
4. The Supplier

Using Policies and Objectives to Communicate Goals

The vehicle through which we'll satisfy our Shareholder is the business operation we've created. As the Company, we will communicate our goals and requirements to the operation through policies and objectives. Policies communicate the long-term goals, establish an operational framework, and clarify functional responsibilities. Objectives communicate the short- and mid-term tactics and results necessary to satisfy the goals. (The role of policies will be fully explored in chapter 6; chapter 9 will look at communicating our objectives throughout the operation.) We will use the above priorities and characterize the content of our policies and objectives on the following basis:

1. Can we meet Shareholder requirements, and support Shareholder goals?
2. Can we create and produce a product that the End-user has defined and will purchase?
3. Have we created an operation that allows the Employee to be successful, thus enabling End-user Satisfaction?
4. Have we created partnerships that permit the Supplier to pros-

per by continuously improving their response to our requirements?

As the Company creates policy and objectives, these characteristics should be examined iteratively until a positive answer is achieved for all four. If you can create policies and objectives that plan to satisfy the prioritized requirements of your Circle-4 Customer, and if you can demonstrate that your actual performance meets those objectives, you have taken the next step toward Circle-4 Quality. These four characteristics should also serve as the yardstick by which the Company measures its own performance.

USING A MODEL TO CREATE POLICIES AND OBJECTIVES

Let's begin building a model to illustrate the process of creating policies and objectives. Later on, we will expand the model to include the entire quality system defined to implement our direction. The company in our model is "EWC," the Electronic Widget Company, Inc. A start-up company just ending its second year, the founder and general manager of EWC is Dr. Joan Rogers, an innovative, if somewhat eccentric, electrical engineer. Dr. Rogers's reputation for eccentricity arose from the agile twists and turns her logic and decision making take as she steers this little corporate ship. A student of quality, she has created a small profit on $11.0M in sales in her second year. She manages with astounding intuition and immediately embraced the concepts of *The Quality-Empowered Business* as the framework around which to structure EWC. We're going to describe her operation in detail as we demonstrate how she is approaching total customer satisfaction.

Let's look first at the results for the calendar year just ended:

Sales, avg. sell price	$11.0M
Selling cost	$ 1.0M
Net sales	$10.0M

Material cost	$6.0M
Operating expenses	$3.9M
Net profit	$0.1M
ROA	1.8%
Inventory	$5.7M
Throughput	$4.0M

Defining the Customer Profile

As a result of their analysis, the EWC senior management team reached the following conclusions about their Customer:

THE SHAREHOLDER

Dr. Rogers and her six managers are equal partners in EWC. They have established for themselves the following goals for the next three years:

1. Increase sales at a 20 percent annual rate.
2. Realize a 10 percent net profit in the third year.
3. Improve ROA to 20 percent.

THE END-USER

1. Average goal of 6 percent annual profit improvement.
2. Goal to expand their served market by 10 percent annually.
3. Requirement for highly reliable product, decreased cost of ownership.
4. Requires on-time delivery in 30 to 45 days after ordering.
5. Requires applications solutions, not black-box products.

THE EMPLOYEE

1. Requires annual salary increase that maintains equity with cost of living.
2. Requires identifiable career paths.
3. Goal to have a challenging job with the opportunity to be rewarded for participation and exceptional performance.

THE SUPPLIER

1. Average goal of 5 percent annual profit improvement.
2. Goal of long-term, profitable contracts with their customers.
3. Goal to provide application solutions during product design process.
4. Requires stability in short-term (under 90 days) requirements.

Establishing Objectives

By iteratively examining the Customer requirements, based on their own priorities, the Company at EWC arrived at the following objectives:

1. Realized sales of $12M.
2. Realized a minimum 4 percent net profit.
3. Created additional product applications for the End-user, with no increase in product list prices for two years.
4. Strengthened supplier partnerships and create incentive to reduce material cost by 5 percent annually. Budgeted a 2.5 percent annual decrease in cost of material. Split all realized material cost reductions equally with the Supplier.
5. Challenged the Employee to reduce operating expenses by 10 percent annually, measured as a percentage of net sales. Budgeted a 5 percent annual decrease in operating expense. Operating expense savings against the budget will be turned over to the Employee.
6. Improved customer delivery to an average of 30 days ARO, and reduce finished goods inventory to an average of 30 days within two years.
7. Maintained product development investment at 12% of net sales annually.

Relating Objectives to Defined Priorities

While there are implications within the objectives that must be understood by all the players, and while a great deal of translation to lower-level objectives remains to be done, have we satisfied the priority characteristics we defined earlier?

1. *Can we meet Shareholder requirements and support Shareholder goals?* If you look at the abbreviated EWC plan in Appendix 1, you will see that they've created a plan that will create 10 percent profit and 20 percent ROA in three years. They have also projected growth at 20 percent per year. The budget requirements specified in the objectives support this plan.

2. *Can we create and produce a product that the End-user has defined and will purchase?* EWC has created the scenario for success. Given the End-user's desire to increase profitability, EWC will freeze the list price of their products and create an advertising campaign around this strategy. EWC has committed to create additional applications for their products, and must involve the End-user in defining those applications. They have also demonstrated a commitment to new product development by maintaining engineering at 12 percent of sales and putting more of a burden for realizing operating expense goals on the other departments. Deciding that EWC's investment areas at this point should be in product development and in improving the company's quality system was a unanimous decision of the Shareholder.

3. *Have we created an operation that allows the Employee to be successful?* Having created objectives with Circle-4 Quality in mind, EWC realizes that its business system requires a lot of nurturing and fine-tuning before it can fully support its profitability goals. During the next business year, EWC will conduct numerous focused internal audits in order to create specific improvement projects. We will follow them through their quality system throughout the remainder of this book. Through the specific wording on the goal for operating expenses, employees are empowered to create profitability within their own departments. As a group, the employees will determine how to disburse any operating expense savings below budget. This program, like all the others, will be carefully focused and measured as the objectives are driven further down the organization.

4. *Have we created partnerships that permit the Supplier to prosper by continuously improving their response to our requirements?* EWC is committed to creating a profit for the Shareholder and rightfully expects some improvement in the cost of material. Also keeping in mind the Supplier's desire to improve profitability, EWC has a goal of creating joint cost-improvement programs with the Supplier. The cost savings begin with the first such project, with the Supplier and EWC sharing equal benefit from the beginning.

While this is just a cursory look, we can conclude that EWC has considered their Circle-4 Customer in creating its business goals—and it has considered them in the right context, or priority. A lot of work remains if those goals are to become reality, but we can say that EWC shows a committed intent to pursue Circle-4 Quality.

PURSUING CIRCLE-4 QUALITY

Now that we've established the priorities for customer satisfaction, we can introduce a complete definition of Circle-4 Quality, thus completing our vision of our new role in running the business, our new paradigm.

Circle-4 Quality is the commitment to work in cooperation with the Circle-4 Customer in the pursuit of a profitable business. By ensuring a return for the Shareholder, solving problems for the End-user, challenging and rewarding the Employee, and proactively involving the Supplier, there can be no result other than profit and growth for the business.

Circle-4 Quality is the consideration of the needs of the Circle-4 Customer in all business activities and decisions. The philosophy of total quality management identifies a variety of customer-supplier relationships throughout the business. These relationships are, in fact, Circle-4 Customer relationships.

Circle-4 Quality is the result of satisfying the prioritized requirements of the Circle-4 Customer. Within the remaining chapters of this book, we'll construct a quality system designed to promote awareness of the Circle-4 Customer throughout our business and designed to enable the continuously improving satisfaction of that Customer. We'll base all our activities, including our decision-making process, on satisfying the prioritized requirements of our Circle-4 Customer. Such a result will ensure our success and profitability, now and in the future.

The application of total quality dynamics begins with the Company. The commitment, leadership, involvement, and participation by the senior management team of an operation is essential to the attainment of Circle-4 Quality and to the realization of a quality system. In the next chapter, we'll talk about creating a quality culture which will support your quality goals.

SUMMARY

1. Our priorities for customer satisfaction are, in order of importance, the Shareholder, End-user, Employee, and Supplier.
2. The goals and requirements for our business are communicated to the operation through published policies and objectives.
3. Objectives must state the required measurable level of performance for a particular requirement over a specified period of time.
4. In order to enable Customer satisfaction, our policies and objectives must reflect the prioritized requirements of our Customer.
5. Circle-4 Quality is:
   a. The commitment to work in cooperation with the Circle-4 Customer in the pursuit of a profitable business.
   b. The consideration of the needs of the Circle-4 Customer in all business activities and decisions.
   c. The result of satisfying the prioritized requirements of the Circle-4 Customer.
6. Our commitment to Circle-4 Quality enables total quality business management.

Quality Applications

1. Using the Customer profiles created at the end of Chapter 3, create a set of annual objectives for your business unit.
2. Review and revise your objectives until you agree that they will enable an affirmative answer to all of the following Circle-4 Customer priorities:
   a. Can we meet Shareholder requirements, and support Shareholder goals?
   b. Can we create and produce a product that the End-user has defined and will purchase?
   c. Have we created an operation that allows the Employee to be successful, thus enabling End-user satisfaction?
   d. Have we created partnerships that permit the Supplier to prosper by continuously improving their response to our requirements?
3. How do your newly created objectives compare with past business objectives? Which set of objectives will enable greater success for the Company?
4. Publish your new business objectives and make sure they are well understood by all employees.

Quality Benefits

1. The objectives of the business unit now reflect a commitment to Circle-4 Quality.
2. The published objectives will direct business operations with the proper customer satisfaction priority and with a clear definition of your expected results.

5

DO WE PURSUE
A QUALITY PROGRAM
OR ESTABLISH
A QUALITY CULTURE?

Let's look at a basic organizational dynamic, the leadership dynamic. Any group of people with a common goal must work through some defined organization in order to focus diverse resources toward the result. Within an organization there exists recognized leadership, which is conferred either by organizational position, exceptional expertise, or individual excellence. In fact, our best leaders are correctly positioned within the organization as a result of their demonstrated excellence and expertise. The dynamics of the operation evolves and coalesces around the *perceived* leaders. It becomes apparent over time that all operations, regardless of business system performance, do "what's important to the boss," the boss being the perceived leaders in the organization. If the boss advocates a course of action contrary to policy, generally the policy gets changed or falls into disuse. This attitude is also supported through the perception of power and authority, which may sometimes differ from leadership. Poor leaders can be given power and authority. Although their abuses are eventually uncovered and corrected, they can wreak havoc on an operation. This recognition of leadership and power and the inherent tendency to do what's important to the boss exist as part of the dynamic of any organized group. As characteristics, they can be positive or negative and should be recognized as two of the necessary constraints of human interaction. Our recognition allows us to consider focusing these characteristics as we create our quality system. Given human tendency to identify, focus on, and satisfy our perceived leaders, let's use it in our favor. Let's deploy leaders who espouse our goals and our values, let's get them working toward our common objectives, and let's make sure we reflect their guidance and direction in our quality system documentation. Let's create leaders throughout the operation who understand the business and work in concert toward defined results.

Is the creation of leadership within our company a *program?* If a program is defined as a series of actions taken toward a specific goal, we would fail if we consider the creation of leadership within our company to be a program. First of all, I don't recall ever seeing or creating a company leadership goal. If you did think about making it a goal, how would you measure the result? What quantifies leadership? Leadership could be specified in our company policies, right? Perhaps, but again only if we quantify the means to assess the attainment of leadership. We can train our personnel in management and supervisory techniques, we can make sure they thoroughly understand our goals and requirements, and we can steer them in the direction of becoming leaders, but whether they ever achieve that status is up to each individual and is contingent upon the perception each creates in the minds of other employees. The sum of experience, the effect of a value system, and individual capabilities and limitations will influence the group perception and recognition of leadership.

Leadership is an example of something we need and desire within our company, but it's something that cannot be directed through company goals or policies. Instead, it is part of that nebulous concept known as the quality "culture." Leadership cannot be created through a program; neither can quality be created through a program. As an additional argument, managers often view programs as "things" that can be delegated. Leadership cannot be delegated, and quality cannot be delegated.

As we begin creating our quality system, we've discussed the need to fully define and understand our Circle-4 Customer and the need to create goals for the Company that strive to satisfy that Customer, in order of priority. We know that these goals and objectives will need to be communicated to the entire operation, in greater and greater detail. We also know that we will need to establish a system that measures our performance against our goals and objectives and that such a system must also have the capability for causing performance improvements. We can see the need for a defined type of behavior that will enhance and fuel our performance. Embodied in the general term *culture*, this desired behavior needs to be addressed by the Company with the intent of establishing a level playing field for success. And because it is creating the playing field, and is not an end or goal in itself, the idea of a quality culture needs to be specifically addressed outside of goals, objectives, and policies. It cannot be, and should not be, construed as a program. It is, instead, the continuous examination of who we are and who we want to become.

HOW TO DEFINE YOUR QUALITY CULTURE

If you do not specifically address the issue of company culture, then you'll live with the outcome of an unfocused agglomeration of values and ideals which reflect the behavior of the leaders that have the strength of personality to surface through the chaos. By merely identifying the company leadership, and by creating an organization that focuses power and responsibility on those identified individuals, you have taken the first step toward creating a culture. You've all participated in molding the culture of a company at least to this extent or you wouldn't currently be part of the management team, the Company. Acknowledging this reality, you can now choose to allow your company's quality culture to evolve in a free form, directed only by individual personalities, or you can be deliberate about your expectations and direction. Let's spend a few minutes describing the *ideal* culture from our perspective as the Company.

Certainly we desire a culture that supports the goals and objectives we've established. In light of our current paradigm, we would like a culture that understands, accepts, and pursues the satisfaction of our Circle-4 Customer. We want our operation to work as a team, with each player aware of their own role as well as those of the other players. We want decision making to be done on a widespread basis in our company, and we want those decisions to made as close to the source of the issue as possible, in order to ensure timeliness and accuracy. We want all our plans and decisions based on the prioritized requirements of the Customer. We encourage honesty and integrity in all business dealings and relationships, and we want an environment where customer satisfaction leads to personal success and rewards.

Establishing a Quality Philosophy

The culture that we envision can and should be formalized in a special policy document, the *Quality Philosophy*. Once you agree on the basic qualities and values that characterize the interaction of your employees with themselves and with your Customer, this agreement will be the cornerstone for operating your business. As such, it will serve as the qualitative standard for individual and group behavior. The leaders in your company will come to be those individuals who most completely embody and exemplify your quality philosophy. An example of such a quality philosophy statement is shown here.

SAMPLE QUALITY PHILOSOPHY

This Quality Philosophy is intended to describe the ideal behavior of our organization. It is our desire to use this document as a behavioral benchmark, realizing that it will take hard work and continuous improvement to fully achieve these traits.

- We take as our basic personal and operational goal the understanding and subsequent satisfaction of the needs of our internal and external Circle-4 Customers, Shareholders, End-users, Employees, and Suppliers.

- All of our employees understand how their work contributes to and impacts business results.
- All of our employees know who their customers are and have developed a partnership with those customers.
- All of our employees accept personal responsibility for rapid and relentless performance improvement.
- The leaders of the organization encourage all employees to take an active role in key issues that affect them.
- Our leaders continually reinforce the core mission of the Company.
- The cross-functional Quality Improvement Team structure of the organization encourages the interfaces required for business success.
- The organization is flexible and "product driven," not department or territory driven.
- All of our employees are involved in problem solving, decision making, planning, and implementation within their circle of influence.
- The values of our organization are well defined, frequently discussed, and widely understood by all employees.
- Key values:

  —The primary indicator of success is customer satisfaction.
  —Decisions will be made closest to the source of the issue.
  —There will be no unnecessary barriers which limit anyone's ability to make a contribution to the organization.
  —Constructive disagreement will be encouraged.
  —People will be rewarded for appropriate risk taking.
  —The customer will always be provided with the best value.
  —Information will be freely shared.

- Our employees are rewarded based on the skills and the work-related knowledge they possess and on their initiative to apply them to improving business.
- Our employees have and use a variety of skills and work effectively in multiple team functions within the organization. They focus on the "work to be done" as opposed to "their job."

- Openness, honesty, respect, and constructive feedback are highly regarded and are demonstrated by all Company employees.

HOW TO IMPLEMENT YOUR DEFINED QUALITY CULTURE

There is a second reason for documenting your quality philosophy. In addition to communicating your cultural and behavioral intent, your philosophy requires implementation and action, as would any other company policy. The implementation will be somewhat different from a tactical, operational policy. The results will not be seen through direct measurements, but rather through interpreting the entire set of performance measurements with which you manage your quality system. Once the quality philosophy has been established, the specific actions which must be taken in order to begin realizing your defined quality culture include:

1. Top management (the Company) commitment to creating a quality culture.
2. Total employee education/training utilizing a course designed to improve human interaction, relationships, and decision making in a business environment.
3. Basic total quality education for all employees, facilitated and administered by the Company.
4. Discussion and agreement on the need for identified Circle-4 Customers.
5. Participation in defining or redefining the quality system.
6. Implementation and/or improvement of quality system elements.
7. Ongoing education programs to improve all necessary business skills.
8. From measured performance, trend analysis for establishing proactive improvement activities designed to prevent, rather than detect, nonconformance to requirements.

This looks suspiciously like the framework of a plan to implement a quality system. It is, in fact, just that. The culture you create is the culmination of all the activity that occurs in the company. The goals you set, the organizational structure you establish, the products you develop, the values you promote and emphasize, and so on, serve to create your cultural foundation. Initially expressed as your quality philosophy, you must take deliberate and positive action to ensure realization of the behavior and interaction you've envisioned as the ideal business operating environment.

If we compare this preliminary action plan to the objectives of our company model from chapter 4, EWC, Inc., we see something missing from their objectives. No mention of a quality system, or a culture, or leadership, or anything. We have here an example of an instance where we, the Company, may want to establish a goal that has not been expressly stated by our Customer. In the context of EWC's mutual expectations, none of their customers has a reason to specifically require them to have a functional quality system. In real life, quite the opposite might exist. The advent of standards and registration for ISO-9000 is an example of the End-user requiring the Supplier to comply with a specific standard. The goal for a quality system may also come from the Shareholder, if you're a division of a larger business entity. It is your responsibility as the leaders of the operation to create additional goals that establish the capability for realizing customer satisfaction. EWC needs a measurable goal that supports the evolution of a customer-oriented culture and operation. Let's create an eighth objective for EWC:

> 8. During the budget period, spend 5 percent of available working hours, from a normal 40-hour week, training and educating our employees so they can define, implement, operate, and improve our quality system.

YOUR COMMITMENT TO CUSTOMER SATISFACTION

The commitment of time and money for training and educating our employees has an immediate cultural impact. Provided that we follow through and actually spend the time and money for training, the Company will be viewed as being serious about quality and as being committed to Customer satisfaction. I've seen companies with haphazard training programs where managers often ranked training below fire drills on their list of priorities. The employees in these companies are exposed to the management "program of the month," accompanied by a lot of hoopla and maybe some real intensive training up front. These programs gradually die from lack of nourishment, devoid of refresher training, skills improvement, and application to daily operations. If you elevate the importance of education and training and place it on your short list of company objectives, you've eliminated a major stumbling block and you've built the forms, so to speak, to "pour" the cultural foundation of your company. The real test of your commitment is the quality and completeness of the education and training you deliver.

Because consistent, high-quality education and training are essential to the establishment of a quality system and prerequisite to the emergence of any quality culture, let's explore education and training requirements in greater depth. The days of the uneducated laborer are long past. Some of us know with glaring familiarity the need to impart the basic skills of reading and writing to our workforce. Some of our workers need to be taught English, or we need to create a bilingual, or multilingual culture. Do we have any reason to believe, based on our experience, that our workers come to us *fully* prepared to function in the business community?

Consider teamwork, for example. Organized athletics is one of the few widespread programs in our public school system that fosters teamwork. In fact, the process of earning a high school diploma or a college degree is a process based on individual performance and recognition, at the exclusion of team performance. Do our new hires then come to us intuitively understanding teamwork? Not where I come from. The most we can expect is that new employees bring with them whatever they have learned about teamwork since leaving school. Given the variety of perspectives and backgrounds that exist among our employees, do we have an obligation to train them in the basics of the style of teamwork we want to prevail in our operation? Fundamental to teamwork are the skills required for people to interact in a structured or group envi-

self-management are important traits for today's team members. Self-management must precede group management.

Our company education and training program should start with instruction in the basic skills of human interaction, goal setting, problem solving, and teamwork. There are many good training courses and seminars available for this purpose. One that has been especially effective and rewarding is the *Seven Habits of Highly Effective People* created by Dr. Stephen R. Covey. In his program Dr. Covey creates the evolution of the individual from one of being dependent, through being independent, and arriving at interdependence. A sign of recognized interdependency is the ability to seek win/win relationships, which we defined in basic terms in chapter 1. Dr. Covey's ultimate expression of successful interdependency is "win/win or no deal," insistence on a mutually satisfying solution as the preferred basis for agreement.[4]

Whichever employee development program you select, you must ensure that all employees are trained, that you adopt the peculiar lexicon of the program into your company vocabulary, that you reinforce and utilize the principles taught during normal business operations, and that you schedule refresher training at least every 12 to 18 months.

Having established a basis for your personal interactions, you also need to train yourselves, and all your employees, in the basic philosophy of total quality and Circle-4 Quality, the structure and framework of the quality system that you envision, and the requirements and expectations you have of your Circle-4 Customer. This needs to be followed with training on the detailed policies, procedures, work instructions, and standards established for the company's quality system operation. You need to refresh this training on a periodic basis in order to reconfirm your commitment and revitalize the improvement process.

A complete training program needs to include consideration of production skills training, technology education/training, product training, and other education and training needs for specific roles and responsibilities. To ensure that you've created the coverage and

---

[4] Covey, Stephen, R., *The Seven Habits of Highly Effective People*, Simon & Schuster, 1989, p. 214.

content necessary, I suggest that you require specific training or proof of training for new hires and new promotions. The managers making up the Company have a responsibility to establish, improve, and participate in comprehensive employee education and training.

Creating a satisfactory quality culture is a never-ending process. Results can be seen in two to three years, if you're consistent and persistent. A quality culture is the final expression of your company goals, objectives, requirements, and values; it embodies what you are as a company. A culture cannot be forced into existence by policy, but it can be effectively steered and evolved through the resolute application of appropriate employee education and training. We'll talk about creating a framework for employee training as we discuss the quality information system in Part 2. Next, however, it's time to unfold a picture of the mechanics of our quality system and to identify those operational elements necessary for us to ensure total customer satisfaction.

SUMMARY

1. A company culture is created through the continuous examination of who we are and who we want to become.
2. Ideal behavior and values are presented in a quality philosophy document.
3. Commitment to extensive and ongoing employee education and training is required to realize the behavior and values expressed in the quality philosophy.
4. We must create a measurable business objective in support of our desire for a customer-oriented culture and business operation.

Quality Applications

1. Through an employee forum, create a Quality Philosophy that expresses the ideal behavior and values of your business.
2. Audit your company training program and implement

improvements to make it responsive to your commitment to Circle-4 Quality.
3. Define a business objective in support of your desired customer-oriented culture.

Quality Benefits

1. Through a well-defined quality philosophy, you have established the requisite control over the values and behavior of your employees.
2. A comprehensive program for employee education and training will permit you to establish the pace of change and improvement for your business.

Within the constraints of your business objectives, the more you spend on education and training, the faster the pace of improvement. I once had the experience of participating in an MRPII (Manufacturing Resources Planning) implementation for a manufacturing company. As part of the project team, we made sure that 90 percent of our employees received at least 40 hours worth of classroom instruction on MRPII and related topics. Our implementation was very successful, resulting in our operation realizing a "Class A" level of systems performance within two years of starting our project. It saddens me to say that within another four years, operating system performance was perhaps at the 70-percent to 80-percent or "Class C" level, at best. While it would be easy to point to corresponding changes in top management and a lack of commitment from those new managers, I can tell you with certainty that the real reason our operating system performance started degrading is because our original implementation plan failed to require and implement an ongoing employee education and training program. The lack of reinforcement through refresher training, together with a few completely untrained new executives, dealt a one-two punch to an excellent operating system which, to this day is only performing at an average level. Without an ongoing, committed effort to educate your employees, your improvement efforts will be doomed to failure

6

DEFINING THE
QUALITY SYSTEM

Circle-4 Quality is the consideration of the needs of the Circle-4 Customer in all business activities and decisions. Our commitment to Circle-4 Quality enables the deliberate application of total quality dynamics to create a system capable of sustaining and assuring Customer satisfaction.

We created a foundation for defining quality by developing an understanding of our Circle-4 Customer. Our Customer-based definition of quality will serve as the bedrock for building an operation tailored to Circle-4 Customer satisfaction. Throughout the remainder of this book we will construct that operation in detail, then we'll examine the process of moving our existing business into conformance with our new model. This chapter introduces you to the basic framework of the operation we're going to define.

When we examined the influence of the Circle-4 Customer on our business operation, we referred to our total business as the integrated business system (IBS). We recognize that we have a responsibility to meet the needs of the Circle-4 Customer, and we also recognize that we exert little actual control over three of the four influence groups. If we draw a boundary depicting the limits of our control, it would encompass the Company, the Employee, the IBS, and a portion of each of the Shareholder, the End-user, and the Supplier. This boundary defines the limits of the quality system. The significance of including a portion of our three external influence groups is that our quality system must extend into, and become part of, the relationships we create with these groups. Only by doing so may we begin to envision an environment that leads to true, mutually beneficial partnerships.

The quality system is comprised of three major operational elements the quality organization, the quality delivery system, and the quality information system. The *quality organization* (QO) represents the manner in which we deploy the resources for which we, the Company, take responsibility. The quality organization should focus on clearly identifying functional responsibility, including showing the specific interface points with the End-user, Supplier, and Shareholder. The QO must create and promote organizational empowerment through an operational network, should define the macro-processes of the business via company policy, and should ensure proper control of all quality (business) documentation. Company policies link the quality organization with the quality delivery system and the quality information system.

The *quality delivery system* (QDS) encompasses those interactive processes commonly associated with the conversion of raw material to finished product. With its structure determined by the product documentation, the QDS also includes the necessary elements of product quality, process definition and integration, and process execution and control. The traditional elements of quality assurance as well as the new cultural concepts of Circle-4 Customer relationships are all within the bounds of the QDS. The output of the QDS is the delivery of products that satisfy customer requirements and the infusion of performance information into the quality information system.

The *quality information system* (QIS) is the component of the quality system that has been dealt with superficially, if not ignored, by many practitioners of total quality. With the goal of establishing a formal, consistent flow of information, the QIS requires the creation of a communications network consisting of four paths. Those

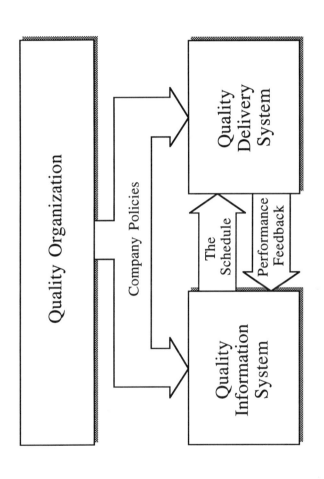

Figure 6.1 Primary links integrating the three major elements of the Quality System

paths are *communicating objectives, performance feedback, recognition, and simulation,* and *customer feedback.* Once the paths are established, and the flow of information is fueled via the decision-making process, the ability exists to continuously improve the entire quality system. Without a formal, structured information system, Circle-4 Quality and continuous improvement become fragmented and compartmentalized.

The end result of communicating objectives is the *Schedule.* The schedule acts as the operational bridge between the QIS and the QDS. The Schedule can be thought of as the four-dimensional representation of the Company's objectives: product, quantity, cost, and time. The Schedule is comprised of all the plans and schedules used to run the business.

The three major elements are shown in Figure 6.1 with the primary functional links that bind them together into an integrated quality system.

The quality system resulting from the creation of a quality organization, quality delivery system, and quality information system may have a different look and feel from one business to the next. The unique characteristics of your quality system will come from the collective requirements and necessary constraints established by your Circle-4 Customer. Building a functional quality system will enable you to achieve lasting customer satisfaction, the realization of Circle-4 Quality.

SUMMARY

1. The quality system includes the quality organization, quality delivery system, and quality information system.
2. The quality organization establishes functional responsibilities, macro-business processes, and an operational network and provides control of business documentation.
3. The quality delivery system encompasses all operational elements for product documentation, product quality, process definition, and process control and improvement.

4. The quality information system structures the flow of company information into four pathways: communicating objectives, performance feedback, recognition and simulation, and customer feedback.

5. The schedule acts as the operational bridge between the information system and the delivery system and includes all the plans and schedules used to run the business.

7

STRUCTURING AN EFFECTIVE QUALITY ORGANIZATION

In examining the requirements for creating a quality organization (QO), we won't dwell on specific organizational schemes which may be advocated by focused management strategies, such as matrix management. Instead, we will establish the characteristics of a complete and functional QO. The exact groupings and interrelationships of your employees is a matter best left to each individual company and management team.

The quality organization must answer the question, "How are we going to fulfill our responsibilities?" The answer to this question needs to include not only our hierarchical structure, but also the salient characteristics of our operation, established as necessary constraints by the Customer. The primary characteristics we want to be sure to include in a defined quality organization are:

1. established functional responsibility,
2. macro definition of business processes,
3. implementation of an operational network; and
4. formalization of the business operation through quality documentation and control.

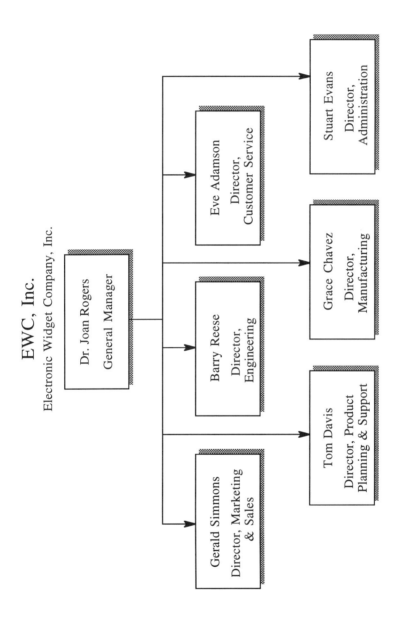

Figure 7.1 Organization for company model.

We have looked at the total business chain within the context of the integrated business system. The total business chain represents those functions necessary to create, produce, and deliver our product or service to the End-user. The major categories we've identified within this chain are *marketing, research, development, purchasing, production, selling, distribution,* and *service.* Your company may include all of these, or only a portion of them, particularly if you operate within a larger corporate entity. The important point is to understand the limits of responsibility given to the Company and to ensure that you have adequate coverage for those responsibilities in your organization. Once you understand your responsibilities, you need to determine how to structure your departments and your management team to create the most efficient operation. This structure is often based on process similarity. Some companies, for example, may extract elements from purchasing and production and combine them into a materials or logistics department. If the operation is large enough, production itself may be subdivided into different departments based on process or product segmentation. The manner in which you decide to cover your responsibilities will be affected by your product, volume, and process requirements.

In our company model, EWC, Inc., we have created a traditional management structure. Marketing and sales, product planning and support, engineering, manufacturing, and customer service cover all the elements of the business system (see Figure 7.1). Administration is added as a necessary function for finance, human resources, and facilities support services.

ASSIGNING FUNCTIONAL RESPONSIBILITIES

Once the general segmentation of functionality is determined, the Company needs to spend some amount of time verbalizing the major responsibilities within each established function. One method of doing this is to conduct an informal discussion and talk a product through its creation, production, sales, delivery, and support. As each step of the process is identified, it should be given to one of the established functions. This is an important exercise for the management team to undertake, because it allows macro-processes to be defined and it also identifies processes which could logically fit under more than one function. For example, which function in the organization should be responsible for the engineering change process? We can create valid, logical arguments for either engineering or product planning and support (product management) in to our company model. When such cases arise, an agreement needs to be reached that clearly establishes the functional responsibility. All Company managers need to commit to the decisions made in these instances in order for the agreement to be considered complete. Well-established companies should consider repeating this same exercise every one or two years. The approach should be, "Let's review our assigned functional responsibilities to see if we can envision any operational efficiencies by changing our structure or shifting responsibilities." This type of regular review is a part of the Company's ongoing responsibility for continuous improvement. Your discussions should be open and honest in portraying the strengths and weaknesses of the interactions that you've created throughout your organization.

You'll notice that our company model does not contain an identified quality department. I hope all of you are comfortable with that. If you're sincere in your commitment to Circle-4 Quality, to create a quality system, and to ensure customer satisfaction, the necessary requirements to create that satisfaction must be built into the responsibility and objectives of each department and each employee, and not enabled through a specific quality department.

The Proper Role of Job Descriptions

By what means should we document and communicate our defined functional responsibilities? A good number of companies put great stock in job descriptions, particularly with the recent enactment of the Americans with Disabilities Act (ADA), which requires employers to include mental and physical requirements within each job description. This seems like an appropriate time to properly categorize job descriptions within our quality system. Job descriptions should be created and used only for the purpose of hiring new employees or determining qualifications for promotion. Job descriptions define the characteristics desired of the ideal candidate for a particular position. Those characteristics may sometimes be couched in terms of "will be responsible for," but this responsibility will be expressed in general terms, not in specifics. Because job descriptions define desired capabilities, they may be used to help create goals for employees desiring promotion in a certain direction. Job descriptions represent the necessary qualifications for an individual, whereas the definition of functional job responsibilities focuses on the characteristics of the function, not the person.

Job descriptions should only be used in the hiring and promotional processes. Outside of these areas, they're relatively useless in helping you create your quality organization. Functional job responsibilities, if defined through separate, discrete documents, are also relatively useless. The appropriate means of documenting and communicating functional job responsibilities is through the approved policies of the company. Job responsibilities take on significance only within the context of your defined organization and assigned functionality. In light of your commitment to customer satisfaction, a stand-alone definition of job responsibility has no relevance. Everyone needs to understand their responsibilities within the interactive business processes, which must be defined through company policy.

MANDATING MAJOR PROCESS CHARACTERISTICS

Once the management team has agreed to, and documented, major functional responsibilities, you have established yourselves as the Company. That is to say, you've created a hierarchal framework that places the management team in the position of running the business unit. Next, you need to define the business processes you will use to carry out your responsibilities. As previously noted, this identification may be facilitated through a "conference room operation," wherein you talk your way step by step through the entire business process, in order to ensure coverage of responsibilities. Accepted practices for internal processes should be defined, in order to establish a foundation for the quality delivery system. Clearly mandating major process characteristics is your responsibility and should be done to support the requirements of your Circle-4 Customer. For example, "We will use MRP (material requirements planning) to develop our production schedules," "We will use JIT (Just-In-Time) to create optimum factory execution," or "The basis for our quality system will be Circle-4 Quality." External standards and practices you need to meet should also be identified, such as ISO-9000 certification, UL or CSA product safety approval, FCC emissions standards, EEOC guidelines and so on. The proper place to document and communicate this macro-characterization of your business processes is also through your company policies.

HORIZONTAL COMMUNICATIONS: ESTABLISHING NETWORKS

The third characteristic of a quality organization is the implementation of an operational network that answers the question, "How will we manage our operation?" You've created functional responsibilities and specified how your major processes will look. Now you need to add the choreography—you need to tell your employees how you want them to behave. An operational network adds to your foundation and supports the company culture you wish to create. A quality policy, quality philosophy, and statements of values and ethics are all examples of the type of policies that begin to create an operational network. The Company should also agree on guidelines for the delegation of responsibility and authority throughout the operation. These guidelines should be documented and applied fairly in order to facilitate organizational empowerment. Your assigned functional responsibilities and defined macro-processes will create logical lines of communication which should be identified, documented, and nurtured. Process-oriented communication is more effective than the "chain of command," as it puts the experts face to face, creating a network. Special attention should be paid to the construction of horizontal communications in your organizations: it's more effective and it gets your experts together, but it must be accompanied by empowered decision making if it's to be effective.

Implementing Effective Decision Making

Decision making is one of the reasons managers exist, right? You'll be more successful if you shift your paradigm and consider that decision making is one of the reasons your *employees* exist. The need for a decision comes from a disturbance in a defined process. If there were never any process disturbances, we'd all happily execute our assignments without ever having to make any decisions. If your quality system is thoroughly defined and implemented, the total number of decisions required on a daily basis will be significantly less than in an operation with poorly documented processes. All decisions, regardless of the disturbance, tend to become more critical with the passage of time. Let's look at an example. An out-of-spec component stops the production line. The line supervisor identifies a lot problem and prepares a requisition to pull correct parts from another lot. The search for the manager's approval signature on the requisition takes over an hour, since the manager is away visiting a customer site. The resulting work stoppage cost the company $36,000.00 in profit for the day. At a competitor's company, a similar disturbance occurred. In this case, the line supervisor had the responsibility to authorize the replacement parts. The line made up the five-minute line stoppage by the end of the day, maintaining daily profitability.

Some decisions take a longer time than others to escalate to criticality, but eventually they all do. Unfortunately, this phenomenon fuels the erroneous view of a few managers that they need to make all the decisions, because they're all so critical. The real lesson is that decisions need to be made as soon as possible after the disturbance and as close as possible to the disturbance in order to minimize cost to the operation. Decision accuracy must also be considered when empowering employees. It's easy to demonstrate that decisions made closest to the disturbance are the most accurate. From our previous example, imagine an alarm ringing in the vice president of manufacturing's office whenever the line stopped. His meetings interrupted, he storms out to the line, listens to the line supervisor's litany on the component specs, commiserates with the technicians, who have run out of work, then tells everyone to use the part as is—it's worked before, it'll work again. Probably not the most accurate decision that could have been made—we'll know the real impact when all the rework comes back from test tomorrow! Had it been made by the line supervisor, the decision would have benefited from real-time knowledge and experience. I don't want to interfere with the delegation of authority and responsibility within your companies, but let me suggest that you try to create an environment for accurate decision making as close to the disturbance as possible. You need to constrain yourselves to those decisions wherein you truly add value to resolving the disturbance.

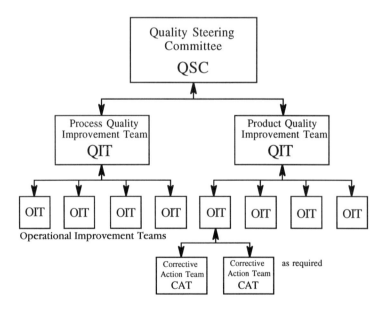

Figure 7.2 Total quality network for EWC, Inc.

How to Maintain a Functional Network

As you begin to create your operational network, you will want to document routine committees, groups, and meetings that need to occur in order to maintain functional communications and operations. There is much to be said for building a network around a total quality structure that encompasses all these interactions. The total quality network used by our model, EWC, Inc., is shown in Figure 7.2.

This network is used by EWC to manage its business. The quality steering committee is the management team, what we've called the Company. They meet routinely to review performance to objectives and to monitor improvement projects. The quality improvement teams are chaired by members of the QSC, creating organizational linkage and responsibility. Both lower-level management as well as QSC members sit on the QITs. The process QIT is concerned with all the objectives and improvement projects for the processes of the business. The product QIT deals with new product creation, management of current products and product support. Both the QITs and the QSC are standing teams, with a documented charter and membership.

The operational improvement teams are also standing teams, with rotating membership. OITs represent smaller segments of the charter of their parent QIT. Linkage is maintained by having QIT members chair the defined teams. In our example, we may have OITs for new product analysis, product applications, product marketing, and configuration management branching out from the product QIT. As branches from the process QIT, we might see OITs for material control, production planning, customer order management, and engineering support. All OITs are cross-functional groups with assigned improvement responsibilities that tie to their functional responsibilities. The decision-making employees responsible for the performance and results of a process represent that process on the OITs. If an OIT decides to investigate a segment of their collective processes, they may involve additional employees by forming a corrective action team. A CAT is constituted for a specific length of time in order to satisfy specific objectives. Each CAT is chaired by an OIT member who makes regular status reports to the OIT.

All meetings are steered by an agenda and are summarized with published minutes. Members of a given team are considered equals during their consideration and pursuit of improving performance to objectives. The entire total-quality network is tied together with a reporting and feedback structure that allows communication of objectives, performance reporting, recognition and simulation, and customer feedback.

USING CUSTOMER-ORIENTED CONTROL TO MAXIMIZE FLEXIBILITY

All of the required analysis and definition we've identified so far for the quality organization cannot be created in one meeting, nor should it be. You should remember to consider the other elements of the quality system, because the quality organization is tightly interwoven with the quality information system and the quality delivery system. The creation of the quality organization will take place over time, following the familiar path of continuous improvement. For this reason, all your decisions regarding functional responsibilities, process definition, and operational networks need to be documented. Further, that documentation must be controlled so that you can be sure it reflects reality.

Let's talk about control for a minute. When some of us think of control, we envision a regimented structure, the very antithesis of flexibility. We believe that controls must be loosened in order to promote agile, efficient reactions to market requirements. Consider for a moment that controls need to be changed, but not necessarily loosened. The fundamental reason for exerting control over a process is to guarantee consistency. "If I want something done right, I'll have to do it myself!" is a time-worn phrase that's driven by the desire for consistency. If we can create consistency through regimented, autocratic control, why can't we create consistent flexibility through realistic, customer-oriented control? Flexibility is characterized by rapid delivery and high quality. End-users are often willing to pay for short leadtime, but not at the expense of quality. The winner of the race will be the company that can maximize flexibility while improving product quality. While we can certainly create rapid delivery through inventory, we all know the evils of having too much inventory. In addition, we'd be restricted in satisfying any special customer requirements. Excess inventory is a very poor quality route to rapid delivery.

Let's expand on our insight of a few moments ago when we concluded that the fastest and most accurate decisions in our business are those that are made closest to the process disturbance. If you mandate that decision making must be assigned and delegated to operational employees, you reduce the overhead associated with chain-of-command decision making. Taken right down to the individual employee, empowered decision making will put the operation into high gear with no loss of quality. In fact, you now have an army of informed, involved decision makers who also have the responsibility for improving the processes they own. Part 2 of this book will discuss how you can maintain control, no, how you can have more control over the operation through established objectives.

Documenting Your Network

By documenting the flexible, empowered operational network you've created, you have the ability to train new employees and to audit yourselves routinely to see that you're still doing it the way you said you would do it. Quality documentation and control encompass the documentation, control, and communication of all essential business operations. Documentation should include, but is not limited to, policies, procedures, work instructions, workmanship standards, product documentation, financial records, customer records, and quality records of the operation. Directed through company policy, your documentation system must allow easy, controlled updating of these documents and must ensure that only the most recent, authorized versions are available for operational use.

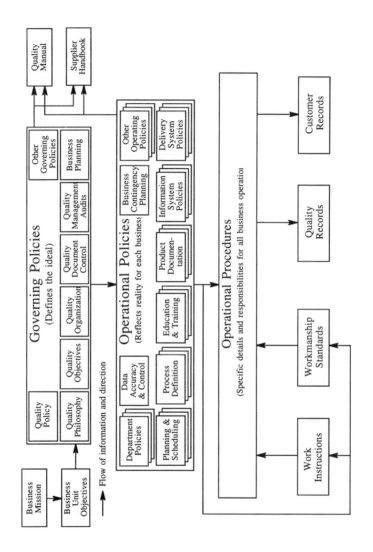

Figure 7.3 Generic quality documentation relationship

The ISO-9000 standard (ANSI/ASQC Q91-1987) provides an excellent framework for creating a quality documentation and control system.

Figure 7.3 illustrates the content and relationships for generic quality documentation. Policies and procedures form the central core of quality documentation. Policies define what must be done and identify functional responsibility. Policies can be either governing or operational. Governing policies serve as the baseline, or standard, for the business and describe the ideal world. The content of governing policies is determined by the business mission, business unit objectives, nature of the company's products and services, and by the experience and expertise of the Company. Typical governing policies are shown and include the quality policy, the business planning policy, and the quality document control policy. Once established and approved, this group of policies will change very slowly, following the evolution of the business mission and objectives.

Operational policies also define what must be done and identify functional responsibility. Nevertheless, operational policies must reflect the current reality of the business. This group of policies will change at a faster pace, following the improvement activities of the business. They are directed in all cases by the governing policies, though not necessarily on a one-to-one basis. For example, the governing quality policy may direct, in part, that each major department is responsible for establishing an employee education/training program and that the human resources department is responsible for maintaining training records for all employees. If the major departments are manufacturing, engineering, and administration, then each of these departments will create an operational policy identifying what is currently being done for employee education/training and which functions are responsible. Human resources will create an operational policy for training records, resulting in a total of four operational policies directed by one portion of the governing policy. Initially, if an operational policy does not fully meet the intent of the governing policy, there is a visible indication of needed improvement. As improvements are made, operational policies are updated until a quality audit confirms that they accurately reflect the intent and direction of their governing policy.

A similar relationship exists between operational policies and operational procedures. Procedures define how a process is to be executed. They must reflect the current reality of the operation and will change much more rapidly than either policy group as continuous improvement activities begin to take place in the business. The accuracy of operational procedures is always assessed against both actual operations and the direction provided by the operational policy.

Other elements of quality documentation as shown in Figure 7.3 include the quality manual and supplier handbook, which are extracted from appropriate business policies. Work instructions and workmanship standards are special documents which describe in great detail how repetitive processes are to be executed and the expected quality of the involved workmanship. Quality records and customer records may include any defined business records which must be accurate, controlled, and retained for a specific length of time.

The portion of the documentation system that most directly concerns the quality organization are the governing and operational policies. Governing policies should follow the established structure of the business unit, and must reflect your decisions for functional responsibility, macro-process definition, and operational networking. They must direct the creation of operational policies, in order to define the QO in greater detail. Policies may be defined with a required format, something which should be decided by each individual business. Appendix 2 contains some policy examples from our company model.

In this chapter we talked about creating a quality organization, thoroughly documented and controlled, which reflects the Company direction for functional responsibilities, definition of macro-processes, and creation of an operational network. This organization will allow us to flex and improve in response to the requirements of our Circle-4 Customer. It will provide us with the basis for creating a culture of involved, satisfied employees who will recognize and address the needs of the Supplier, End-user and Shareholder. A quality organization will permit the realization of efficient, value-added processes and consistently high-quality products, allowing all of us to "make more money now and in the future."

In Part 2 of *The Quality-Empowered Business,* we will turn our attention to the second major component of the quality system, the quality information system. Now that we've built our machine, so to speak, we've got to give it some fuel. We've created our structure, defined our processes, and decided how we're going to behave and how we've going to relate to one another. Now we have to get our operation into action by telling it how much to build, how fast to build it, and how much it should cost. Exactly what to build, the product, will enter the picture in Part 3, when we discuss the quality delivery system.

SUMMARY

1. The quality organization answers the question, "How are we going to fulfill our responsibilities?" and includes functional responsibilities, macro-definitions of business processes, a defined operational network, and control of quality documentation.
2. All elements of the quality organization are documented and communicated through company policies.
3. Job descriptions are useful only as guidelines for hiring and promotions.
4. The steps necessary to determine functional responsibility include:
   a. Outline all requisite business functions, from product/service creation through and including after-sales support and customer service.
   b. Assign each function to a member of the management team.
   c. Document the assignments within company policies written to direct the mission of each major company department.
5. Once identified, requisite business functions must be given specific, macro-characteristics based on Company direction.

These descriptive characteristics are also included within the policies that direct the mission of major departments.

6. Accurate decisions are those which are made as close to the disturbance as possible.

7. An operational network that maximizes horizontal communication and local decision making throughout the business process must be formally defined.

8. Consistent execution of business processes enables quality. Control of quality (business) documentation enables consistent process execution and permits process flexibility.

9. Documentation must be controlled to ensure the following:
   a. Use of only the most current version.
   b. Accurate and timely incorporation of revisions.
   c. Formal authorization and approval.

Quality Applications

1. Create a detailed flowchart of your business by talking a typical product or service through its life cycle. Using the flowchart, answer the following questions and take appropriate action to formalize your quality organization:
   a. Are all major functions assigned to a member of the management team (the Company)?
   b. Does your current organization chart accurately reflect the management teams' assignments?
   c. Have you identified the characteristics of each major function or process (for example, "Production scheduling will be accomplished using MRP software XYZ.")?
   d. Do your company policies clearly communicate the assignment and characteristics of major processes and functions?

2. Beginning with the flowchart created above, discuss how your business actually operates today. Focus on how requirements are communicated, both within and among departments, and on how problems are dealt with and decisions made. Answer the following questions and take appropriate action to begin to optimize your operational network:

    a. Is horizontal communication between processes and departments encouraged and fostered rather than chain-of-command communication?

    b. Do teams or groups meet on a routine basis to monitor and manage the interface points between major processes and functions? Are these teams aware of their "customer-supplier" roles within the business?

    c. Do the employees responsible for specific processes routinely make decisions to quell disturbances within that process? How are those decisions communicated?

    d. What are your overhead performance baselines? How long does it take to schedule delivery of a customer order? Change the production schedule? Requisition material? Create an invoice? Close a fiscal period?

    e. Is the manner in which you communicate, solve problems, make decisions, and operate the business reflected in your company policies and procedures?

3. Review the means by which you create, maintain, update, and control company policies, procedures and other business documentation. Answer the following questions and take appropriate action to improve your quality document control:

    a. Have you defined in detail what company documents will be controlled?

    b. Is there a clearly defined process for creating, updating, and distributing those controlled documents?

    c. Is there a document review and approval process prior to publication or revision?

    d. Does your documentation accurately reflect the business, and do your employees access and use that documentation?

Quality Benefits

1. Beginning to create a formal quality organization allows the Company to pursue Circle-4 Quality in the most rapid and efficient manner: by ensuring control and visibility over the basic definitions of business operations.

2. Formal control of company documentation will permit rapid and controlled changes and updates to that documentation which will be necessary in the evolution of a complete quality *system.*

In an example from my professional experience, when we dusted off our quality documentation system several years ago, the management team gravitated toward two main points of discussion. First, how could we restructure the system so that company policies didn't become outdated and ignored, as was the current situation? Second, was it more accurate and valid for operational policies to reflect reality or to reflect the ideal intentions of the governing policy? We resolved the first issue fairly quickly by requiring that each policy have an expiration date. The expiration date was automatically set for one year after the last date of issue or revision. Upon expiration, the authorizing manager reviewed the policy for accuracy, made any required changes, and approved the policy for reissue.

The second issue took longer to resolve since the management team was evenly divided in opinion. We decided to run a test case and issued several operational policies which reflected the ideal, with instructions to the process owners to use the policies to develop their operational procedures. After a month, we discovered that operational procedures had indeed been written to satisfy the intent of the policies, but that both policies and procedures were not being used, and instead were collecting dust in a file cabinet. The process owners informed us that, in their ideal state, the documents were unusable because they did not represent how things were actually being done. When we reversed our test case and allowed operational policies and procedures to reflect the reality of the business, we discovered that the documents were used consistently and were updated routinely as process improvements were implemented. We succeeded in proving to ourselves that operational documentation must reflect reality if we expect our employees to use it and keep it current.

PART 2

DEFINING A CLOSED-LOOP QUALITY INFORMATION SYSTEM

8

UNDERSTANDING THE RELATIONSHIP BETWEEN INFORMATION, DATA AND DECISION MAKING

Our businesses are drowning in data. I spent several years managing a business unit which delivered about $25M in electronics equipment annually. We dealt with an average of 50 customer orders each week. Those orders specified equipment configurations from a selection of over 600 various features and options. The forecast for the features and options pulled an average of 500 work orders through the factory each month. The requisite subassemblies required MRP to process in excess of 1,500 manufactured items on a weekly basis. Component purchasing extracted 15,000 active components from a database containing over 52,000 part numbers. Can you envision the size and breadth of the reports that were available just to manage production planning and factory scheduling? If so, it's easy for you to understand why most of the reports went unread straight into the recycling barrel and why most of the data passed into obscurity, unseen by human eyes.

What is *data?* What is *information?* How are they different? In *The Haystack Syndrome,* Dr. E. M. Goldratt eloquently describes the difference and puts both data and information in their proper perspective within the business system. Data are raw material, a collection, or string, of characters that describes something about our reality. Information can be data, depending on who's looking at it. For an engineer, the scheduled delivery date on a customer order is data, to the customer, the scheduled delivery date is information. According to Dr. Goldratt, "Intuitively we understand information to be that portion of the data which impacts our actions, or if missing or not available will impact our actions."[5] One person's data may be another person's information. Throughout our lives, our actions are governed by decisions, decisions we make ourselves or decisions that are made for us. When we reach a decision point, a point where a choice is required to maintain forward momentum, we look for data that are useful in helping us reach our decision. Useful or required data can help us answer questions about the options we're facing.

Using Data to Make Accurate Decisions

For example, I want to reduce my personal operating expenses, so I decide to investigate riding the bus to work. If I can be convinced that it's just as fast, just as convenient, and it costs less than driving alone, then I'll try taking the bus. In order to get the right data to make my decision, I'll ask the following questions:

1. What are the bus schedules from my home to my workplace?
2. How many times do I have to transfer during the 32-mile round trip?
3. How long will it take, compared to driving myself?
4. How much will it cost compared to gas/oil for my car?

Once I get the data required to answer these questions, I can deduce whether or not taking the bus satisfies my requirements. Because I want my deduction and consequently my decision to be accurate, I've made my data requests very specific. I've also identified my expectations: convenience, time, and cost. The first two questions address convenience, the third time, and the fourth cost. Once I receive the data, I'll begin the process of assessing the impact of deciding to ride the bus. If I'm satisfied that it's no real

[5] Goldratt, Eliyahu M., *The Haystack Syndrome*, North River Press, 1990, p. 4.

inconvenience, costs less, and only takes 10 minutes more than my normal drive time, I may decide to give it a try. If the decision appears inconclusive, I may ask for more data or I may consult with someone who's riding the bus.

OK, I've decided to give it a try. At this point I'm only about halfway through the process of extracting information from data through decision making. Based on the data given me by the bus company, I've decided to become a customer for their service. As a customer I now have to confirm, or disconfirm, my decision through my own experience. If the bus company performs to my expectations, then I've confirmed my decision and verified the accuracy of the information I was given. If they don't perform as advertised, then I've reached a corrective action decision point. Do I change my expectations, reverse my decision, or try and get them to improve their service? My experience will provide the conclusive evidence at this point. My decision will be based on the severity of their nonperformance and the ease with which I can pursue alternatives. The process I've gone through in total provides the body of information to answer my initial question, "Should I ride the bus to work?" So, if data are a collection of symbols that defines something about our reality, and if it can only become information through a decision process, it stands to reason that information can be defined as the answer to the initial question asked.

As soon as we realize that information is the answer to the question asked, we begin to see information in its proper perspective relative to data. As Dr. Goldratt explains, "The minute we define information as the answer to the question asked, it means that information is not the input to the decision process, it is the output of the decision process." Data extracted and processed via the decision-making process becomes information.

Defining Basic Information System

If data become information through the process of making decisions, it follows logically that information cannot exist without decisions. If we want to create a useful information system, it must include a useful decision process. If we want accurate, timely, and useful information, we need accurate, timely, and useful decision making. Accurate, timely, and useful decision making is possible only through accurate, timely, and useful data.

What we've constructed through the bus example is a decision-making process that constitutes a basic information system. If we review the process in general terms, we can derive the following steps:

1. Establish the need to make a decision.
2. Identify alternatives based on existing constraints.
3. Determine expectations for the desired outcome.
4. Request data with specifically worded questions.
5. Convert received data into information through deductive reasoning.
6. Determine course of action.
7. Confirm decision and information accuracy through experience.
8. Determine required corrective action.

Let's see if we can apply these rules within the context of our business operations. Given normal, ongoing business operations, the need to make a decision usually arises from a disturbance within a process. These disturbances can be called constraints, bottlenecks which measurably deter the outcome of a process. Constraints have the same affect on both serial and parallel processes. The eventual outcome of the process is limited by the performance of the constraint. If the performance of the constraint is poor enough, the need for a decision arises. Companies with *reactive* business systems wait until the disturbance is manifested physically, then make decisions for corrective action. *Proactive* quality systems routinely analyze process performance, looking for trends that could escalate into constraints, and take preemptive action to prevent their occurrence. Our goal is to develop a proactive information system.

When our business system discovers a constraint requiring a decision, the next step is to brainstorm alternative courses of action to quell the disturbance and relieve the constraint. These alternatives become the apparent choices we'll have when we make our decision. We begin to assess our alternatives by first weighing them against our expectations. Every process has a Customer (Shareholder [boss], Employee, Supplier, and End-user). What are their collective expectations regarding the outcome of our process? Which of our alternatives will allow improvement toward satisfying those expectations? We know enough at this point to request specific data that will allow us to fully characterize the constraint in comparison to the expectations of our Customer. Our questions must require evidence of performance against the defined requirement.

Once we've collected the evidence, deductive reasoning will inform us of how much improvement is required to satisfy the requirements, and at what cost. We will select the alternative that offers the most acceptable outcome to the Customer. The best quality systems will simulate the decision before putting it into practice, perhaps using one of the many operational software models available today. Simulation can reduce the risk of a decision or it can safely permit analysis of very creative alternatives before a final decision is implemented. The true test of our final decision is through its implementation, followed by performance measurement and customer feedback. Negative results or feedback necessitate additional analysis and corrective action. This process continues and becomes an iterative cycle of improvement, provided that customer requirements are kept in clear focus.

IDENTIFYING BASIC ELEMENTS OF YOUR QUALITY INFORMATION SYSTEM

Our basic information system is tailored to an identified process. We need to make some slight modifications in order for it to apply generally across the quality system. If we change our entry point into the cycle so that customer requirements come first, and if we group our process steps into four general categories, we can arrive at the following road map for our company information system:

1. Communicate objectives.
   a. Determine customer expectations and formulate business unit objectives.
   b. Translate objectives into the requirements for process performance based on quality system constraints.
   c. Communicate performance objectives throughout the organization.
   d. Request data with specifically worded questions.
2. Generate performance feedback.
   a. Convert process performance data into information through calculation and deductive reasoning.
   b. Confirm previous decision and information accuracy through experience, simulation, trend analysis, and comparison to the objective.
   c. Establish the need to make new decisions.
   d. Identify alternatives based on existing constraints and objectives.
   e. Decide course of action.
   f. Report performance and corrective action decisions.
3. Provide recognition and request simulation.
   a. Advise Customer of performance results.
   b. Demonstrate support for actual performance and improvement decisions.
   c. Suggest possible future improvements.
   d. Request feedback for suggestions and ability to consistently meet existing objectives.
4. Accept and process customer feedback.
   a. Analyze feedback for suggested improvements.
   b. Analyze trends and feedback for existing objectives.
   c. Determine any changes necessary to business unit objectives.

You'll notice we've also changed the order of some of the steps. This was done in order to create a proactive, rather than reactive, process. Our goal is to create an information system that can anticipate and prevent system constraints as well as establish corrective action for the disturbances that do occur.

The four categories we've created form the basic elements of our quality information system (see Figure 8.1). The QIS depends on well-documented, structured processes in order to create accurate data, leading to accurate information. Beginning with business unit objectives, communicating objectives takes place throughout the operation, moving through the department level down to the individual employee or work team and culminating in the detail of the businesses plans and schedules. Process execution creates performance feedback, which travels back up through the organization and is reported as performance against objectives at each level until the Company reports against business unit objectives. The Company has the responsibility of initiating recognition of performance and requesting simulation for potential performance improvements. Recognition fosters ownership among the Circle-4

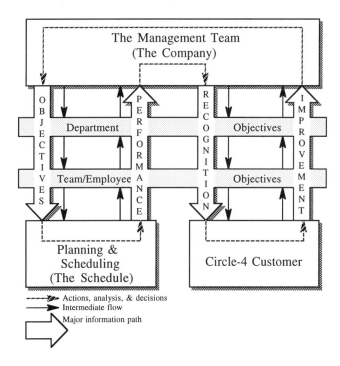

Figure 8.1 QIS information flow.

Customer, which enables true customer feedback of improvement ideas. The cycle is completed as customer feedback is used to validate and improve business unit objectives by the Company. Establishing and maintaining the flow of information throughout the system is realized through decision making. Each of the four categories will be explored in detail in following chapters. In Chapter 9, we'll formalize decision making and explain how objectives are translated down through the organization. Before we do that, let's expand our overview and describe the four elements of the QIS from the point of view of the Company, within the quality system.

BEGINNING THE INFORMATION CYCLE

When we created our quality organization, we assigned functional responsibilities, defined our macro-processes, created an operational network of empowered employees, and ensured the control of our documentation. Now we begin to tell our organization *what* we expect them to do. When we communicate objectives, we start with the requirements of our Circle-4 Customer and we create a list of results which would satisfy those requirements. This list of results, or objectives, should be *complementary* in nature, and it should provide for quantitative measurement. We translate these objectives throughout our operation by first identifying the constraints which exist in our defined processes. We then calculate the performance required from each constraint if we're to meet our business unit objectives. The constraint and its required level of performance are expressed as departmental objectives or work group objectives. At each level, decisions are made so that operations and processes are structured to satisfy that objective.

The culmination of translating objectives through the operation is the Schedule. The schedule provides the fuel for the quality delivery system. Most of the constraints we'll measure will be within the QDS, and most will involve measuring either products themselves, or measuring the planning and execution of the schedule.

Schedule execution creates a flow of information back into the

QIS, performance feedback. Data are collected for actual constraint performance, then compared against expectations. Any deviation creates the need for a corrective action decision. Alternatives are identified, supporting data collected, simulation conducted, and the decision made. A regular report sent up through the operational network includes performance results, supporting evidence, and improvement decisions. At each objective level, lower-level results are consolidated in order to report against own objectives up to the next level. Lower-level results may be requested or included as supporting evidence. When performance feedback reaches the Company, an assessment is made against overall business unit objectives.

If we want to confirm correct behavior and communicate overall business results, recognition is a necessity. Consisting of a series of nested loops, recognition must be given from each objective level back down to its supporting levels and employees. Recognition may include rewards, and special accomplishments may be elevated to Company-level recognition. Recognition should be accompanied by request for simulation: "what-if" questions that refresh the change process, keep people thinking in terms of change, and point out weak or potentially weak areas of the process as seen from a broader perspective. Recognition and simulation are done, within context, for all four major customer groups.

The customer feedback we receive as the Company is required data for planning our future. We will examine the feedback in light of future business alternatives and use it to determine how to improve our goals and business unit objectives. Understanding the evolving expectations of the Customer will allow us to begin the information cycle again, completing our quality information system.

SUMMARY

1. Data are a collection of symbols that describe something about our reality.
2. Data become information through the process of making decisions.

3. Accurate, timely, and useful decision making is possible only through accurate, timely, and useful data.
4. Decision making creates a flow of information.
5. The quality information system consists of four structured flows of information:
    a. Communicate objectives.
    b. Generate performance feedback.
    c. Provide recognition and request simulation.
    d. Accept and process customer feedback.

Quality Applications

1. Discuss how decisions are made in your company. Are all employees trained in a uniform decision-making process? Are accurate data routinely collected and analyzed prior to making decisions? Are employees accountable for their decisions?
2. Review the reports distributed by your data processing department. What percentage of the reports are actually read and used to make decisions? Are the data and information contained in those reports routinely audited and their accuracy reported?

Quality Benefits

1. Focusing on establishing a uniform, consistent decision-making process throughout the business will begin to give the Company confidence in the accuracy and validity of the empowered decisions made by their employees.
2. Accurate data to run the business are essential. Only accurate data will allow accurate decision making. Only accurate decision making can lead to a profitable business operation.

9

INITIATING THE FLOW OF INFORMATION BY COMMUNICATING OBJECTIVES

In Part 1, we defined the process of identifying customer motivation, goals, and requirements. We saw how we can turn the requirements into complementary objectives for the Company. In defining our quality organization, we established the functional responsibilities, business macro-processes, an operational network, and the document control required to permit satisfaction of our objectives. Now we need an accurate, real-time quality information system, to steer our quality system performance ever closer to the established objectives. The first step in developing the QIS is to translate and communicate business unit objectives throughout the operation, so that all employees understand very specifically the results expected from them. Your success in translating objectives throughout the operation depends upon an accepted definition of "objectives," an understanding of your process constraints, and an understanding of your empowered functional responsibilities.

How Objectives Help You Measure Performance

You've created complementary business unit objectives and you're confident that their realization will lead to Circle-4 Customer satisfaction. As you consider lower-level supporting objectives within the quality system, what characteristics should they have? Objectives are short-term, quantitative customer requirements and business results. They provide the motivation for measuring performance of the system. In order to fulfill their purpose, objectives need the following characteristics:

* All objectives are established or approved by the Company.
* At the business unit level, objectives must be complementary.
* Objectives set expectations within a time period.
* Objectives must be quantitative and measurable.
* Objectives require evidence of compliance.
* By defining the expected result of one or more processes, objectives ask for specific information about process performance.
* Objectives must fall within assigned functional responsibility.
* Objectives are expressed in terms of the process constraints.
* Objectives are provided for all employees.

Let's take a brief look at each of these characteristics so we have a common perspective. All objectives are established or approved by the Company. Throughout this book, we will continue to talk about empowered decision making while at the same time clarifying the responsibilities that belong to the Company, which cannot be delegated. We've discussed your responsibility to understand your Circle-4 Customer, create business unit objectives, and establish your quality organization. You also have an obligation to ensure that the objectives communicated to every employee do, in fact, support your business unit objectives. This responsibility itself involves some empowerment.

The Company is responsible for defining and agreeing to departmental objectives. Department managers, who should be part of the management team, are responsible for translating objectives into their responsible areas of the operational network. Department objectives are really department manager objectives. Each department manager is responsible for the performance of assigned processes within the quality system. Since no process exists as an island, each must be managed by a cross-functional team. The cross-functional teams are responsible for the performance and improvement of their assigned processes. Each team member becomes responsible for a segment of the process. The team members may come from different departments, but they share the same objectives, based on the role of each within the process. The department manager responsible for the overall process acts as the Shareholder for the team. So, while the department manager is responsible for developing objectives for assigned processes, the Company needs to understand and take ownership of these objectives. This enables all managers to support in total the objectives of their employees, since many serve on other crossfunctional teams.

Reviewing Objectives

We already talked about complementary business unit objectives in chapter 3, so we'll just do a quick review. All objectives established by the Company for the business unit must complement one another. The success of any given objective must support the achievement and success of all other objectives. For example, objectives concerning "increasing market share" and "improving profitability" might not be complementary unless each objective is carefully worded to consider the other. If this consideration is not given, market share might increase at the expense of profitability.

Objectives must clearly indicate the time available for results. Generally, objectives are determined for a defined fiscal period, often a year. In some special cases, corrective action teams may be given very short-term objectives to analyze or solve a particular process disturbance. Objectives should never be changed within the specified time period unless there is unanimous agreement between the owners of the objective and their Circle-4 Customer.

Consider the following two objectives:

A. Ensure on-time delivery of purchased parts.
B. Create and maintain an improving trend of purchase part quality and delivery to attain a level of greater than 95 percent on-time delivery with 100 percent part acceptance.

Which of these objectives puts the Company in charge of business results? If Objective A is satisfied to the material manager's expectations, how can we be sure the expectations of the Company's business unit objectives are satisfied? Objective B makes the requirement crystal clear. Defined for the current fiscal year, Objective B is interested in an improving trend, with a specific expected outcome. Objectives that cannot be measured are worthless. Objectives must be quantitative and measurable.

If an objective is measurable, then actual performance must be monitored against that expectation. If we don't measure it, we can't manage it. Evidence of compliance needs to include not only the measurement, but also supporting evidence showing data, information, and performance history of the constraints controlling the objective.

By establishing your quality organization, you have accepted ownership of the responsibilities you've assigned and the processes you've defined. In translating objectives throughout the operation, you're interested in knowing the performance results of a process and you're interested in the positive evolution of the process. Remember, your basic goal is to make more money now and in the future. You need specific information, again as supporting evidence, about process trends, or you won't be able to predict future process performance.

Objectives must fall within assigned functional responsibility. This is almost a no-brainer. It's hard to achieve expected results if you assign product management objectives to accounting, for example. No arguments here, right?

HOW TO LOOK AT CONSTRAINTS AS OPPORTUNITIES

Objectives must be expressed in terms of process constraints. This is one of the most important concepts for successful translation throughout the operation. Let's carefully explore the idea of process constraints. Any defined process has limitations. Process limitations may become bottlenecks, constraints to process performance. Because constraints can determine the performance of the process, they may be viewed as the controlling factors of that process. The performance of a process can never be any better than the performance of its most influential constraint. Constraints can be created through policy, wherein process limits are specifically structured and identified. Constraints can be created as a result of how the process is defined in detail within the policy limits. Constraints can also be created through the performance of the employees and machines executing the process. If properly identified, measuring constraints is equivalent to measuring the process. Improvement activities need to look at constraints as opportunities for improving policies, improving process definition, and improving employee performance, all in an effort to satisfy the given objectives.

Using the Company Model to Show Constraint Analysis

Perhaps the best way to show how objectives are expressed in terms of the process constraints is through example. Let's check in on our company model, EWC, Inc. In chapters 4 and 5, EWC created the following business unit objectives:

1. Realize sales of $12M.
2. Realize 4 percent profit in the current year, as a percentage of sales.
3. Create additional product applications for the End-user, with no increase in product list prices for two years.
4. Strengthen Supplier partnerships and create incentive to reduce material cost by 5 percent annually. Budget a 2.5 percent annual decrease in cost of material. Split all realized material cost reductions equally with the Supplier.
5. Challenge employees to reduce operating expenses by 10 percent annually, measured as a percentage of net sales. Budget a 5 percent annual decrease in operating expense. Operating expense savings against the budget will be turned over to the employees.
6. Improve customer delivery to an average of 30 days ARO, and reduce finished goods inventory to an average of 30 days with-

in two years.

7. Maintain product development investment at 12 percent of net sales annually.

8. During the budget period, spend 5 percent of available working hours, from a normal 40-hour week, training and educating our employees so they can improve the quality system.

Let's take one of these objectives and work through the process of translating it throughout the operation and expressing that translation in terms of process constraints. To employ a straightforward example, let's use objective 1, "Realize sales of $12M." As we'll soon discover, this objective will translate into schedule performance within the organization. In order to identify the constraints on a given process, a simple question must be answered: "What factors limit our ability to realize the objective?" If we start from the top down, from the general and work toward the specific, what factors can limit our ability to realize sales of $12M? The results we expect to see are that actual sales equal planned sales. The two most important initial factors are whether we can get orders and whether we can deliver orders. The first major constraints for realizing our objective are customer orders and the factory schedule. Now the question is repeated from the point of view of each identified constraint. What factors can limit our ability to book customer orders? What factors can limit our ability to fully execute the factory schedule? Customer orders can be limited by order availability and by our order management capability. The factory schedule can be limited by schedule accuracy and schedule execution. The next level of subdivision will result in a decision tree as shown in Figure 9.1.

The process constraints driving order availability include product expectations, cost expectations, and delivery expectations. Order management is driven by delivery requirements and existing product definition. Schedule accuracy can be no better than planning accuracy, maintenance accuracy, and timefence accuracy. Schedule execution will be limited by our ability to start on time and finish on time, and our ability to create fit-for-use products and services.

Appendix 3 shows this decision tree subdivided from the general down to the specific to reflect all process constraints in deter-

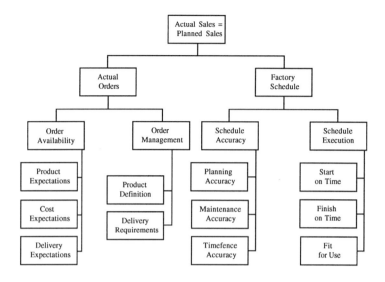

Figure 9.1 Process constraint decision tree.

mining whether actual sales equal planned sales. This may seem like a tremendous amount of detail for just one business unit objective, and the others may certainly be as complex. However, if we fail to understand our defined business processes in any less detail than this, we effectively relinquish control of the business. In fact, I realize that our example for EWC may not have *enough* detail for some of the processes. A road map of this type must be kept current and used frequently to analyze the business. The benefits of conducting a routine constraint analysis include enabling translation of objectives throughout the operation, identification of customer-supplier relationships within the operation, and visibility of process performance interdependencies.

Grouping the Constraints by Owner

Once all constraints are identified, each should be assigned to a manager within the Company, based on previously established functional responsibility. This is also shown in Appendix 3. Even though in our example manufacturing has a majority of the responsibility, enough diversity exists to illustrate the constraint analysis process. Beginning at the bottom and working our way up, you'll notice as we near the top, some constraints do not have clear ownership. These constraints belong to the Company; they comprise the body of information we want to collate and use to assess business unit objectives and to provide as performance recognition to our Circle-4 Customer. If we group the constraints by owner, then eliminate all but the highest level in any given branch, we see the assigned constraints as follows:

1. The Company
   A. Base objective: realize sales of $12M.
   B. Actual orders
2. Director, Manufacturing
   A. Factory schedule
3. Director, Marketing
   A. Order availability
4. Director, Product Planning and Support
   A. Order management
   B. Inventory plan
   C. Mix percentage Forecast
5. Director, Engineering
   A. Product structure
   B. Product release
   C. Part specification

The factory schedule is common to all constraints belonging to Grace Chavez, EWC's Director of Manufacturing. Therefore, she'll be measured against the performance of her assigned functions through an overall factory schedule measurement. Her operational teams and employees will be assigned the constraints below factory schedule. The Company owns two constraints, the basic business unit objective and actual orders. Because the responsibility for obtaining and processing customer orders is more or less evenly split between two managers, rather than make an arbitrary decision for responsibility, we assign the constraint to the Company, with the two managers assigned one of the two major constraints controlling actual orders. You will also notice, that since BOM (bill of material) accuracy appears twice, we only consider it under its higher-level constraint, product structure.

The constraints identified for product planning and support and engineering appear within those owned by Manufacturing, implying that these two managers report to manufacturing insofar as managing their assigned constraints to achieve the sales plan. This is absolutely the case; however, you would be better served to consider the relationship one of a clearly identified Circle-4 Customer relationship and to stay away from the notion of "reporting to," or implied subservience. For issues regarding product structure and product release, for example, engineering needs to consider manufacturing as its End-user, and establish the relationship accordingly. Similarly, manufacturing is the End-user of product planning and support for issues concerning order management, inventory planning, and mix percentage forecasts. The ability to clearly see some of our Circle-4 Customer relationships is another reason to keep current process constraint models. We can also see process performance interdependencies from our constraint model. For example, because of the indicated hierarchal relationship, factory schedule starts can be no more accurate than the vendor performance which precedes it. Followed down to the lowest constraint levels, it becomes evident that basic data accuracy exerts a fundamental influence on the accuracy of all process performance measures.

Identifying the Desired Results

The constraints we've assigned EWC's department managers now need to be analyzed and restated in the form of objectives. The basic question to answer when beginning this analysis is "What result do we desire from this constraint, in order for it to support the higher-level objective?" The answer becomes the performance benchmark for the constraint, against which we compare actual performance. Part of answering this first question is considering the limitations of both the constraint and the process. We may want to make some test measurements of actual performance, if we're not already measuring it, in order to understand the actual state of affairs. Our desired result should anticipate a realistic, but aggressive, improvement over actual performance. If current performance is only 50 percentage of the ideal, don't expect to reach the ideal in one year. As you'll see in a moment, we can account for both variables, our ideal result and our realistic expectation, through the wording of the objective.

Let's review the constraints which were assigned to EWC's department managers for the business unit objective "Realize current year sales of $12M." This time, let's include below each constraint our expected results. EWC came up with the following:

1. The Company
   * Base Objective: Realize Sales of $12M.
     —Result: Actual Sales = Planned Sales.
   * Actual Orders
     —Result: Actual Orders = Planned Orders.
2. Director, Manufacturing
   * Factory Schedule
     —Result: On-time Customer Order Delivery.
3. Director, Marketing
   * Order Availability
     —Results: Actual Bookings = Planned Bookings
4. Director, Product Planning and Support
   * Order Management
     —Result: Booked Orders = Delivered Orders.
   * Inventory Plan
     —Actual Inventory = Planned Inventory.
   * Mix percentage Forecast
     —Customer Order Mix = Forecast Order Mix.
5. Director, Engineering
   * Product Structure
     —Result: Actual Product Structure = Documented Structure.
   * Product Release
     —Result: Actual New Product Engineering Releases = Planned Releases.

  * Part Specification
    —Result: Multiple Sources of Supply for All Components.

Once we define expected results, we can restate each constraint in the form of an objective. We need to keep in mind the characteristics of objectives as previously outlined. The objectives derived from our constraint analysis are:

1. The Company
   * Base Objective: Realize Sales of $12M.
   * Book and deliver 100 percent of the customer orders required by the Business Plan. (Actual Sales = Planned Sales)

2. Director, Manufacturing
   * Deliver 100 percent of scheduled customer orders on time according to customer requirements. (On-Time Customer Order Delivery)

3. Director, Marketing
   * Book 100 percent of the customer orders required by the Order Intake Plan. (Actual = Planned Bookings)

4. Director, Product Planning and Support
   * Ensure that 100 percent of booked orders are delivered to customers as defined. (Booked = Delivered Orders)
   * Ensure that 100 percent of actual inventory equals planned inventory, by product line. (Actual = Planned Inventory)
   * Establish and maintain product mix forecasts that predict 100% of actual demand. (Actual = Forecast Order Mix)

5. Director, Engineering
   * Maintain and control Product Documentation which reflects 100 percent of the current configuration products. (Actual = Documented Product Structure)
   * Ensure 100 percent on-time release of new products and engineering changes vs. development plans. (Actual = Planned Product Release)
   * Ensure that 100 percent of the active purchased components have more than one manufacturer. (Multisourced Components)

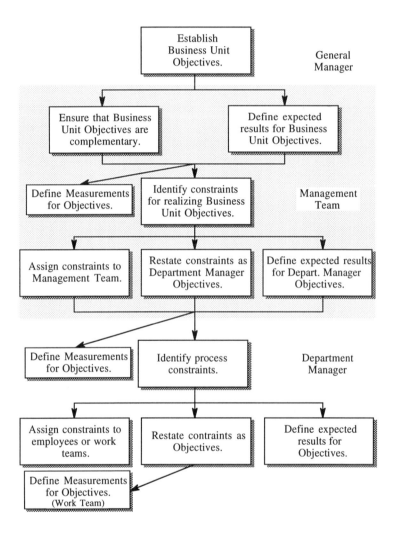

Figure 9.2 Process for translating business unit objectives
throughout the operation.

How to Establish Your Own Results

I've used the expected result of 100 percent performance in all defined objectives for the sake of simplicity and to avoid discussion of what constitutes "world-class" performance. You need to establish your expected results based on current actual performance, realistic improvement expectations, and customer requirements. I personally believe that performance should continue to be improved and that 100 percent conformance to all requirements is the ultimate measure of business success.

Department managers now have the responsibility of assigning constraints and objectives to their employees and cross-functional teams. This process must continue until every employee understands how they're expected to perform. Figure 9.2 depicts the process of communicating objectives through constraint analysis. It also indicates the step of defining measurements for the objectives, which we'll discuss in detail in chapter 11, as we consider performance feedback.

Keep in mind that our examples have dealt with the translation of a single business unit objective. An identical process must be used for the remaining business unit objectives. Constraint analysis for all objectives will result in assigned responsibility and accountability for all business functions. Next, we're going to take a close look at the end product of communicating objectives throughout the operation, the Schedule.

Summary

1. Objectives are short-term, quantitative customer requirements and business results that provide the motivation for measuring the performance of the quality system.
2. In identifying their characteristics, it can be stated that objectives are:
   a. approved by the Company;
   b. complementary;

     c. for a stated period of time;

     d. quantitative and measurable;

     e. process oriented;

     f. expressed in terms of process constraints; and

     g. provided for all employees.

3. Constraints are limitations to process performance and can arise from policy, employee performance, or machine performance.

5. Lower-level objectives are defined from business unit objectives through constraint analysis, by successively identifying those factors which limit the performance of the next-level process.

6. Process limits, or constraints, are expressed as lower level objectives by defining them in terms of expected results.

7. Translating objectives throughout the operation, using constraint analysis, must be repeated at least annually.

Quality Applications

1. Using the business objectives you developed at the end of chapter 4, create a process constraint model for each objective. Express each constraint as a measurable lower-level objective. Use Figure 9.2 and Appendix 3 for guidance. The basic logic for constraint analysis can be simplified as follows:

     a. We will achieve Objective A if our results are X.

     b. X will be determined by the performance of B and C (constraints).

     c. Result X can be achieved if the result of B is Y and the result of C is Z.

     d. State lower-level objective B in terms of Y results, and state lower-level objective C in terms of Z results.

     e. Assign ownership to objectives B and C.

     f. Repeat steps a-e for objective B and then for objective C.

     g. Repeat the process for all business unit objectives until all lower-level objectives are defined and assigned ownership.

2. Communicate objectives to all employees so they understand the specific results expected from their process.

Quality Benefits

1. All employees are working toward specific, measurable objectives.
2. All objectives are expressed in terms of local process performance.
3. All objectives are derived from and linked to the overall business unit objectives.

The positive effect these three benefits will have on employee morale, process performance, and process improvement will be immediate and noticeable. Several years ago, when we were implementing MRPII (Manufacturing Resources Planning), we began measuring the standard performance indicators of systems effectiveness, such as bill of material accuracy, master schedule accuracy, material requirements accuracy, and inventory record accuracy. We noticed after a couple of months that the relatively general measurements, such as purchasing accuracy, gave rise to frequent arguments about who was responsible for creating the poor performance indicated by the measurement. As a result, we took each measurement and subdivided it into lower-level measurements that could be assigned to specific individuals and teams. In the case of purchasing accuracy, for example, we assigned delivery date accuracy and quantity accuracy to each individual buyer for their commodities. The accuracy of the actual material requirements driving purchasing was assigned to the material planners, and so on. Once the employees felt that they were accountable for the specific performance of their area of responsibility, we began to see consistent improvement in the lower-level measurements and in the general MRPII measurements. Performance measurement became a matter of pride for our employees, in part because they knew they would only be held accountable for process results within their control.

10

THE ROLE OF THE SCHEDULE IN THE QUALITY SYSTEM

As we complete the task of analyzing process constraints and translating objectives throughout the operation, the *Schedule* becomes our final destination. By definition within our quality system, the Schedule is the complete, integrated set of plans and schedules defined for the operation of our business. If we review the analysis we did for one of EWC's business objectives, "Realize sales of $12M" (see Appendix 3), we see that 63 percent of the identified constraints involve factory schedule planning or execution and another 11 percent encompass the performance of the development schedule. Constraint analysis for other business unit objectives will result in a similar dependency on other plans and schedules within our business, such as the product support schedule, the order intake plan, and the operating budget. Before we discuss some of the desired characteristics of its constituent plans and schedules, let's put the schedule in perspective within the total business.

THE RELATIONSHIP BETWEEN A PLAN AND A SCHEDULE

In chapter 7 we discussed the quality organization and concluded that it must establish functional responsibility, define macro-processes, and create an operational network. A major subset of the macro-processes that we define through company policy are the planning processes. As we all know, planning is crucial to our success and to our continued operation. Since the inception of your business, which was preceded by a proposed business plan, you have accepted the need to create plans. What should your plans encompass? How do they interrelate? What's the relationship between a plan and a schedule, and how are they related? Books have been written on business planning, and since I don't want to stray too far from our quality system, I'm not going to wade through the fine details of different types of planning or how to create plans. Good managers know how to plan. However, planning is such an important part of the business "front end" that a brief overview is in order.

The purpose of planning is to predict what we *think* we can accomplish based on what we *perceive* to be the internal and external influences on our business. Plans are preceded by our business mission and goals, which are refined into required short-term detail by business unit objectives. For all intents and purposes, we can say

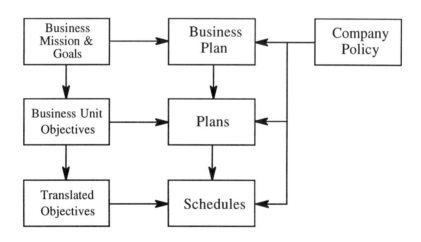

Figure 10.1 Business planning matrix.

that a plan is the expression of our goals and objectives over a defined period of time.

As we can see from Figure 10.1, company policy establishes the need and defines the format for our plans, while goals and objectives drive the quantitative input. The output of the planning process is the plan itself, an expression of our desired results over time. Implementation of a plan, any plan, leads to the creation of a schedule. Schedules provide additional, specific details that enable action and subsequent realization of the plan. For example, a revenue plan may require shipments of $1M per month for Product Line A. The factory schedule derived from the revenue plan requires the production of specific quantities of the end-items comprising Product Line A. This schedule also requires these quantities to be completed on specific dates. Think of a schedule as a detailed four-dimensional representation of a plan. The four critical dimensions are *product, quantity, time,* and *cost.* Figure 10.1 shows that the end result of planning and establishing business unit objectives are the schedules. A plan must be implemented through a schedule. Our business processes are galvanized to action by schedules, not by plans. Our desired products or services are available to our End-users as a result of schedule execution.

In most businesses, the business plan is the overall, encompassing plan for the business unit. It's the "mother of all plans," to use a well-worn phrase. The business plan expresses the expected result of all planned quality system activity in terms that satisfy the requirements of the Shareholder. Depending on your particular business, results may be expressed as net profit, return on investment, return on assets, earnings per share, or some other form of "bottom-line" performance. The business plan is often presented as projected income statements and balance sheets over a covered horizon. Because it contains very general, results-oriented information, it is usually accompanied by a variety of supporting plans as evidence of business direction and intent and to thoroughly communicate requirements to the organization. For these reasons, the business plan needs to be viewed as the aggregate representation of all the business units' plans and schedules, which are summarized through the income statement and balance sheet.

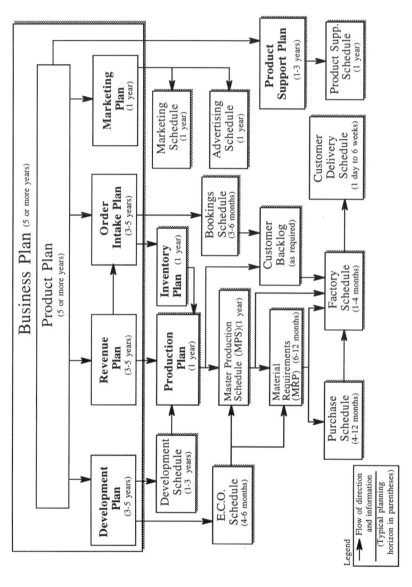

Figure 10.2 The relationship of typical business plans and schedules.

Figure 10.2 shows the typical relationship of plans and schedules within a business. While the exact relationships may be somewhat different in your business, let's examine the common characteristics and dynamics which apply generally.

DETERMINING THE LEVEL OF DETAIL NEEDED IN A SCHEDULE

Just as goals and objectives become more specific as we translate them throughout the operation, plans and schedules become more specific as they branch out from the business plan. The requirement for an increasing level of detail is driven by the results expected within communicated objectives and by the complexity of the processes affected by a schedule. If we have an objective for 100 percent on-time delivery of customer orders, we create the need for a customer delivery schedule that can respond to very specific delivery requests. Such a delivery schedule must identify and communicate customer delivery requirements down to the day, or sometimes even the hour within the day. At the other extreme, if our objective requires that we deliver only within 90 days of the date requested by the customer, we don't need a very specific or controlled delivery schedule. (We probably won't have many repeat customers either!) The need to satisfy Circle-4 Customer requirements creates the need for increasing levels of detail in our schedules, as well as the need to maintain schedule accuracy.

We can see in Figure 10.2 a typical planning horizon for each of the indicated plans and schedules. Generally, the longer the horizon, the less detailed the plan. Conversely, the shorter the horizon, the more detailed the schedule. Another characteristic of plans is that, within themselves, detail increases as the horizon approaches the present. Within the Revenue Plan for example, years 3, 4, and 5 may be in annual time periods, year 2 may be expressed in quarters, and the current year is always expressed in months. Schedules, on the other hand, are characterized by a uniform level of detail across their horizon. A one-year master production schedule has the same level of detail in all twelve months. A Development Schedule, which may extend two or three years in some businesses, has the same level of detail throughout its horizon. Specific characteristics of the various plans and schedules identified in Figure 10.2 are available in Appendix 4.

How Processes Are Reflected in the Schedule

In addition to expected results, the other major determinant for the amount of detail necessary in a given schedule are the processes which have been established to execute that schedule. A process can be defined as a specific sequence of actions which must be repeated on a regular and consistent basis within the business operation in order to achieve a defined outcome. Processes are commonly documented as operational procedures and exist for almost every facet of a business. We'll explore process definition thoroughly in chapter 18. For now, let's look at those process elements which must be reflected in the schedule detail.

Every process is characterized by conditions, actions, and results. Conditions identify the input necessary for the defined actions to take place. Conditions can be information, physical material, human resources, machines, or a combination of these elements. Actions are the sequence of operations required to achieve the results. Our schedules need to know the identification of each step in the sequence and the amount of time each requires to perform its function. Overall process results can be finished, or partially finished, products, reports, product designs, or even plans and schedules themselves. Results must be identified to the extent that the process outcome is clear and unambiguous. Within the quality system, the results of a given process quite often satisfy the conditions or provide input necessary for other processes. Expressed in general manufacturing terminology, conditions, actions, and results become material/capacity requirements, leadtimes/costs, and finished products. This level of detail allows each schedule to evaluate the demands of our plans and business objectives against our defined capabilities, in terms of product, quantity, time, and cost. This evaluation culminates in a detailed schedule output which directs business activity in terms of what to do, when to do it, how much to do, and when to finish it. The integration of detailed information about our plans and about our capabilities permits schedules to act as the critical interface between the quality information system and the quality delivery system.

Viewing a Schedule as a Process Model

Because we require information about a process in developing a means to schedule it, a schedule can also be viewed as a type of process model. We'll talk about the relative accuracy and effectiveness of a schedule as a process model in a minute, but for now let's address the implications of our statement. If a schedule models a process, then we should be able to move the schedule anywhere in time and have it retain its modeling ability. If we tell the schedule we need 10,000 pieces finished during the month of April three years from now, it should have the ability to move our process model forward three years, look backward through the process and tell us how much raw material to start into the process, and when to start it. From there of course, we can tell the purchasing schedule when the raw material must be available. The purchasing schedule can look back through component leadtimes and tell our buyers when to place the material on order. This is a traditional back scheduling algorithm. Conversely, we can tell the schedule when the purchased material will be available and ask it to predict the finished product completion date. A third common scheduling practice creates a "window" with predefined start and end dates and requires the schedule to spread the necessary operations between the two. This ability to predict the actions and timing necessary to satisfy our plans and objectives gives us confidence that we understand what needs to take place in our business over time.

Limitations of Scheduling Algorithms

The ability of a schedule to model a process has limitations. Most project and factory scheduling algorithms are implemented through computer software, and most of them concentrate on subdividing the process into the smallest possible segments. Each segment is characterized by material requirements, capacity requirements, standard costs, and leadtimes. Material requirements consist of correct part numbers and quantities. Capacity requirements include man-hours, machine hours, and the correct sequence of steps necessary to realize a finished assembly. Cost standards are laboriously subdivided into material, labor, and various overhead categories. Traditional cost accounting has outlived its usefulness and today creates a cumbersome business overhead in its pursuit of seemingly endless factory cost categories. The fourth variable, leadtime, has also been subdivided *ad nauseam* into setup, run, move, queue, and wait times.

In traditional delivery systems, product and material definition is an engineering responsibility, product quantities are mandated by the production plan, capacity limits are set by the operating budget, and standard costs are tightly controlled by finance. As a result, the easiest schedule parameter for the factory itself to control and influence is the leadtime parameter. This tends to focus factory schedule management and control toward leadtime management and control, since the other major process characteristics are not viewed as factory responsibilities. Consequently, we see a policy-imposed limitation on the effectiveness of the traditional factory schedule as a realistic process model. From the factory point of view, this primary emphasis on leadtimes comes at the expense of controlling and managing material, capacity, and standard costs. Leadtime management and control is a worthy endeavor and can lead to significant quality improvements. However, leadtime management should not preclude other avenues of process management.

Another limitation of most current scheduling algorithms is their inability to recharacterize a process over time. As we plan process improvements or changes, it is not possible in most cases to reflect those changes out in the horizon where they will take effect. For example, if we wish to automate our process of loading printed circuit boards, the product and data structures used by our scheduling software will not allow us to reflect a direct time-phased cutover for this improvement. Instead of showing manufacturing "cell A" changing over time and taking on new characteristics, we're forced to create a manufacturing "cell B" for our future automated process, then manually manipulate the product structure in a sloppy effort to properly reflect our intended cutover. The majority of process-specific characteristics that are utilized by scheduling software are uniformly static. While it's possible to change these characteristics, any changes are immediately reflected across the entire schedule. Most scheduling algorithms do permit time-phased changes for defined components or raw material, but I have yet to see the ability to make time-phased changes to process characteristics. This severely restricts our ability to model planned, continuous improvements via computer regenerated schedules.

Inflexibility surfaces again when we look at defining resource requirements, where traditional schedules demonstrate remarkable tunnel vision. Standard costs are normally converted into setup and run hours for each operation within a process. Not only are these hours difficult for factory personnel to change, but most scheduling software does not allow operation hours to influence the actual scheduling algorithm. As the algorithms drive down through the product structures, they're very adept at netting material requirements, provided that inventory and work-in-process records are accurate. As product build leadtimes are passed through process leadtimes, little or no influence is exerted by the resulting resource loading. Resource requirements are only accumulated and made visible to planners and factory personnel through capacity requirements reports. Another way of stating this limitation is to say that most scheduling packages assume the infinite availability of process resources; man-hours and machine hours. The result is a significant requirement for manual schedule manipulation to alleviate capacity constraints, an exercise which is nullified by the next material requirements plan (MRP) or schedule run. This tunnel vision also extends to the simplistic manner in which resources are scheduled, most often in a serial fashion as dictated by the product structure. While this may be ideal for some businesses, most factories routinely move partial quantities or run parallel operations in order to more efficiently utilize and control limited resources.

Our intent in pointing out the common limitations of today's scheduling software is to put current schedules, most notably factory schedules, in proper perspective within the quality information system. You must be realistic about your expectations from your schedules and about their ability to accurately model your delivery system processes. The technology continues to be advanced, however. There are available, the best at considerable cost, a number of software packages that focus on accurately and thoroughly modeling processes and/or factory operations. They're worth a detailed evaluation as you pursue complete and accurate information with which to make complete and accurate business decisions.

HOW THE SCHEDULE LINKS YOUR QUALITY INFORMATION SYSTEM AND YOUR QUALITY DELIVERY SYSTEM

The Schedule provides the link between the quality information system (QIS) and the quality delivery system (QDS) by providing the greatest level of detail about our objectives and how we're planning to achieve them. This link is crucial to proper execution of the QDS. The plans contained within the Schedule must accurately reflect the objectives established for the business. Operating schedules derived from the plans must accurately reflect both their parent plan and the capabilities of the processes they're directing. Because complete and accurate linkage between the QIS and QDS is so critical to business performance, and because it has the limitations noted previously, it is very important for you to closely monitor and manage the complete Schedule.

Process constraint analysis will identify areas requiring schedule management. First you need to satisfy yourself that all schedules truly reflect the requirements of their plan. Does the schedule equal the plan? Strict conformance to policies governing plan and schedule creation and updating is necessary to manage this variable. Process leadtimes should establish the horizon for plan changes, schedule changes should be driven only by plan changes, and both should require authorizing signatures which testify that all changes have been properly defined and are within the bounds of current business objectives. Second, since you're providing a link into your delivery system, each schedule must also reflect process capability, including what is actually occurring during process execution. Does the schedule reflect reality? Your operations must allow for updating all schedules as close to "real time" as possible. Accuracy improves with frequency of use. A factory schedule that's only updated with actual process information on a weekly basis will not be used by the process owners to manage their operations. Whatever occurred yesterday must be reflected in today's schedule. Whatever occurred an hour ago must be reflected in this hour's schedule. Your schedule management policies must demand that the outcome of actual process execution be reflected within the schedule as rapidly as possible. Finally, you need to ensure complete accuracy of the data and information provided to all schedules. Because you only have four major scheduling parameters, product, quantity, time, and cost, each exerts considerable influence over schedule accuracy. If you were using ten major scheduling parameters instead of only four, each of the ten would exert proportionally less influence on overall schedule accuracy. To avoid creating and using an invalid schedule, the accuracies of each parameter must be separately monitored, measured, reported, and improved. Let's consider a simple example.

A Model for Handling Schedule Accuracy

During the past two years, EWC has been improving their total quality system. They created the operational network we described in chapter 7, and their operational improvement teams have been busy identifying and pursuing improvement opportunities. This effort has been accompanied by real pressure from the marketplace to reduce widget prices, precipitating a related cost-reduction program. With admirable intent, Dr. Rogers, the general manager, combined the two objectives by requiring improvement projects that could result in cost reduction. However, the need to cut costs was perceived as a higher priority by her management team, who saw their jobs in jeopardy if the business started losing market share or if profits decreased. Grace Chavez, the director of manufacturing, saw total quality as beneficial, but adding to the manufacturing overhead "burden" she was determined to reduce. Consequently, she decided to eliminate the overhead of minutely measuring schedule accuracy and performance in favor of allowing the improvement teams to operate with more flexibility. She reasoned that she could still measure her objectives at the department manager level, and since the OIT's were going to be constantly changing their processes, the old schedule measurements would cease to be valuable anyway. Having a number of years experience in manufacturing management, Grace was also convinced that the best way to control direct labor costs was through efficiency and utilization. Keeping those parameters in line would minimize the direct labor contribution to the overhead. In addition, she continued to measure on-time customer delivery, inventory value, and department expense levels.

After a year of this combined emphasis on cost reduction and total quality, manufacturing is exhibiting some interesting results. On-time delivery, measured against the factory's original quoted ship date, is running around 85 percent, utilization 87 percent, efficiency 98 percent, and operating expenses are 95 percent to budget, all slight improvements over the previous year. However, inventory is growing, factory material shortages are tracked on four different manual lists, and customer delivery complaints seem almost constant. Grace finds herself in the position of reacting to a crisis almost every day of the week. She is becoming convinced that the effort required by total quality is decreasing her employees' available delivery system management time. What is happening to her factory? Are her employees pursuing total quality at the expense of business objectives? Let's look at some of the now less visible activity and performance indicators.

Grace's production manager, Bill Simon, has also been in manufacturing for years. True to the maxim, "Tell me how you'll measure me and I'll tell you how I'll behave," Bill knows exactly how to ensure top performance to his assigned objectives. Operating expenses are no problem, since he can control the amount of direct labor transferred out of his budget. Objectives for efficiency, utilization, and on-time deliveries provide easy targets to hit. His first order of business at the beginning of the year was to convince his boss and his colleagues that they ought to be measuring customer delivery against the original ship date the factory established for each order. Customers, he reasoned, don't understand some of EWC's leadtime requirements, and often request one- and two-week delivery for systems that normally take four to six weeks to configure and test. Having made a convincing argument, Bill took steps to ensure that the order scheduling process was extremely detailed in determining availability of features and options, followed by precisely calculating system test time. He also requires the schedulers to account for routine order processing time and kitting time, in addition to the calculated configuration and test time. He's pleased with the resulting 85 percent delivery performance, up 5 percent from last year. What he's failed to recognize is that measuring against customer defined delivery requirements is really the *only valid measurement*. His deliveries are averaging 45 to 60 days ARO (after receipt of order), while marketing continues to say that customers are demanding 30 to 45-day ARO delivery. No wonder customer complaints are increasing. One basic schedule failure in this example comes through injecting inaccurate data into the schedule by ignoring the real customer required delivery date. The schedule reacts predictably, but not in a manner that promotes Circle-4 Customer satisfaction.

Bill has also pegged efficiency and utilization. First, he allows no indirect labor charges without his personal approval. He restricts himself to approving only total quality activities, and causes work orders to be created for categories like rework and refurbishment, since he knows that charges to work orders are considered direct charges and would therefore reflect favorably on his resource utilization. Second, since he knows customers regularly change their order configurations before shipment, causing many schedule changes, he understates his resource availability in the schedule work center file. If he actually has four people in a manufacturing cell, he tells the work center file he only has two, causing work to be scheduled across a greater number of days. He does pay close attention to his standard costs, making sure that his people are trained and can achieve the aggregate scheduled setup and run hours. What he's done is give his crew more calendar time within which to do the actual work, thus allowing for the routine schedule interruptions and expedite requests. What he doesn't realize is that as the schedule deals with this inaccurate data, overall manufacturing leadtimes *increase*, causing order availability analysis to predict longer customer delivery dates for new orders.

We can also point out similar actions within the manufacturing logistics and materials processes that fail to provide accurate data for the scheduling process. It's no wonder that EWC's schedule is straying farther from reality, that the employees believe in it less and less, and that they consequently spend more of their time using hot lists and shortage lists that tell them the "real" story.

MAINTAINING ACCURATE SCHEDULES TO AVOID ERRONEOUS DECISIONS

Because the Schedule represents the intersection of the quality delivery system and the quality information system, it must accurately represent both sides. The slightest discrepancy from reality in the data representing product, quantity, cost, and time that are utilized by the Schedule, will result in future erroneous decisions within both systems. The means to maintain a high level of accuracy for these parameters is through identifying the constraints they represent, establishing desired results or objectives for these constraints, followed by measuring actual process performance and comparing it to the objectives.

In addition to maintaining accurate schedule parameters, it's also very important to give consideration to process constraints that are not reflected through the Schedule. The most important of these within our QDS is product quality, followed closely by product documentation, process documentation, and employee readiness, or training. In the next chapter's discussion of performance feedback, we'll include these areas in our recommendations, as well as the schedule parameters just discussed.

We've learned that the Schedule is the set of all plans reflecting our business objectives together with the lower-level schedules derived to execute those plans. We understand that the Schedule defines the product, quantity, time and cost for all quality delivery system activities. We realize that all schedules have inherent limitations that must be considered in properly defining management and control. A high level of accuracy is required for the data supplied to the Schedule, both to ensure an accurate interface between the QDS and the QIS and to minimize the potential damage of rapidly spreading inaccuracies. The Schedule is an important part of our quality information system as the culmination of translating and communicating our business objectives throughout the operation.

SUMMARY

1. The Schedule is the complete, integrated set of plans, and lower-level schedules defined for the operation of our business.
2. A plan is the expression of our goals and objectives over a defined period of time.
3. The business plan is the overall, encompassing plan for the business unit.
4. A schedule is derived from a plan and provides product, quantity, time, and cost details which enable action and subsequent realization of the plan.
5. The level of detail required in a given schedule is determined by the results demanded by its plan and by the complexity of the processes it directs.
6. All processes are characterized by conditions, actions, and results.
7. Schedules have a limited ability to model processes.
8. The integration of detailed information about our plans and about our capabilities permits schedules to act as the critical interface between the quality information system and the quality delivery system.
9. All plans and schedules, as well as the data and information they use, must be maintained with a high degree of accuracy.

Quality Applications

1. Using Figure 10.2 as a guide, create a chart showing all the plans and schedules, and their interrelationships, used for your business operation. Discuss the overall importance of the schedule to your business.
2. Review your planning and scheduling policies. Do your policies provide adequate control for the timing, content, and accuracy of schedule management?
3. Select one of the schedules used in your business. Conduct a detailed audit of that schedule by answering the following questions:
   a. Does the schedule accurately reflect the requirements of its plan? How is this accuracy routinely measured?
   b. How effectively does the schedule model the processes which it directs? Is it accurate enough to simulate potential future activity?
   c. How often is the schedule updated to show actual process performance? Do the process owners trust and rely on their schedule? Why or why not?
   d. How accurate are the data and information used by the schedule? What evidence of accuracy do you have?
   e. What steps should you take to improve the overall accuracy and management of this schedule?

Quality Benefits

1. All plans and schedules are derived from business objectives.
2. Policies and procedures are in place to ensure proper control and management of the Schedule.
3. All schedules are kept current and the information used by all plans and schedules is maintained with a measured degree of accuracy.

The quality benefit of maintaining schedule and data accuracy cannot be overemphasized. The previous EWC case study is taken from a real company, and I can cite dozens of similar cases. If your factory scheduling suffers from "nervousness," where MRP requirements and schedule due-date recommendations appear to change extensively on a daily or weekly basis, don't look for quick fixes like "freezing" your schedule, or changing the regeneration to every two weeks instead of weekly. Instead, take a close, hard look at the accuracy of the data being used by your scheduling software. I'll guarantee you a realistic, executable schedule if you invest the effort to make all your data excruciatingly accurate; don't let up until you achieve 100 percent data accuracy!

11

UNDERSTANDING EFFECTIVE PERFORMANCE FEEDBACK

The often-used phrase, "you can't manage what you don't measure," illustrates the importance of measuring performance, even outside the context of Circle-4 Quality and the quality information system. *Keeping score* is an integral part of everyday life, whether we do so in an organized, methodical fashion, or in an informal, subjective manner. For example, sporting activities would be boring, aggravating, and pointless if we didn't keep score. On the informal side, many people compare their dress and grooming to the usually unwritten norms established by the world around them.

Keeping score in business provides you with the opportunity to avoid surprises, identify problems, focus on trends, and target improvement areas. Only through measuring business performance are you able to throw off the chains of reactive crisis management, and become a proactive decision maker, in control of your own destiny. Measuring the results of business operations not only gives you the ability to properly manage the business, it also signals your employees and reminds them how you expect them to behave. I have repeatedly seen a 5 to 15 percent improvement in process performance just because we started to measure it on a regular basis! If you'll recall our example in the last chapter, EWC's production manager was very creative in achieving the performance required by the few objectives he was given. Implicitly told he could ignore other operating parameters, he looked for and found the path of least resistance for achieving the highest score for his given objectives. People will behave according to how they're measured and graded, or as is the case in many businesses, people will behave according to how they're *not* measured.

PERFORMANCE FEEDBACK: THE RULES OF THE GAME

The first pathway of our quality information system established measurable objectives throughout the operation. These objectives are determined by looking for more and more detail in defining the constraints on satisfying business unit objectives. Whether or not the objectives you've established are exactly the ones you should be measuring is not a major issue. By beginning to measure performance, the results will steer you toward other constraints that are limiting process performance.

Performance feedback is the second information pathway in our QIS, and the first feedback pathway from the Company perspective. In order for this path to function fully, you must define measurements for each objective, begin making regular measurements, allow improvement decisions to be made based on those measurements, and construct the means to report performance up through the organization until it reaches the Company.

ESTABLISHING FEEDBACK

Before we begin defining measurements, let's put the whole issue of performance feedback in perspective within the business. When we defined our quality organization, we established our business intentions through goals and objectives. We committed ourselves to establishing the means to fully satisfy our Circle-4 Customer. We further implemented our intent by creating policies to define our macro-processes and functional responsibilities and to establish an operational network. Once our business unit objectives have been translated throughout the operation, each department has the responsibility for ensuring that their assigned processes, defined via controlled departmental policies and procedures, are capable of meeting their objectives. Just as objectives will tell our employees how they will be measured, policies and procedures will tell them how they're supposed to execute their assigned responsibilities. We cannot have one without the other. It is unacceptable to tell employees how we're going to measure them if we haven't already told them how they should act in working toward that result. If your company does not operate using approved policies and procedures for all processes, don't bother measuring performance in those delinquent areas where policies and procedures are outdated or nonexistent. Do first things first. *Your employees must understand the rules of the game before you give them an objective and ask them to keep score.* This maxim also points out the underlying premise of performance feedback, "How well do we do what we said we would do?"

HOW TO DERIVE MEASUREMENTS FROM OBJECTIVES

Knowing that we've fully documented our processes, and knowing that we keep our policies and procedures meticulously accurate, let's get on with the business of measuring performance. The measurements themselves need to be defined by the employee or group assigned the objective, with that definition confirmed and supported by the next level of management. The process of deriving measurements is straightforward and repeatable for all types of objectives. The constraint analysis conducted to translate our objectives is a useful tool in helping to determine accurate measurements.

What evidence can be extracted from the process to demonstrate compliance with the objective?

This should be a fairly straightforward question to answer, provided your objective has been specifically worded. Let's extract an example from the EWC constraint analysis in Appendix 3. For the purchased material constraint beneath material availability, the following current-year objective was derived and presented to the purchasing supervisor: "Create and maintain an improving trend of purchase part quality and delivery to attain a level of greater than 95 percent on-time delivery with 100 percent part acceptance." In reality, this objective is probably going to be subdivided amongst the buyers, but for our purposes we'll allow the supervisor to fully construct a performance measurement. The wording of the objective is precise and unambiguous. EWC's management is interested first and foremost in seeing an *improving trend*, an important point when we begin to construct the feedback report. The requirement for an improving trend also assures the supervisor, a motivated former buyer named Gladys, that one-time satisfactory results are not desirable, in fact they're unacceptable. The evidence that needs to be extracted from the purchasing process can be derived clearly and specifically from the objective. She needs to see evidence for on-time purchase order receipts, and for quality acceptance of those receipts.

What data and information most accurately represent evidence of compliance to the objective?

There are several different ways for Gladys to measure on-time delivery and quality acceptance. She must choose the most accurate, in terms of reflecting the impact of the process on the quality delivery system. EWC is an electronics manufacturing company, and they routinely order hundreds or thousands of components on a single purchase order line item. Gladys can choose to measure on-time delivery based on total quantities of components received or she can measure line items received. Which is more accurate? Our goal is to have *all* required material available by the MRP required date, therefore the quantity of different part numbers is irrelevant for this measurement. We need to measure against our instructions to the vendor, deliver this line item by this date. The most accurate measurement, and the most objective evaluation of process impact, is through measuring received line items, with the stipulation that any partial delivery of a line item is counted as a late delivery. Before we talk about the quality of the received parts, let's finish identifying on-time delivery data by looking at delivery dates. Some purchasing systems maintain a bewildering variety of delivery dates, including the MRP need date, the original vendor promised date, the latest vendor promised date, the date the delivery date was last changed, and on and on and on. Which date is the most accurate baseline for this measurement? Purchasing has an End-user in the factory expecting the parts on the date reflected by the MRP run. Regardless of when the vendors say they can perform, purchasing must measure itself against the End-user's expectation. The only accurate delivery date against which to measure actual deliveries is the MRP required date.

Identifying the most accurate data or information for measuring the quality of received parts necessitates looking again to the End-user. The factory desires 100 percent quality acceptance of all parts. It's immaterial to them whether the 10,000 parts they require tomorrow came in on one line item or 10,000 line items—they're looking for 10,000 "fit-for-use" parts. Therefore, part acceptance should be measured against total received quantities, not against "lots" or line items.

What's the standard against which we judge the quality of received parts? We could allow ourselves to get deeply involved here and permit this chapter to overrun the book if we're not careful. There are numerous ways to structure a receiving inspection operation from visual inspection through and including 100 percent functional testing. The correct answer is found again by identifying the Circle-4 Customer requirement. Based on the design of the product, engineering defines the quality expectations of the component parts. Received parts should be inspected as defined for your business, against the part specifications approved by engineering.

Define the measurements required by the objective.

Gladys now has enough information to identify the measurements she needs to make. The objective is specific enough to indicate the format for expressing the measurement, percent acceptable compliance. Gladys has determined that the two most accurate measurements to show compliance to her objective are:

- percentage of purchase order line items received on the MRP need date (vs. all received line items); and

- percentage of acceptable parts (vs. all parts received).

There are three additional questions to answer before Gladys can say she's completely defined her measurements.

What supporting data and information are required to permit accurate evaluation of the measured performance?

Gladys has the responsibility to not only measure her process, but to also determine improvements that facilitate an improving trend toward the stated objective. If she regularly receives the measurements defined above, will she have enough information to identify improvements? The answer is no; she needs additional information. This additional information, or "supporting evidence," serves to characterize the measurements within the entire process and allows visibility on the pervading influences that created the measurement. In our example, Gladys determines that it's not enough to only see the on-time delivery measure. She wants to see early deliveries, late deliveries, and on-time deliveries, both in total and subdivided by vendor. In addition, she also wants to see delivery performance against the vendor promised date as well as against the MRP need date. Now she feels she will have enough information to begin focusing on any causes of poor performance for on time delivery of purchased parts. When she considers the quality acceptance measurement, Gladys decides she wants the measurement broken down by vendor, and she also wants the nonconforming parts grouped into causes. Armed with her supporting evidence, Gladys can begin accurately evaluating corrective action and improvement alternatives.

What is my responsibility for the required data or information?

Now that she has a body of information containing the measurement, required data and supporting evidence, Gladys needs to understand clearly where her responsibility lies and where her performance is influenced by someone else's responsibility. This understanding will further characterize her improvement actions and decisions. For example, we've already identified part specifications, the baseline for quality acceptance, as an engineering responsibility. If a received part does not routinely meet the specification, Gladys has an obligation to involve engineering in the analysis and solution of the problem. If measurements show a lack of performance by a particular vendor, she has an obligation to include that vendor in any improvement discussions. Responsibilities can be clearly identified by identifying the Circle-4 Customer of the process being measured, followed by determining which players within each influence group have contributed to the measured performance requiring improvement. Clarifying Circle-4 Customer responsibilities is documented within the operating procedures and sets the stage for approaching process improvement by involving the right people for the right reasons.

What is the accuracy of the required data and information?

As the final step in defining her measurements, Gladys needs evidence of the accuracy of the data and information she's using as supporting evidence, in addition to making the measurement itself. This becomes particularly important as measurements move farther away from the QDS and become consolidated measurements such as overall schedule execution or product quality. The accuracy of performance variables affect one another algebraically. For instance, if performance measurement C is based on data A and B, if A is only 80 percent accurate, C can be no more than 80 percent accurate if B is 100 percent accurate. If both A and B are 80 percent accurate, then C can be no more than the product of the accuracies of A and B, or no more than 64 percent accurate. In a very complex set of interrelated processes, such as a typical manufacturing business, this effect has serious implications. As the Company, you may be presented with measurements consolidated from three, four or more lower-level measurements. If a consolidated measurement consists of three measures, and each has an accuracy of 95 percent, the accuracy of the consolidation can be no more than 85.74 percent. The implication is that two out of every ten decisions you make based on this measurement will be wrong!

Just as we talked about the need for schedule accuracy in the last chapter, you have a responsibility as managers to mandate data accuracy. Partially done through the wording of objectives, you need to ensure understanding of the requirement through a performance measurement policy that specifically defines data accuracy. Product data, including product structure, product documentation, and part specifications must be 100 percent accurate, or as close as you can possibly get. Process data, including schedule dates, quantities, costs, and leadtimes must be more than 95 percent accurate. If Gladys is serious about achieving her objective, she needs to be keenly aware of the accuracy of the data she's using. This of course, can and should lead to performance measurements of data accuracy. For instance, as she measures on-time delivery against MRP need date, what percentage of the open purchase order line items reflect the latest MRP need date as the required delivery date? The answer to this question can have a significant impact on the validity and success of her improvement actions. If her vendors are delivering against dates that are only 80 percent accurate compared to MRP needs, they could be achieving 100 percent on-time delivery from their perspective, when Gladys sees only 80 percent performance. Without knowing the accuracy of the required delivery dates, Gladys may waste her resources if she looks at improving vendor performance through additional education and training or through more frequent calls for purchase order status.

With Gladys's help, we've established the process you need to follow to define measurements that support your objectives, collect supporting evidence, confirm data accuracy, and establish the basis

UNDERSTANDING EFFECTIVE PERFORMANCE FEEDBACK **141**

for accurate decisions for improvement or corrective action. In summary, the six steps of this process are:

1. Extract evidence from the process to demonstrate compliance with the objective.
2. Define the data or information which accurately represent evidence of compliance to the objective.
3. Define the measurements required by the objective.
4. Identify the supporting data or information required to permit accurate evaluation of the measured performance.
5. Clarify the Circle-4 Customer responsibility for specific process performance.
6. Validate the accuracy of required data and information.

What Is Statistical Process Control?

Before we move on from the subject of defining performance measurements, let's mention a specialized type of performance measurement that's become very useful in many companies. Statistical process control, or SPC, has a definite and useful place within our quality system. Although it is used mainly with the repetitive processes of the factory, SPC is an effective tool to use when large and/or diverse sets of data are involved, or where analysis appears complex and ambiguous. Keep in mind that SPC does not define the measurement, but instead identifies the methods of making defined measurements.

HOW TO DETERMINE MEASUREMENT FREQUENCY

Now that Gladys has defined her measurements, she needs to begin measuring. How often should she measure? At the risk of being flippant, the answer is based on the measurement being taken. Should Gladys measure purchase delivery and quality once a year, just before her annual review? She can see that annually is not often enough. Well, what about the other extreme? Gladys really wants to maintain control of her vendors, so maybe she should measure delivery and quality on an hourly basis. What do you think? That might be a little bit too often for a moderately complex measurement. Her people would spend all their time measuring performance. Both extremes certainly appear incorrect. What basis should be used to determine measurement frequency? There are no hard and fast rules, but the following guidelines will help you determine measurement frequency:

1. Measure more frequently than you report.
2. Measure at least as frequently as the cycle of the process being measured.

In a minute we'll talk about reporting format and reporting frequency. You need to measure your process more frequently than the reporting requirement in order to allow for evaluation and decision making toward improvement. Gladys is required to report performance against her objective to Grace Chavez at the end of each fiscal month. If she only makes a measurement to coincide with her reporting requirement, any improvement decisions she makes, which also need to be reported, will most likely be made in haste, and with an eye to the reporting deadline. Gladys needs to measure more often than monthly. Looking at the second guideline, there are two major process cycles that affect Gladys' purchasing process. First, EWC runs MRP on a weekly basis in order to update the factory schedule. Second, EWC is working toward a JIT factory, with the expectation that daily vendor deliveries will supply the factory within a year. Today, however, planned work orders are kitted weekly, usually with no more than one work order per specific assembly per week. Given this information, Gladys reasonably concludes that she needs to measure her performance at least weekly, but should give some serious consideration to daily measurements as the factory gets closer to Just-In-Time. As measurement frequencies are defined and implemented, don't be deterred by the apparent need to make frequent measurements. Rather than forego measurements because the resource impact appears high, instead try and automate the measurement. With the exception of some top-level performance measurements, the business operating software ought to be able to extract the data and report the measurement to your satisfaction. If data processing tells you it's not possible, or that it will take a zillion hours of programming, remind them who the customer is (you!) and make your expectations clear. A programming investment on the front end is far more cost effective than tying up ongoing resources manually extracting data and reporting measurements.

Identifying Improvement Opportunities

Determining actions to improve process performance involves detailed analysis of the measurement data and supporting evidence. One of the most straightforward approaches to identifying improvement opportunities is to begin with the measured result and ask "Why?" five times. Let's see how Gladys makes this work. Presented with an on-time delivery rate of 75 percent for last week, she asks, "Why was our delivery performance only 75 percent?" She discovers that two vendors are delivering at 30 percent and the remainder are above 95 percent. "Why are two vendors delivering at 30 percent?" Both are the newest vendors and are required to deliver fairly standard components. "Why are the two newest vendors delivering so poorly?" Gladys determines that EWC started buying from them prior to conducting a supplier quality audit. "Why did we fail to do an audit for these vendors?" As it turns out, both vendors are big-name, nationwide distributors for their component lines. So far, Gladys has only asked why four times and she has a pretty good idea what needs to be done as an improvement activity. She's probably going to start with a supplier audit and with some vendor education so both new vendors understand EWC's expectations.

Deciding on an improvement action is only the first half of the improvement process. The second half is identifying the changes required in the quality documentation to assure everyone that the constraint being lessened or eliminated will not resurface, or at least will not resurface easily. The improvement action is complete when the defined corrective action has occurred and the requisite process changes have been documented. Following the supplier audit and vendor education, Gladys will review purchasing policies and procedures to ensure that these activities are required before purchases are made from any new vendors. Gladys will then retrain her buyers, even if the documentation is found to be correct, and document the training in their ongoing training records.

GENERATING COMPLETE AND INFORMATIVE REPORTS

The requirement to report performance back through the quality organization will complete this second pathway of the information system. Generally, reporting frequency is mandated by the next level of management. Format and content of the report may also be mandated. If it is not, there are a few simple guidelines to follow to ensure a complete and informative report.

1. The measurement is reported in the form identified by the objective.
2. Trends are important whether or not they're specified in the objective. Trends are presented in graphical form, covering a horizon pertinent to the objective. For valid trend analysis, a minimum of six prior reporting periods should be visible on the graph. If it's possible to view results that cover a year or more, so much the better. Longer visible trends will allow evaluation of seasonal cycles and other low-frequency performance influences.
3. Improvement decisions are always mentioned, citing applicable supporting evidence as the basis for the decision. Subsequent reports will show the status of ongoing improvement activities until they are completed and considered closed.
4. Required data, supporting data and information, and data accuracy will be collected, controlled, and maintained at the local level and only included in the report if required.

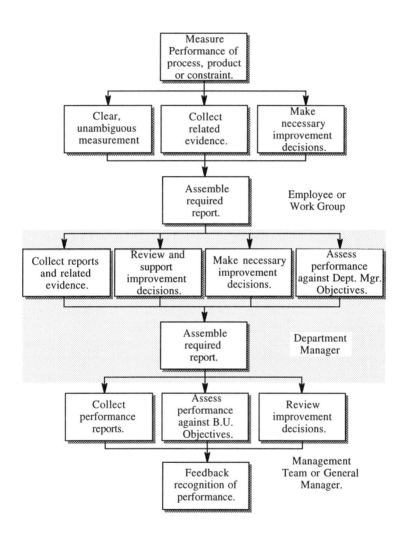

Figure 11.1 The process of managing through performance.

Management is the Shareholder for performance reports, and as such, their expectations should be solicited and satisfied.

Creating performance feedback from your communicated objectives involves defining the measurements, making the measurements, identifying, implementing, and documenting improvements, and making regular reports to management. This pathway in the quality information system stimulates ownership and accountability throughout the operation, and permits the Company to routinely and accurately monitor the lifesigns of the quality system. Figure 11.1 depicts this process of managing through performance from the employee level up through and including the Company.

In the next chapter the Company takes a more active role in "closing the loop" for the information system as you become involved in the process of recognition and simulation.

SUMMARY

1. You can't manage what you don't measure.
2. Performance feedback is the second communication path of the QIS and requires the following:
   a. Define measurements for each objective.
   b. Make regular measurements.
   c. Make improvement decisions based on the measurements.
   d. Report performance to management.
3. Measurements are defined from objectives using the following steps:
   a. Extract evidence from the process to demonstrate compliance with the objective.
   b. Define the data and information which accurately represent our evidence of compliance to the objective.
   c. Define the measurements required by the objective.
   d. Identify the supporting data or information required to permit accurate evaluation of the measured performance.
   e. Clarify the Circle-4 Customer responsibility for process performance.

f. Validate the accuracy of required data and information.
4. Performance measurements should be made more frequently than the reporting requirement and at least as frequently as the cycle of the process being measured.
5. Management is the Shareholder for performance reports. General format guidelines include:
   a. Report in accordance with the objective being measured.
   b. Include trend analysis.
   c. Cite improvement decisions and provide status for prior decisions.
   d. Include supporting data only when requested.

Quality Applications

1. Evaluate your performance feedback information flow using the guidelines in this chapter and by answering the questions below. Based on your answers, discuss improvements for your performance feedback.
   a. Are all communicated objectives measured on a regular basis?
   b. Is the accuracy of each measurement traceable and routinely verified?
   c. Do you have visibility for business performance trends?
   d. Are quality system improvements driven by performance measurements?
2. Discuss the importance of identifying and involving the Circle-4 Customer at all levels of your business as a part of regular performance feedback.

Quality Benefits

1. Performance feedback has become the recognized method of verifying operational performance against communicated objectives.
   Just beginning to measure performance will guarantee you an

improvement in results. I have repeatedly seen immediate performance improvements of 5 percent, 10 percent, and 15 percent brought about solely because we started measuring. The measurements are seen by the employees as what's important to the boss, and they almost subconsciously begin to do a better job in those areas.

2. Quality system improvements are identified and pursued as a result of regular, accurate performance feedback.

   Because you now have a performance feedback system which is totally linked to your business unit objectives, you have the visibility to trace the source of exemplary, or unacceptable, performance back to specific process areas. Further, you know instantly what action has taken place to create exemplary results, or what action is taking place to improve unacceptable results. This total visibility simplifies daily business management, allowing you to spend more time on strategic issues.

3. Recognition and understanding of Circle-4 Customers is accepted as a prerequisite to identifying any quality system performance improvements.

12

THE IMPORTANCE OF RECOGNITION AND SIMULATION IN THE INFORMATION SYSTEM

The third important path in the construction of the quality information system is *recognition and simulation*. It may be viewed as the most controversial, but also most potentially beneficial, element of the entire quality system.

Your goal in creating a quality information system is to establish a formal, consistent flow of information within the quality system. Your intent in creating the QIS is threefold: First, you want all employees to receive, understand, and accept specific business objectives that reflect the requirements of your Circle-4 Customer. Second, you want your employees to routinely assess performance against their objectives, determine necessary improvements, and provide feedback to you, the Company. Third, you want to create ownership and involvement within the Circle-4 Customer toward directing the future success of the business. The information path of providing recognition and requesting simulation of potential improvements will help create and sustain such ownership and involvement.

IDENTIFYING YOUR MANAGEMENT HABITS

As the Company (the management team), we need to recognize within ourselves a resistance to change our own behavior. We are, after all, managers. It's our destiny to shape and mold our organization into an efficient vehicle for success. We have the answers, the solutions to the problems; we have the "big picture." *We* don't have to change, we have to change our operation. If you don't believe that this is the attitude, deep down, of most managers, let's look at a typical monthly management meeting within a typical company of today. The business has been working on improvement for years. They started with MRP back in the 1970s, they played with just-in-time, and now they're enthusiastically pursuing total quality management. They promote employee involvement, they have empowered employees, they have work teams and quality improvement teams. Once a month the management team meets to review the business performance from the previous month. They review process performance measurements from each department, the status of ongoing improvement projects, and business unit results. Convinced they understand the numbers and the problems, they end the meeting by assigning action items for improvement to each of the team members. Satisfied that they've done their job as managers, the management team adjourns the monthly meeting.

I can almost see you scratching your head and asking, "So what's wrong with this picture? They did their jobs as managers, didn't they?" Of course they did, if you use the old management paradigm. Some of our management habits and paradigms are so deeply entrenched that any suggestion that they might represent incorrect behavior is often met with emotional resistance and disbelief.

If we truly and fervently believe in Circle-4 Customer satisfaction and if we sincerely desire the re-creation of our business into a total quality operation, a quality system, we must accept that 95 percent of the problems that occur within the business result from management problems. It is absolutely imperative that we examine ourselves and our actions and change our own thinking and our own behavior if we expect to see lasting continuous improvement in our business. For six years, I was a senior manager for a company now owned by Philips, the big Dutch conglomerate. There was an inside joke at Philips about a managing director who died and went to heaven. He was met by St. Peter, who proceeded to give him a tour of the facility. Midway through the tour, they entered a huge room where clocks covered all four walls from floor to ceiling. Seeing that each clock was labeled with the name of a corporation, the managing director said, "These clocks must show the time at each headquarters." "No," St. Peter explained, "these clocks advance only when the company management makes a mistake." The managing director looked about a little more intently before asking, "Where's the Philips clock? I don't see it here." St. Peter answered, "It's not here. We needed a new exhaust fan in the kitchen!" Philips of course, has been making a tremendous effort to improve its business management and quality practices since Jan Timmer was appointed president in 1990. This story can be told in any boardroom, using any company name, and the knowing chuckles and nods of agreement will all be the same.

Creating a Climate for Quality

The essence of this chapter is the creation of a win/win relationship between the Company and the Customer, realizing Circle-4 Quality. Up to this point we've established a valuable foundation. We've identified our Circle-4 Customers and their requirements. We have established a quality organization to satisfy those requirements and we've communicated their requirements as objectives throughout our operation. We've set up the means to measure and report the performance of our processes against the objectives. We've given our employees the responsibility to identify and implement improvements based on measuring themselves, and based on understanding their Circle-4 Customer. We stand now on the threshold of being able to empower not just our employees, but to truly empower our Customer. We cannot risk this breakthrough by clinging to an archaic management paradigm. In our monthly management meeting example, the management team clung to old habits by directing actions in areas for which responsibility and authority had been previously delegated.

CREATING OWNERSHIP THROUGH RECOGNITION

When we talked about the motivation and goals of our Customer, we recognized that all are driven to "make more money now and in the future." In considering such a motivation as we construct win/win relationships with our Circle-4 Customer, we cannot overlook the importance of job satisfaction. While the basic motivation to do a good job may be to make more money now and in the future, the measure of accomplishment is contained both within the paycheck and the relative assessment of job satisfaction. Job satisfaction is many things to many people. I once had an engineer working for me who accepted an offer from another company. He wouldn't listen to my counter offers, saying he was enticed by the prospect of a more *challenging* project. I've known people who regularly received promotions and pay increases but were overwhelmingly unhappy with their jobs. On the other hand, I've also known people who never seek a promotion and are happy as clams following the same routine day in and day out. The common denominator in these examples seems to be a personal sense of "contribution." Have I made a difference? Is the company better because I'm here? Do I leave work each day with a satisfying sense of accomplishment? The basic motivation to make more money now and in the future can only be sustained over time through this sense of contribution. A better term for a sense of contribution is *ownership.*

The desire to succeed springs initially from the basic motivation to make more money now and in the future. The desire to succeed is sustained and revitalized through a sense of contribution, a sense of ownership in the outcome and results of the business. A feeling of real ownership can only be created through recognition. While there are a very few people who can revitalize themselves through their own personal awareness of their accomplishments, most of us yearn for and need external confirmation that our efforts have been worthwhile. The unwitting disaster which occurred in our management meeting example was the disconfirmation of ownership by making decisions for those areas where responsibility had ostensibly been delegated. What the management team was effectively saying to their subordinates was, "We'll give you responsibility until we see the need to make a decision for you. We don't really trust you to run your operation."

CREATING A NEW PARADIGM FOR YOURSELVES

As managers, we need to create a new paradigm for ourselves in this new world of total customer satisfaction. We must determine what type of behavior supports and sustains our foundation for Circle-4 Quality. Let's take a look at the monthly management meeting in a different company. Our company model, EWC, Inc., has as many problems as any other company, but they are making a concerted effort to try and change their management habits. Let's look at how they deal with their monthly operational review.

Recalling the operational network described for EWC in chapter 7, the Company meets monthly as the Quality Steering Committee to review business results from the previous month. The meeting is chaired by the general manager, Dr. Joan Rogers, and always follows a specific agenda. Minutes are taken and published within 24 hours following the meeting. Department managers distribute their monthly performance reports two days before the meeting to give the committee an opportunity to review the information and prepare questions. The meeting generally takes an entire morning and is always fast paced and informative.

Dr. Rogers begins the meeting with a summary of EWC performance against the business unit objectives. She reviews the previous month and year-to-date results. Actual trends against plan are graphically displayed and discussed.

Each department manager then presents their performance against objectives. Following the same basic pattern, they identify previous month and YTD performance, followed by a look at unfolding actual trends. Each manager then presents the results of any completed improvement projects and the status of ongoing projects aimed at improving performance trends. Members of operational improvement teams or corrective action teams may be invited to present the results of their own work. Mention is made of any significant or noteworthy accomplishments which should be singled out for special recognition. Finally, each manager projects their performance to objectives for the next 90 days based on trends, current improvement projects, and other pertinent influences.

Wrapping up the first half of the meeting, before the coffee break, the Company determines any special performance recognition. This recognition can be targeted at any individual or group within any of the four influence groups of the Circle-4 Customer, who has demonstrated particularly exceptional performance during the previous month.

The second half of their monthly meeting has two purposes. First, guided by Dr. Rogers, they project overall future business results based on the trends they've just discussed. They brainstorm potential courses of action and pose "what if" questions to ask targeted groups or individuals within their Circle-4 Customer. Instead of directing specific action, they ask for advice from the responsible experts. For example, if they observe inventory increasing for Product Line B due to lower than expected sales, they may decide to ask two "what if" questions. The operational improvement team responsible for product marketing may be asked to investigate and recommend special promotions to boost sales. The material control OIT may be supplied with specific sales history and projections and asked to determine ways to realistically bring inventory trends back under control if booking trends don't improve. These simulation requests are communicated to the responsible parties separately from routine business feedback. "What if" requests are specifically worded, and a very short deadline is identified, usually 48 to 72 hours. Simulation requests for areas where management team members have direct responsibility are handled in the same manner; no corrective action decisions are taken during the QSC meeting.

The final item on the agenda is to outline the communication, the recognition, to be given to each major group of the Customer. Each member of the Company has a specific responsibility in this area. Dr. Rogers is responsible for holding a meeting with all employees within 48 hours of the QSC meeting. She will inform them of business performance and expectations and will recognize individuals or groups for their special accomplishments. These meetings usually last 30 to 40 minutes and are eagerly anticipated by the employees.

The directors of manufacturing and engineering are jointly responsible for issuing a quarterly bulletin to EWC's major suppliers. Each bulletin highlights significant business and supplier performance, recognizes exceptional suppliers, and provides a compilation of collected information about EWC's market and the electronic components market in general.

The directors of marketing and sales, customer service, and product planning and support are responsible for a similar quarterly bulletin issued to all of EWC's End-users. Highlighting sales trends and product information, each bulletin also includes items of interest about suppliers, company operations, and any significant product creation partnerships between EWC and specific End-users. Product application notes and tips collected from the user base are included as well.

Stuart Evans, the director of administration, is responsible for preparing the official monthly report documenting the minutes of the QSC meeting, business results, and performance trends. Since EWC is a corporation owned by the management team, this report constitutes the report to the Shareholder.

We can learn a great deal about the new way we need to behave as managers from EWC's monthly Quality Steering Committee meeting. Perhaps the most important lesson is that the Company is very careful not to usurp or override the responsibility and authority they've delegated, via policy, to the operation. The goals of their monthly management meeting are to understand the results and the trends well enough to recognize accomplishments and request investigation or simulation for potential courses of improvement and corrective action. This is not a demonstration of weak, diluted management, as you might initially conclude. Rather, this is an example of proactive management at its best: steering the company by viewing the operation from the high ground, and encouraging the process experts to examine and decide on course corrections that support business unit objectives. Let's take a closer look at the human equation.

INSTILLING OWNERSHIP THROUGHOUT THE COMPANY

Through the creation of the quality organization you created functional responsibility in your company. By translating business objectives throughout the operation you motivated performance, established accountability, facilitated distributed decision making, and required performance feedback. By recognizing the decisions made and the performance achieved, you have confirmed and sustained the responsibilities previously delegated, thereby instilling ownership throughout the operation. Once you've recognized and validated past performance, you create the climate for soliciting creativity from your operation through requests for simulating various courses of future action. At this point, your employees feel truly empowered, in charge of their destiny, and in control of their assigned processes.

By following this progression, and by changing your habits as managers, you have opened the door for solid win/win relationships with your Circle-4 Customer. You have taken your operation from a stage of dependence, where you directed responsibility and objectives, through independence by recognizing and fostering ownership, to a climate of interdependence, where your employees feel truly empowered and part of the team. The beauty of this model is that it also allows you to involve the End-user, the Shareholder, and the Supplier. Though you certainly don't establish their policy or objectives, by recognizing their requirements in your objectives, and by including them in your recognition of past performance, you instill a sense of ownership in their behavior, empowering them to work together with you, since they see a realization of their objectives in so doing. This is an exciting concept and one which, if applied consistently, will elevate your operation toward Circle-4 Quality, the commitment to work in cooperation with the Circle-4 Customer in the pursuit of a profitable business. Figure 12.1 shows the dynamics we've just described, and shows also that the realization of empowerment is the only way to enable meaningful Customer feedback and cooperation. Responsibility, performance, and accountability take place between the Company and the Employee. Recognition, ownership, empowerment, and customer feedback take place between the Company and the entire Circle-4 Customer.

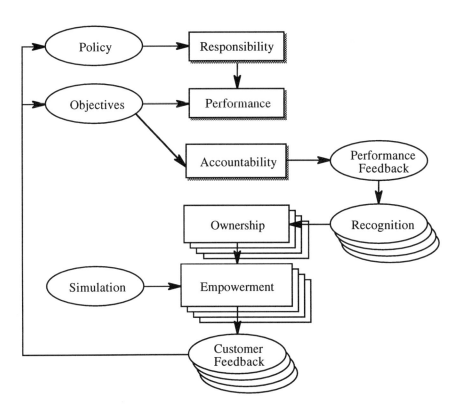

Figure 12.1 The dynamics of empowering the Circle-4 Customer.

HOW TO REINFORCE ACCEPTABLE BEHAVIOR

Recognition can take many forms. It should place performance and improvement within the context of achieving business objectives, and it should encompass a defined reward system. Rewards should be devised to fit the culture and nature of the business. Small monetary bonuses, perks accompanying "Employee of the Month Awards," and profit sharing are just some examples of potential rewards. Rewards should be applied consistently and should closely follow performance achievements. Rewards reinforce acceptable behavior and tangibly support recognition. While companywide reward systems such as profit sharing are valuable and should be applied where appropriate, special recognition such as Employee of the Month, should be administered and determined by peer groups and not by management.

Simulation can also take many forms, from the simple to the very complex. Simple analysis questions such as the ones asked in our EWC management meeting example can lead to complex simulations that ascertain the impact of introducing new product lines or entering new markets. This is a vital element of achieving complete customer satisfaction, especially since it allows the operation to visualize its future without actually impacting operations. Unfortunately, as mentioned during discussion of the Schedule, today's business system software packages do not readily and easily support simulation. You should all strive, as part of your new proactive management ethic, to continually improve your ability to model your operations and simulate the impact of alternative trends and decisions. Given the shortage of realistic computer models, it's possible to conduct macrosimulations in a conference room environment, wherein each expert brings their process constraints to the table, and through brainstorming towards "what if" objectives, the group talks its way through the possible dynamics.

You should use all of your experience and creativity as managers to construct recognition and simulation tools within your operation that foster ownership, create true empowerment, and result in real customer feedback. You've all been schooled in using a variety of problem-solving techniques and methods. Your past mindset has caused you to apply these techniques to solving problems that have already occurred in your operations. How exciting it will be for you to apply your knowledge and skills in a proactive manner, seeking to anticipate and prevent problems before they impact your business. These same tools also need to be extended to the Circle-4 Customer in a consistent, proactive manner in order to generate ever-improving levels of customer satisfaction.

SUMMARY

1. Providing recognition and requesting improvement simulation will promote ownership and involvement in business success on the part of the Circle-4 Customer.
2. Recognition of decisions and performance toward business objectives instills ownership.
3. Recognition must take place consistently and must include a defined reward system.
4. Ownership creates a climate for innovation and creativity, allowing requests for simulation of potential future courses of action.
5. Simulation allows the business to visualize its future without impacting current operations, and it instigates customer feedback.

Quality Applications

1. Review the performance feedback for the last fiscal period. Identify specific instances of exceptional performance from your Circle-4 Customer. Discuss ways of recognizing this performance.
2. Predict potential business results from current performance trends. Which performance trends need to be improved in order to achieve the best possible prediction? Identify the process owners for the targeted performance trends and struc-

ture specific investigative questions which will cause them to evaluate alternatives for improving their performance. Give them a defined, short period of time to make their evaluations and reports.

Quality Benefits

1. Commitment to recognition and simulation is the proactive method of fostering Circle-4 Customer ownership and a climate of creativity in pursuit of Circle-4 Quality. If your employees are doing a good job of making improvement decisions as part of their performance feedback, you may find your simulation requests covering much broader subjects, or extending out into the long-term horizon of the business. This is exactly where you want to find yourselves. You may also wish to assemble temporary teams of experts to evaluate some of your simulation requests. You will have willing and enthusiastic participants when they realize you're involving them in determining the future course of the business.

13

CLOSING THE INFORMATION LOOP USING CUSTOMER FEEDBACK

Substantive customer feedback is required if you hope to accurately influence and evolve your business unit objectives and keep them directed toward Circle-4 Customer satisfaction. Is it really necessary to execute the processes defined thus far for the quality information system in order to obtain valid customer feedback? Isn't there any easier path to follow? We may be able to answer these questions if we define the customer feedback your business requires and look at possible means for obtaining it.

Every influence group within the Circle-4 Customer, the Shareholder, the End-user, the Employee, and the Supplier, looks to the Company to provide solutions to their problems and meet their requirements. The Shareholder is looking for the means to generate return on their investment and you must be able to offer a better alternative than other investments. The Supplier is also trying to create profitability by supplying specific goods and services, and you need to provide a supportive market for their endeavors or they'll look for more amenable customers. The Employee is looking for a satisfying, challenging career and the opportunity to periodically improve their financial position. If you cannot establish such an environment, your employees will become distracted looking for other opportunities that meet their needs, and as a result will become less efficient, adding cost instead of value to your operation. The End-user is not interested in your products and services themselves. Very few companies have the luxury of marketing a totally unique product. End-users are interested in your ability to help them be successful, to solve their problems, through the informed application of your products and services.

MAKING A COMMITMENT TO CUSTOMER EXPECTATIONS

When we engaged in the process of identifying Circle-4 Customer requirements in chapter 3, we mentioned the possible need to commit ourselves to action if the Customer raised any immediate issues in the current relationship. The presence of unresolved expectations will always block any discussion or feedback about future needs and requirements. At one of my previous companies, our central copier was the product of a well-known leader in the copier industry. The reliability of our copy machine was so poor that we often joked about giving the repair technicians an office and putting them on the payroll. Their service response time was excellent, and most of the repairs were expedient, but the continuing low mean time between failures left us with the uncomfortable feeling that we'd bought a lemon. When we began analyzing our future copier requirements, we got quite a sales pitch from this company. We really didn't even want to talk to them; as far as we were concerned we'd learned our lesson. They didn't understand and meet our immediate expectation for reliability as well as performance and prompt service. We essentially told them, "Based on our past relationship, we don't even want to talk to you about our future needs. You haven't met our expectations, so why should we think you can start doing so now?" Needless to say, we bought their competitor's copier.

The Customer will always tell you to put first things first. "Meet my needs today or don't bother talking to me about tomorrow." The quality information system is structured to do just that. Your business objectives represent today's customer expectations. You communicate them throughout the operation and then require performance feedback to measure the effectiveness of your processes in meeting customer requirements. By recognizing performance and making that information available to the Customer, you're involving them in the understanding that you are improving and that you do have a commitment to their expectations. If you're successful in your performance and in communicating that performance, you can begin to request the meaningful dialogue necessary to keep your objectives current and accurate.

For the sake of discussion, let's suppose that you're meeting the current expectations of the Customer. How do you go about obtaining worthwhile feedback concerning their future expectations? We touched on the front end of the process in the last chapter when we talked about requests for simulation, asking your Customer to give their expert opinion for alternative courses of future action.

How to Establish Regular and Substantive Feedback

Let's explore Customer feedback in more detail, looking at each influence group of the Circle-4 Customer.

Getting End-User Feedback

The End-user is the center of your universe, as far as evolving Company strategy. Depending on the nature of your business, End-user feedback can take a variety of forms. You're interested in evolving your products and services so they continue to meet the requirements of the End-user. You may consider establishing a customer hotline to allow End-users to call in with application questions and product problems. If you do so, you must be prepared to follow through with at least interim solutions to *all* issues that arise. Statistics must be kept on questions and problems that are raised through the hotline, even to the point of polling a broader market sample to determine the pervasiveness of some of the issues. Those with general applicability will be infused into your objectives and your product plan.

Another major issue confronting the Company when considering the future requirements of the End-user is the evolution of technology. Far too many companies allow technology to drive their product evolution, often to the point where they create products looking for a market. A good example of this misplaced priority is the creation of high definition television (HDTV) within the professional video industry. HDTV, which has yet to become a commercial reality in the U.S., and is far from being seen as the solution to a problem by consumers, is an industry attempt to rejuvenate a stagnant segment of the electronics industry. New technology can be a wonderful asset, provided it fills a need. As you participate in the evolution of your technology, it is imperative that you involve the End-user in determining whether realistic applications of new technology will support *their* long-range goals and objectives. This involvement can come through product development partnerships, trade shows, user groups, and product application conferences. While you should certainly help the End-user envision future possibilities, you must be very careful not to create solutions for nonexistent problems.

Getting Supplier Feedback

Your primary windows for viewing the evolution of the basic technology used in your products and services are through your own research, the activities of your competitors, and feedback from the Supplier. In our old operating paradigm, the Supplier was an untapped goldmine. "Captive" suppliers, or ones that exist for the benefit of a single company, are the exception rather than the rule. Captive suppliers should be treated as employees or as distinct departments within the business. The majority of suppliers are not captive and provide raw material to a variety of customers and thus can be an invaluable source of information. In addition to keeping you apprised of the long-range availability of their particular raw materials, they can also tell you how other companies are applying their products and how overall demand is steering the evolution of their products, technology, and services.

If you fail to foster this communication, the impact on your business could be disastrous and costly. I know of several instances where our company specified a state-of-the-art electronic device in a new product, only to have the supply eliminated six months into product launch because we were the only user and we didn't create sufficient demand for the Supplier. Or, in several other cases, we specified a new device only to have it eliminated because the supplier couldn't economically resolve technical performance and manufacturing problems. The best forum to create meaningful feedback from the Supplier is not in the purchasing department, but in product development. Suppliers know this, by the way. They're always trying to get in to see the engineers, often bypassing purchasing in the process. Purchasing should always be involved in these communications, and you must take deliberate steps to educate the Supplier to prevent them from only trying to sell you a product rather than trying to help you solve the problems of your End-user. Once you've cultivated Suppliers who meet your current expectations, and once they're satisfied with the business relationship, you need to be open with them about your new product plans and expectations. Involving the Supplier right from the start of the new product creation process can result in lower development costs and faster time to market. A win/win relationship with the Supplier will allow you to benefit from their experience and knowledge.

Getting Employee Feedback

Customer feedback from the Employee, among other things, allows the Company to utilize process experts to improve and evolve the mechanics of creating and producing products. You need to continuously nurture this creativity by giving employees the opportunity to visit similar operations, participate in professional organizations, and attend trade shows and seminars. Employee development should be encouraged by supporting higher education and by providing abundant training opportunities for everyone, including yourselves. I would suggest that a minimum of 5 percent of the available working hours be allocated to education and training activities. By exposing your personnel to the most progressive business and operations concepts, you're giving them the tools to create effective continuous improvements within their operations. Other types of training should be planned and administered on a cyclical basis. Refresher training on the company quality system, total quality philosophy and methods, teamwork, personal interrelationships, and values serve not only as reminders but also reconfirm your direction and commitment to the Employee.

Feedback from employees may come from directions other than as responses to simulation requests. Employee suggestion programs, regular "think tank" sessions, or informal department or team meetings are potential vehicles to encourage thinking and creativity. One of the most important concepts to remember as you foster real creative dialogue between the Employee and the Company is allowable risk taking. Employees need to understand the potential outcomes of their ideas and suggestions, but they also need to feel unthreatened by the possibility of failing or making mistakes. Risk taking should be encouraged, mistakes should be viewed as learning experiences, and in no instance should an employee be chastised, reprimanded, or dismissed for making an honest mistake. The day that occurs, you've set back your total quality efforts by years.

Getting Shareholder Feedback

Perhaps the most difficult area of Circle-4 Customer feedback to manage is feedback from the Shareholder. The Shareholder may be very close to your business unit, as is the case with EWC, or very distant. In all cases, the Shareholder is the boss and calls the shots. The primary interest is in the bottom line and improvement of profitability from one year to the next, along with reasonable growth of the business. As the Company, you have an obligation to give the Shareholder a realistic, comprehensive summary of the business on a regular basis. It is important within that view to clearly communicate your best analysis of the future, based on historical trends and on analysis of feedback from the End-user, Supplier, and Employee. If this feedback is missing or incomplete, the preponderance of your evidence for the future will be based on trends and past history. Without meaningful Customer feedback, you may be blindsided by an emerging dynamic within one of your influence groups. You cannot effectively communicate with your Shareholder without having reliable and accurate feedback from your other influence groups. You also need to keep abreast of any other dynamics that influence your Shareholder, and you need to be sensitive to their current motivation. Is there a requirement for greater short-term profits in order to support a new start-up elsewhere? Will a potential new market for you complement or compete with their other interests? Open and honest communication with your Shareholder will give you these insights and will allow you to present business information in a manner designed to solicit ongoing support and commitment.

Once you've established regular and substantive feedback from the Shareholder, based on your own recognized performance and your analysis of future alternatives gleaned from feedback from the Customer, you have succeeded in closing the loop within the quality information system. You now have a clearly established strategic direction, one which you will continuously monitor and fine tune, and one which you will publish and communicate by regularly updating your business unit objectives.

SUMMARY

1. Customer feedback is required in order to accurately influence and evolve business unit objectives.
2. Meaningful customer feedback is only possible if current customer expectations are met.
3. Mutually beneficial relationships with the Circle-4 Customer will enable regular forums to be established for customer feedback.

Quality Application

1. Discuss potential forums to obtain customer feedback from your Shareholder, End-user, Employee, and Supplier. Identify the kinds of information from each group which would be most beneficial to you for validating and/or improving your business

unit objectives. Are there any unresolved issues that prevent you from establishing your defined forums and seeking the identified information?

2. Quantify allowable risk taking within your company. As your employees seek to improve products and processes, what limits will you impose on their creativity? What factors govern the identified limits? Do you have an action plan to ease or broaden the limits thus encouraging more creativity?

Quality Benefits

1. Understanding and recognizing that beneficial customer feedback is only possible within a structured quality information system.
2. Realization that only meaningful customer feedback can lead to real improvement of business unit objectives.

14

CREATING A FLOW OF INFORMATION THROUGH QUALITY DECISION MAKING

We've described the elements of a functional quality information system. We've translated and communicated business unit objectives, which reflect the requirements of the Circle-4 Customer, throughout the quality organization. We've catalyzed performance feedback and we've empowered our employees by recognizing their performance. By providing recognition of our quality system performance to our Customer, thus showing them our realization of their requirements, we've created ownership and established an interdependency that has provided us with valid and substantive feedback. We've completed the cycle by influencing and improving business unit objectives with the feedback we've received.

The flow of information within our information system is fueled by decision making. The timing of information flow is dictated by our processes, and hence by the policies we've established to create those processes. The quality of our information is directly proportional to the quality of our decisions. Let's take a closer look at both decision timing and decision quality.

THE CIRCLE-4 CUSTOMER GUIDES EVERY PROCESS

When you established the macro-processes of your quality organization, you reflected in those processes certain characteristics as dictated by customer requirements, through your business unit objectives. By delegating process responsibility, you made your employees responsible for further defining their assigned processes, via detailed procedures, and for creating schedules which are characterized by product, quantity, time, and cost. As we examine any correctly defined process within your operation, we should see a reflection of the most important characteristics of your global quality system. The macro should be reflected in the micro. The most important characteristic is the presence of a Circle-4 Customer as the guiding influence for every process. In order for it to mesh completely within the quality system, each defined process must have a Shareholder, an End-user, a Supplier, and an Employee. Within the universe of a particular process, the Shareholder defines the mechanics of the process and the expected results via policy; the End-user defines the process output in terms of quantity, quality, and timing; the Supplier provides the necessary raw material at the proper time, and the Employee works the process "machine" to convert the raw material to the expected output. Teamwork among

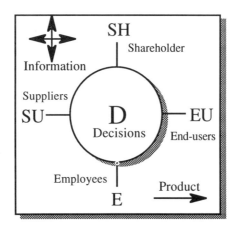

Figure 14.1 A Customer-oriented process.

the four involved parties and the process owner results from decisions made within the process boundaries. This concept includes,
but expands upon, the Circle-4 Quality view of customer-supplier
relationships. This view includes the need to create information, as
well as product, in each of your processes. We might visualize a
process fueled by decision making, as shown in Figure 14.1.

This model also allows us to accurately visualize interconnec-
tions between processes, as illustrated in Figure 14.2. Always looking at the world from within the process, the End-user elegantly
links to the Supplier, and the Employee links to the Shareholder.

From the point of view of process C, process A is the

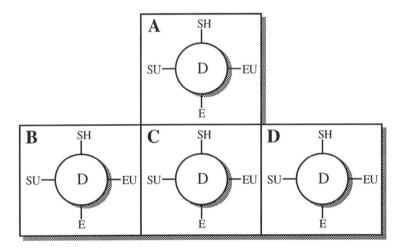

Figure 14.2 The interconnection of Customer-oriented processes.

Shareholder, B is the Supplier, and D is the End-user.
Correspondingly, from the point of view of process B, process C
is the End-user, and so on. The Circle-4 Customer for a given
process is identified within the procedure created for the process.
Within the same procedure, reference to the directing policy
establishes the Shareholder. The Supplier is identified by specifying prerequisites, or conditions necessary for process execution.
The End-user is characterized through the required results, and

the Employee through defined process actions. End-user requirements are further defined through the schedule that fuels process activity.

Determining Information and Decision Timing

Information and decision timing required from each process are determined by the End-user and Shareholder of the process. The End-user determines the quality, quantity, and timing of process output and the information that must accompany this output. Consequently, information must flow at the same speed to the Supplier in order to match the supply of raw material to the required output. The Shareholder demands periodic information about actual process characteristics. This timing is usually a multiple of process iteration, in order for a sample or a trend over time to be visible. This information will precipitate process improvement decisions, which will be defined and applied to the process by the process owners, and which is again measured after an appropriate number of iterations. Information timing progresses in this fashion up through the quality system until consolidated information reaches the Company.

In general terms, information and decision timing is at its fastest the closer you are to the quality delivery system, the production of your products and services. Production information and decisions can occur minute by minute, depending on required throughput. Information is passed up through the various Shareholders as defined by policy. Consolidated production results may only reach the Company weekly or monthly. Recognition may take place monthly or quarterly. Customer feedback can occur at a variety of intervals, depending on the forum. Product partnerships may result in relatively rapid customer feedback; employee suggestions may be processed weekly or monthly, feedback from the Shareholder may only be requested quarterly or semi-annually. Business unit objectives are normally only influenced by total customer feedback on an annual cycle, correspondingly, objectives are retranslated throughout the operation on an annual basis as well. The exact timing of information flow through your operation will largely depend on your defined quality organization, your products and services, and your End-user requirements.

DEMANDING EVIDENCE OF ACCURACY FOR QUALITY DECISIONS

The quality and accuracy of your decisions are major factors in the quality and accuracy of your information. In fact, since data become information only through the decision process, you can conclude that, other than availability of accurate, valid data, the only influence on the accuracy of your information is the accuracy of your decisions.

Quality decisions have the following characteristics:

1. They're made as close to the process disturbance as possible.
2. They consider the Customer.
3. They demand accurate data.
4. They ease constraints rather than become constraints.

The need for a decision is created by a disturbance in the process. These disturbances, which can also be viewed as constraints or bottlenecks, are best evaluated by someone with detailed, intimate process knowledge. As one becomes further removed from the process, either organizationally or by time, decision accuracy is significantly reduced. It's obvious that a person who's been outside of a particular process for ten years will not make accurate decisions for disturbances that occur today. Why then should a manager who was promoted six months ago continue to make decisions regarding his former process, even if the process is still within his department? He shouldn't: As vice president of operations, he has no business making production decisions; he hasn't been the production manager for years. This validates the need to delegate responsibility and emphasizes why you should never override the decision-making authority of those delegates. You should absolutely offer your advice and your experience when asked, but you should not make the decision unless you *directly* own the process.

Quality decisions consider the needs of the process Customer. Since the underlying goal of any process is to accomplish its task as efficiently as possible, harmonized teamwork among the process influences is mandatory. As the requirements of the process are considered, priority must be given to the Shareholder and to the End-user. The needs of the Supplier and the Employee are important but subordinate. Considering the Circle-4 Customer in process decisions is so important, that in the past I've required process End-users to approve procedures before they're considered official. The need to consider the Customer in all decisions is not indicative of a mandate to make team decisions. The process owner may want to directly involve the Customer in some decisions, but most can be made in light of the objectives. Communicated objectives given to process owners reflect the prioritized requirements of the Customer. If a process owner determines that the decision supports the realization of the given objectives, group discussion is not necessary. Where the potential decision may impact the Customer, an appropriate discussion and analysis should take place, with the final decision made by the process owner.

There is no way to make a good decision using bad data. One of the first questions any decision maker should ask is, "How accurate are the data?" Demand evidence of data accuracy. Look at how often and by what method the accuracy is determined. If we're using information derived from data, demand evidence of accuracy for both the information and the data used. If you cannot confirm data accuracy, stop the decision-making process until the data are measured and their accuracy confirmed. Too many potentially great decisions have turned into great blunders because data accuracy was assumed or estimated rather than measured. As mentioned in chapter 11, basic company data must be excruciatingly accurate if you have any hope of maintaining reasonably accurate schedules and achieving reasonably accurate business results. In fact, we can go so far as to say that inaccurate data are the result of poor management and undisciplined employees. There are no other causes.

You must demand accurate data before you make decisions—your job depends on it.

Decisions must be made with the expediency demanded by the process. To do otherwise constitutes foot dragging and results in the unmade decision becoming the major constraint. This symptom is most apparent in companies that refuse to delegate or refuse to live by delegated responsibility. This is often a cycle of poor management that feeds upon itself. Some managers insist on making all decisions themselves. However, since they're far removed from the process, they often don't feel like they have enough data or information to make an expedient decision, or they're faced with the need to make so many diverse decisions that they procrastinate and delay, thereby becoming part of the problem. Unmade decisions pile up on desks, convincing these managers that their company is out of control, when in reality, only management is out of control.

The process of making decisions has been discussed in several previous chapters, will be discussed again in chapter 22, and should be well understood by good managers. Keep in mind that your QIS, however well structured is fueled by your quality decisions. Those decisions create a flow of information, they create process improvements, and they must be documented within your policies and procedures if they're to be well understood and consistently followed.

The quality information system you create today won't be—shouldn't be—the quality information system you have a year from now. You need to make the QIS a living, dynamic entity, collecting and sharing information from your Circle-4 Customer and allowing you to realize corrections and improvements to your business that lead you closer to the goal of Circle-4 Quality.

SUMMARY

1. Within the quality information system, the flow of information is fueled by making timely, accurate decisions.
2. Decisions must be made in consideration of the Circle-4 Customer, which exists for every process defined for the business operation.

3. Decisions must be made by those closest to the disturbance, with the expediency demanded by the process and only in the presence of accurate data.

Quality Applications

1. Based on your discussion following chapter 8, discuss whether your identified decision-making process will benefit from the consideration of a Circle-4 Customer in all processes and in all decision making.
2. Conduct a random survey of your process owners. Do they know their Circle-4 Customer and routinely involve them in process-related decisions? How do they feel about their process management since involving the Customer?

Quality Benefits

1. Information flow is understood to be fueled by decision making.
2. Quality decisions are understood to be those based on accurate data and involving the Customer.

Benefits of this nature can often be better understood and accepted through an example of the cost and impact of not following the prescribed course of action. I recently heard about a well-known medical electronics company which was pursuing some major cost-reduction activities. One of the activities involved reducing overall component purchase prices. One of the components used extensively in their products is a specialty device with a single source of supply and a per-unit cost of several thousand dollars. When the single-source vendor refused to lower the purchase price, the vice president of finance mandated that a second source be located immediately and that the first source be cut off completely for not cooperating. A second source was located who promised the part for 15 percent less, a significant potential savings. All orders were immediately canceled from the first vendor and placed with the new source. Having depleted their inventory of this expensive component, the factory eagerly awaited delivery from the new vendor. Because of compressed leadtimes, the first lot received was immediately installed into products representing an entire month's delivery. Not one of the components worked. Surprise! I won't share with you the bloody details of what followed. In the aftermath it was discovered that the original vendor did not want to lower the purchase price because they were only realizing a 70-percent yield manufacturing the part, and unbeknownst to their customer, they were hand-selecting parts in order to deliver 100 percent quality components. The company went back to their original single-source supplier, who promptly raised their price by 15 percent! Would you care to estimate how much money this company could have saved by involving this supplier meaningfully in the cost-reduction discussions and by making a different, quality decision based on Customer understanding and accurate data and information?

PART 3

CHARACTERISTICS OF AN EFFECTIVE QUALITY DELIVERY SYSTEM

15

DEFINING THE QUALITY DELIVERY SYSTEM

We're now going to turn our attention to the third major element of the quality system, the quality delivery system (QDS). The QDS can be envisioned as all the activities directly involved with the creation, production, delivery, and support of our products and services. It is the part of our operation with which we're most familiar. Usually defined as the sequence of processes necessary to manage our product from cradle to grave, the QDS encompasses product definition, creation, logistics, production, sales and marketing, and support, as shown in Figure 15.1. Figure 15.1 also shows that the system is normally segmented into major responsibilities by department. Product management is shown, not as a distinctly defined process within the QDS, but rather as an oversight management activity for the entire delivery system. In order to fulfill their traditional assignment, product management must be aware of, and exert control over, all processes within the QDS. That control is not usually mandated through organizational hierarchy but is established through the product documentation and through the plans and schedules which drive the business.

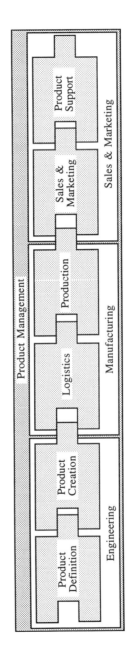

Figure 15.1 The major processes and responsibilities for a quality delivery system.

Figures 15.2, 15.3, and 15.4 depict representative delivery systems for the major areas of engineering, manufacturing, and sales and marketing. In reality, there is significant additional complexity to the process interrelationships. Within engineering, for example, many processes may occur concurrently or design reviews may exist more frequently within the system. The delivery system's interconnection to all necessary plans and schedules has also been simplified in order to focus on the subject at hand; the sequence of processes required to deliver our products and services. Actual definition, structure, and sequence of your processes are highly dependent upon your product and upon the requirements of the End-user.

The fundamental intent of the quality delivery system is to transform 100 percent of End-user requirements into reality, while striving to satisfy the prioritized needs of the Shareholder, Supplier, and Employee. Within the engineering segment of the QDS, the requirements come from the product specification, which must be 100 percent transformed into product documentation. Product documentation, along with the quantification provided by the Schedule and by customer orders, provides the requirements for the manufacturing delivery system. The product documentation again, along with actual availability of products and services, provides the requirements for the sales/marketing delivery system. In an ideal world, all of our systems would function with 100 percent accuracy and 100 percent on-time, ensuring that the End-user receives products and services exactly when needed. Unfortunately, ours is not an ideal world, and in addition to the mistakes and inaccuracies inherent in all processes, we also have to contend with that ageless nemesis of all managers, Murphy. If something can go wrong, it usually will, often at the most inopportune time. Because our world is imperfect, our quality delivery system must be equally concerned with establishing processes intended to meet the defined requirements and with establishing the ability to control those processes by measurement, feedback, and improvement toward the ideal.

Because the defined processes for your quality delivery system will be dependent on your unique products and services, we'll not

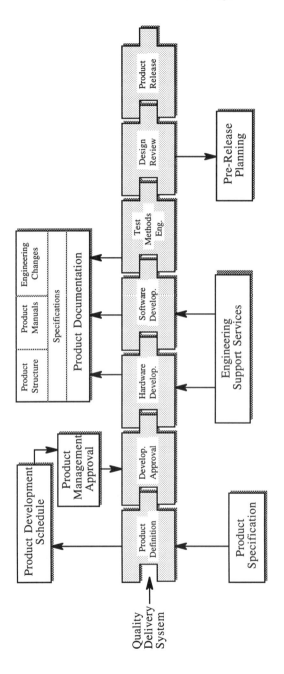

Figure 15.2 A typical engineering delivery system.

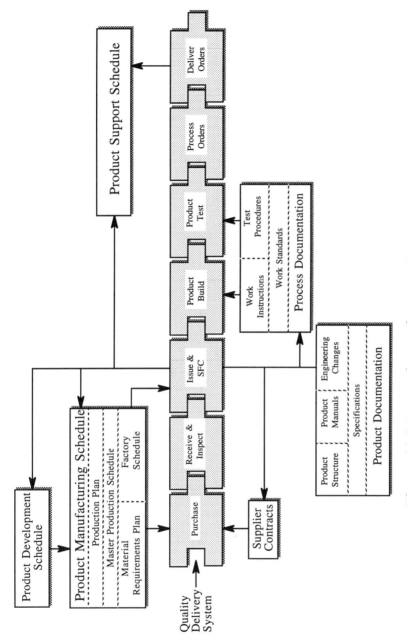

Figure 15.3 A typical manufacturing delivery system.

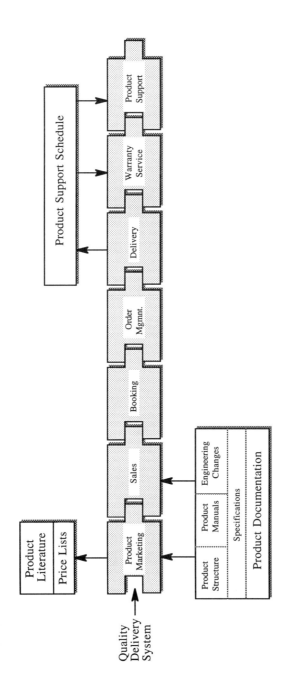

Figure 15.4 A typical sales and marketing delivery system.

advocate or attempt to define any particular QDS structure or process. While we will use our company model, EWC, Inc., to illustrate various concepts throughout Part 3, our major focus will be to define and explore the characteristics of the quality delivery system that must be present in order to enable Circle-4 Customer satisfaction through the various, specific processes defined for your business. The major elements we will address are product quality, product documentation, process definition and integration, and process execution and control.

SUMMARY

1. The quality delivery system encompasses all activities directly associated with the creation, production, delivery, and support of the products and services of a business.
2. Actual product-related processes must be defined by each individual business.
3. The major elements characterizing the quality delivery system are product quality, product documentation, process definition and integration, and process execution and control.

16

UNDERSTANDING THE SOURCE OF PRODUCT QUALITY

Every process has, as the result of its execution, a product. To ensure Circle-4 Customer satisfaction, all processes must be created with the ability to:

- respond to Customer requirements;
- supply the product required by the End-user; and
- integrate with other business processes.

In this chapter, we're going to consider product quality from the perspective of the Company by defining two critical processes which permit the pursuit of high-quality results and products throughout the quality delivery system. Those two critical processes are the creation of the product specification, followed by the product definition.

When we consider the assurance of product quality within our QDS we need to consider all the requirements of the Circle-4 Customer. One of those requirements will almost certainly be translated into objectives requiring the Company to operate the most efficient, cost-effective business possible. A logical extension of this requirement is that we define the most cost-effective methods to assure the highest possible level of product quality.

Back during my days as a quality engineer, we used to justify the early detection of quality defects with the following rule of thumb: A defect that costs $1.00 to detect in a receiving inspection, will cost the company $10.00 if it's found in the assembly operations, $100.00 if it's found in product testing, and $1,000.00 if the customer finds it. While we now focus more on preventing rather than detecting quality defects, the intent of this rule of thumb is valid today. The most economical point in a given process to prevent quality defects is at the beginning of the process. The most economical point within our quality delivery system to assure product quality is at the beginning of the QDS. The very beginning of the QDS is the point of product specification, which must precede product creation.

The ability to attain and sustain a high level of product quality is directly determined by the quality of the specification. If a new product is created from an incomplete or incorrect product specification, no amount of process control or inspection will overcome the deficiency. We're not going to talk about product quality in the factory. The factory builds what they're told to build, how we tell them to build it. We're not going to talk about product quality in purchasing, or in material control, or in product testing. All of these processes do what they're told to do, how they're told to do it. We are going to talk about *creating* product quality, not just *assuring* quality products. Product quality can only be *created* within the product specification. Any attempt at creating quality after the product specification will result in a magnitude of additional cost and diminished success.

DEVELOPING THE PRODUCT SPECIFICATION

The product specification is the initial product document that provides a thorough, detailed, unambiguous description of the product or service expected by the End-user. Teamwork is the key to preparing a complete product specification. It is prepared by a team of experts appointed by the Company from product management, sales, marketing, and engineering. While team members are assigned to detail certain elements, the specification is the result of the combined synergistic expertise of the entire team. The need to create a new product specification may arise from any new product idea submitted to and reviewed by the Company. New product ideas may come from customer feedback, end-user forums, employee suggestions, planned evolution of current products, or other knowledgeable sources. We will discuss the necessary elements of the product specification, and then we'll talk about how to obtain them.

Identifying the Customer Benefit

The most important aspect of any new product, and one which must be considered first, is *customer benefit*. You must clearly identify and verbalize the End-user problem you're trying to solve and the benefits you expect to provide your users through the product being specified. If you cannot define real benefits, benefits which can be validated and confirmed by the End-user, the success of your product idea will be at risk. The assertion that you will sell thousands of units, since no equivalent product is currently on the market, is not a benefit. The observation that development will be a fast, inexpensive evolution of a current product is not a benefit. A customer benefit proposes to make the End-user's business operation more efficient or profitable. A product that combines the accepted functionality of several current products, and does so in less physical space, for a lower End-user investment, and is easier to operate, *may* be a customer benefit if validated by the End-user.

Defining Form, Fit, and Function

Once you've established the underlying benefit of the proposed product, *form, fit,* and *function* are the next basic elements in the product specification. Form defines the look of the product: What does the End-user expect the product to look like? It may look similar to competitive products, or there may be enough dissatisfaction with current products to warrant a completely new look. The fit identifies precisely how the product is expected to interact within the End-user environment: Will the product be a component of a larger system or will it be used in isolation from other products? If it is part of a system, what crucial interfaces are required? Is there a common operational strategy that must be understood and followed in order for your product to integrate? Function of course, specifies the particular operating features and options which will characterize the product. A feature is an inherent operating characteristic that the End-user expects to be present in the product. An option is a product characteristic that the End-user may choose to purchase, based on the required application. You certainly need to understand End-user perception of necessary product features and which product options they feel are needed both now and in the future. Future features and options can scrve to direct the manner in which you physically create the product. If you anticipate providing a particular capability in the future, you may investigate lowering the cost and time to market for that enhancement by creating "hooks" within the initial product offering.

What is the anticipated *product life*? When in the future does the End-user expect to physically replace your product? Between now and that replacement, do they expect regular enhancements or upgrades in the performance of the product they purchased? Are they willing to pay for those upgrades, and if so, how much? Will evolving technology shorten the product life? This type of product life information is essential for defining product manufacturing processes as well as for steering certain physical characteristics of the product. A product that is seen as consumable by the End-user does not need to be designed with any thought toward future features enhancement. Correspondingly, manufacturing processes may be defined using much more specific and therefore, cost-effective tooling if no product evolution is planned. From here, you can draw a direct correlation to selling price; products requiring more expensive product and process "hooks" for future improvement will carry a higher purchase price. End-users will only pay the higher price if they understand and support future product upgrades.

Scheduling Delivery

Delivery is an expectation that isn't often considered as part of a product specification. In fact, understanding delivery expectations is a crucial prerequisite to defining manufacturing and stocking strategies. Does the End-user expect the product to be on the shelf, waiting for their order? Or do they recognize that the complexity of potential product options may require a configuration and order processing leadtime? If your customers expect a make-to-stock product, and you create a make-to-order product, you're going to have serious customer relations problems. Expected delivery may also bear on the form of the developed product. Short delivery times will either require finished goods inventory or a product form that lends itself to rapid manufacturing. Delivery is an important part of product quality, and a definition of required delivery belongs in the product specification.

Complying with Standards and Regulations

The last element that is mandatory for any product specification is *standards and regulations*. Are there any government, safety, communications, radiation, emission, or environmental standards with which your products must comply? A detailed understanding of required standards and regulations, including the cost of compliance or noncompliance, is a necessary part of any product specification in order for the required standards and regulations to properly influence all the elements already identified and in order to correctly estimate development and product costs. If standards and regulations are addressed after the fact, after the product creation process begins, the impact may be so severe as to kill the product completely.

HOW TO VALIDATE YOUR PRODUCT SPECIFICATION

All product specification elements should be treated with equal importance. Understanding End-user expectations for each identified element will allow a complete, in-depth description of your product or service. It may not be possible for the End-user to directly answer each element of the product specification. Market research, especially the kind you do yourselves, is a valuable tool in creating a specification. Market research should always be confirmed by at least one other quantitative source. Your research should be corroborated against market data from a reliable second source. Differences should not be dismissed or changed out of hand. Rather, you need to analyze reasons for the differences and either confirm or modify your results. You should expect to identify your own market trends based on your own complete and unique picture of End-user requirements. Your competitors may have very similar pictures, but none will be exactly like yours, because your end result will be defined to satisfy the requirements of your Circle-4 Customer, not just your End-user. As you define the elements in the product specification, have them validated by your End-user. Again, as you did with market research data, any differences that arise through your validation process should not be dismissed out of hand. Upon further investigation, you may conclude that you have a more forward-looking view for a particular element, or you may decide to modify your specification. Before finally adopting an element that is not completely End-user validated, assess the impact its adoption will have on all other elements and on End-user support. Complex market trends can be difficult to identify and track, and true new product direction is only possible through a synergistic relationship between the Company and the End-user. Seek to understand one another and to share views on products, technologies, and trends, intending always that the final product specification is a win/win specification. Continuous and regular feedback through the quality information system will allow you to set in motion an ongoing program of product trend analysis, product market research, and End-user validation of your resulting product specifications.

Using Benchmarking

Benchmarking is an analytical tool useful in preparing a specification. In fact, I would narrow the focus of many practitioners by suggesting that the only useful application for benchmarking is the comparison of your products and services with those of your competition. In order to create an efficient and successful delivery system, you must stay focused on your product. The processes required to produce your product are derived from the product specification and subsequent product definition, which we'll address in a minute. If you look at the business systems employed by the "best in the business," as some would suggest, you'll be looking at processes which are successful within the context of their products and their customer satisfaction requirements. Successful business processes in the environment of a different business may not be successful in your environment, for your products, and for your Customer. By all means, stay current on evolving process technology and consider appropriate investments in light of your improvement goals and product requirements.

For true benchmarking, apples-to-apples comparison of performance and characteristics, restrict yourself to measuring competitive products and services. Your approach to benchmarking should be complete and thorough in order for your product quality to benefit from the effort. Profile products from all your competitors, not just the heavy hitters. Maintain your profile over time, so you can see and understand competitive product evolution. It's worthwhile to see how the competition views the need for new options or new models with advanced features and performance. Look at minor, as well as major players to bring to light interesting and innovative product directions, which you can validate or invalidate with the End-user. Product benchmarking provides the opportunity to establish a well-rounded, complete picture of your market, including the current positioning of your products. A thorough understanding of competitive products will allow you to consider customer problems in light of all available solutions. If you're open and honest with your End-user in your assessment of their needs against available solutions, they'll be much more open to providing substantive feedback for your product specification. As mentioned previously, this type of dialogue is only possible if your End-users are convinced that you're satisfying their current requirements.

In order to lay a firm foundation for product quality, be thorough and aggressive in preparing your product specification. You don't want to become entrapped in "paralysis from analysis", but you do want to feel a high level of confidence in the accuracy of each element of the specification. When the specification is complete, you've reached the point of thoroughly understanding the new product characteristics and requirements. The next step toward creating product quality is identifying all the detail affecting product cost in order to determine the viability and potential profitability of the new product idea. This next step is carried out through product definition.

DEFINING PROCESSES AND COSTS THROUGH PRODUCT DEFINITION

Product definition is a product management responsibility, although concentrated participation by a team of engineering, purchasing, production, sales, and product marketing experts is required to ensure a complete and thorough result. The team usually includes the members of the product specification team, plus the identified experts from the manufacturing disciplines. Team members are again assigned responsibility for specific elements, with product management ensuring the preparation of a complete, integrated definition. Team members must have the authority, on a confidential, nondisclosure basis, to involve knowledgeable experts from their Circle-4 Customer. The minimum elements within the product definition include product configuration, the product development schedule, a manufacturing strategy, marketing strategy, estimate of product costs, and a proforma product business plan. Product definition is done as a separate exercise from product specification in order to maintain the proper priorities for product planning. The objective of product specification is the complete and thorough description of the new product. The objective of product definition is the definition and estimation of the processes and costs required to develop, produce, sell, and support the specified new product. This separation can be maintained by the requirement for Company approval of the product specification. Once you're satisfied that the specified new product fits within your mission, goals, and objectives, your approval will trigger the creation of product definition.

Creating the Development Schedule

Since product development will be the next step in the life cycle of the new product, a complete *development schedule* is the most extensive component of product definition. In addition to the product specification, *product configuration* detail is a prerequisite for creating the development schedule. Because the elements detailed in the specification may be implemented in a number of different ways, additional definition pertaining to product architecture and technology goals are first defined under the category of product configuration. Product configuration will identify internal and external product construction, materials, and technology to be used in that construction, and it will assess the risks of employing the proposed technology. The technology risk assessment plays an important role in both the development schedule and in assessing the viability of the overall product business.

As the most detailed component of product definition, the development schedule must completely and realistically identify the content and sequence of product development tasks required to realize the specified product and must also identify the resources and costs necessary to carry out all proposed development activity. Resource allocations include assignment of specific engineers and engineering support services. The actual schedule is best prepared using one of the available software packages for project planning. An estimated start date should be agreed upon, to allow actual current allocation of resources to properly impact the proposed schedule. The estimated start date is that date on which the proposed new product business will either be approved or disapproved by the Company.

The development schedule, based on the start date, identifies a timetable of tasks, each having a task description, start date, and end date. All tasks are assigned a responsible party, following which a critical-path analysis is conducted for the complete schedule in order to identify potential bottlenecks, refine the timing of the development tasks, and elevate visibility on the critical paths of the project. Current capital assets are allocated as identified resources within the project, required new capital assets are also allocated but are separately identified as necessary, timed investments. The completed development schedule includes the time-phased tasks, a responsibilities matrix, the critical-path analysis, timed costs, and timed investments. The engineering team members have the primary responsibility for creating the development schedule, with the advice and participation of product management.

Establishing Manufacturing and Marketing Strategy

Identifying a *manufacturing strategy* sets the stage for creating a delivery system model which defines how you're going to produce the product. Devised primarily by the manufacturing team members, and based on the product specification and the defined product configuration, the manufacturing strategy may be relatively brief. Describing the general make-versus-buy tactics for the proposed product, the strategy gives consideration to proposed architecture, specified standards, regulations, technology, and product delivery. The need to accommodate, implement, and protect proprietary technology is clarified within the strategy. When completed, the manufacturing strategy provides a written description of the envisioned factory delivery system, impact on current operations, technology impact, estimated capital investment, and overall risk assessment for manufacturing the proposed product. The strategy will aid in the preparation of product cost estimates for the proforma product business plan, and will serve as the framework for fully defining the manufacturing delivery system when the product business is approved.

Marketing strategy provides similar estimates for the sales and marketing delivery system, and is prepared by team members representing sales, product marketing, and product management. Using the product specification, the marketing strategy must define selling methods, estimate sales volume over the product life, propose a pricing strategy, identify marketing and advertising opportunities, recommend proposed product warranty, support, and service, and define cost of ownership for the proposed product. The overall expense born by the End-user in purchasing, using, and maintaining your product is cost of ownership. Cost of ownership, which can be one of your greatest marketing tools if you understand and manage it, includes all the costs an End-user may encounter by being your customer. Warranty, training, reliability, MTBF (mean time between failure), and repair costs all need to be considered, along with purchase price, in determining total cost of ownership. Finally, and perhaps most importantly, the marketing strategy must assess the impact of the proposed product on current product business and on the current and foreseeable product business of the competition. The new product may force the obsolescence of, or may necessitate changes in sales volume, pricing, or support for some current products. You might also devise a deliberate strategy to market the product in a manner which has the greatest negative impact on the competition.

SETTING THE STANDARDS AND LIMITS FOR PRODUCT QUALITY

The elements defining product configuration, the development schedule, manufacturing strategy, and marketing strategy lay the groundwork for the final two mandatory elements of product definition, which are preliminary product costing and preparation of a proforma product business plan. In addition, you may have noticed that all the product definition elements create a framework describing the quality delivery system necessary to develop, produce, sell, deliver, and support the proposed new product. This framework, together with the product specification, establishes the standards and limits for product quality.

Preliminary product costing is conducted by the product definition team and consists of aggregating cost estimates extracted from the preceding definition elements. Cost estimates should be grouped into general categories of recurring, nonrecurring, and capital investment costs. Recurring costs are those which will occur repeatedly as the product is produced, sold, delivered, and supported. Manufacturing labor, raw material, overhead allocations, packaging material, advertising, selling expense, warranty allocation and service expense are examples of recurring costs. Recurring costs must be refined into "per unit of product" estimates. Nonrecurring costs include engineering and engineering support labor, developmental material, documentation preparation, market research, certification to standards, product field testing, plus any manufacturing start-up costs. Capital investment cost estimates should be grouped into the major departments of engineering, manufacturing, and sales and marketing. At the point of a complete product definition, these costs will be the best available estimates based on your product configuration, development schedule, manufacturing strategy, marketing strategy, and the past experience of your business and your Customer.

As you assemble preliminary costs, it's advisable to build a data set which shows the cost variables as a function of product sales volume. This relationship is necessary information for product management to accurately calculate potential product line profitability. Product costing estimates contained in the product definition serve as initial cost targets for engineering as they develop the new product. During actual product development, the quality delivery system model will be refined and estimated data will gradually be replaced with actual data or more accurate estimates. At the conclusion of the development cycle, the final product and process definition, including all costs, becomes part of the product documentation.

The development schedule must include milestones where the current state of the product is evaluated against the product specification and where the current state of actual and planned costs is evaluated against the product definition. Deviations outside of initially established limits, in either category, will trigger an automatic reevaluation of the proposed product and product business. A regular comparison of actual costs versus the cost estimates contained in the product definition will continue as the new product is manufactured, sold, delivered, and supported. Every effort will be made to ensure that actual costs are equal to or lower than estimated costs. Throughout the product life, regular addenda will be made to the product definition, keeping definitions current and analyzing actual profitability versus the proposed profitability identified in the proforma business plan.

The Role of the Proforma Business Plan

Once the team has completed defining all other elements of the product definition, product management will extract the necessary data into a proforma product business plan. Basically a business plan for the proposed new product, the proforma plan will propose an income statement for each year of the projected product life. It may take several iterations, trying various combinations of time versus volume, until the most realistic, profitable plan is reached. Perceived market entry windows will be assessed against the development schedule. Investment timing and investment return will be calculated and integrated into the final proforma plan. The final plan also includes a summary of the various risks identified within the detail of the product definition. At the appropriate time, the completed product definition, including proforma product business plan is submitted to the Company for review. Approval of the proposed product business triggers the execution of the product Development Schedule.

COMMITTING TO YOUR PRODUCT QUALITY LIMITS

The combined front-end processes of product specification and product definition will determine the achievable limits of product quality. Once product definition is complete, it should be audited against the product specification to ensure that all definition elements accurately represent the specified new product. Any and all discrepancies must be corrected before approval is given to start development. You must be committed to devote as much time as required to the preparation and completeness of these two documents. Too often we feel such a sense of urgency to get product to market that we shortcut the product specification and definition processes.

As general manager of a high-tech electronics company, my team and I uncovered some very interesting dynamics as we started looking for total quality and for opportunities to improve our operation. Historically, our new product development took 24 to 36 months. As we began to look at and measure the constraints apparent in our processes, it was like peeling layer after layer from an onion. At the core we discovered very general and cursory product specifications, followed by incomplete development schedules and cost projections. We justified this state of affairs by rationalizing that it allowed us to "remain flexible in a rapidly changing technology." We created a self-fulfilling prophecy. We were so flexible, and we "improved" the product definition so often, that engineering was constantly shooting at a moving target. Four and five prototype cycles were normal, with a final one disguised as a "first article" or preproduction run. Engineering added their own version of feature creep by routinely suggesting additional features for little added cost. Since product release dates changed so often, we severely strained End-user relations when we booked orders in anticipation of product release. Irate customers and backlog pressure forced engineering to shortcut the development process, resulting in six to eight months of intensive engineering changes following product release. Over time, we stopped talking to sales, since we had little credibility in launching new products, and our End-users had little confidence in our product or delivery performance.

We really had a rude awakening at a major trade show in 1991, when a relatively new competitor introduced a product that sold for just over half the price of our newest model. Our product, which had every feature known to man, and was based on a 10-year old architecture, was introduced only the year before. We knew we had to do something, and do it fast. We wanted to leapfrog the competition with new, customer-defined technology—and with rapid development of a thoroughly customer-specified new product family. Resolving to create a thorough and complete product specification and product definition, we appointed a new product review board (NPRB) and gave them specific product objectives.

The team included members from engineering, purchasing, finance, production, and sales and was chaired by product management. Each member was assigned specific tasks, the results of which were analyzed and, if found acceptable, included in the specification. We benchmarked competitive products and involved several key End-users to help us evaluate the necessary elements of our product specification. The management team met routinely to review and steer the progress of the NPRB. There were some rather heated discussions amongst the team regarding the necessity, or the proposed implementation, of various features and options.

It took four months to create a specification and definition which were acceptable to the management team. We gave engineering approval to begin development at the end of August, 1991. We met all our defined milestones for product, cost, and time, and delivered the first production unit on June 15, 1992. Because we did the right job specifying our required product quality on the front end, we cut our development cycle time in half. Manufacturing also had consistent release dates to plan around, allowing us to deliver over $5.0M worth of products during the first six months after release. We were not perfect by any means, but it became crystal clear to management where product quality really begins and ends. Product quality can be no better than the product specification and product definition.

Using Controlled Quality Documents to Communicate Product Quality

Your entire quality delivery system is focused around the assurance of product quality. Once you approve a new product business, the product specification and product definition become controlled quality documents. All future product and process characteristics must be traceable to the product specification and definition in order to ensure consistent, total product quality. Periodically throughout the product life, you will audit the product against these approved standards. Areas of nonconformity must be expediently corrected, either by correcting the discrepancy, or by approving controlled changes to the specification or definition. Following specification and definition, the product development team records the results of their development efforts as additional product documentation, which also become controlled quality documents. Engineering, and engineering support staff, are predominant on the product development team, which includes product management, purchasing, production, and any other functions required to concurrently develop the complete delivery system for the new product. Product documentation is the next critical characteristic of a functional quality delivery system. In the next chapter, we'll determine how we can create and maintain quality product documentation.

SUMMARY

1. Product quality can only be created at the beginning of a product's life through a complete and accurate product specification, followed by a complete and accurate product definition.
2. The product specification is the thorough description of a new product, driven by the Circle-4 Customer, including at least the following elements:
   a. customer benefit
   b. form, fit, and function
   c. product life
   d. delivery
   e. standards and regulations
3. Product definition is derived from the product specification and describes the processes and costs necessary to create and produce a new product. Product definition includes at least the following elements:
   a. Product configuration
      —Product architecture

—Technology goals
—Technology risk assessment
b. Development schedule
   —timed development tasks
   —engineering responsibility matrix
   —critical-path analysis
   —timed development costs
   —timed capital investment
c. Manufacturing strategy
   —factory delivery system
   —operations and technology impact
   —estimated capital investment
   —manufacturing risk assessment
d. Marketing strategy
   —proposed selling methods
   —sales volume through product life
   —pricing, marketing, and advertising strategies
   —service/support cost estimates
   —cost of ownership
   —market impact assessment
e. Aggregate product cost estimates
   —recurring costs
   —nonrecurring costs
   —capital investment
f. Proforma product business plan
   —annual income statements over product life
   —aggregate risk assessment
4. Following approval, the product specification and product definition become controlled documents. All product and process activity must be routinely audited against these standards.

Quality Applications

1. Audit your most current product against the product specification by answering the following questions:
   a. Is your product specification a controlled document?

    b. Does the product you're currently delivering conform 100 percent to the specification?

    c. How have development delays, start-up problems, and engineering changes affected your new product introduction? Could these problems have been avoided with an improved product specification?

2. Discuss your new product creation process. Are you satisfied with the accuracy and completeness of your specifications and definitions? Are you satisfied with the ongoing control and influence of this information? Define potential improvements for your new product creation process.

Quality Benefits

1. Product quality must begin with the first step in the product creation process.
2. Product quality can never be any better than the product specification and the product definition.

The positive impact this concept will have on reducing development cycle time and improving product line profitability cannot be overstated. A product specification that's ambiguous or that changes continuously can do escalating damage throughout the entire product business life cycle. Faced with unclear requirements, the engineers create the product they think is required, constantly adding features and options, until some senior executive finally forces the completion and release of the product. Plagued by numerous engineering changes and poor documentation, initial production is costly—and usually late. Later on, additional features and options are readily approved, since no stable specification exists to define the limits of product capability. These additional features and options create an expensive configuration control nightmare for the factory and for customer service.

It is almost impossible to overcome the problems created by a poorly prepared product specification and product definition. On the other hand, the benefits of a well-prepared product specification and product definition can be immediate and positive. In the example I cited above, we reduced our development cycle time from around 24 months to 10 months. I'll even throw in the 4 months it took us to create the specification and definition, and say 14 months for the entire cycle. Although we did factor in a shorter development cycle in our proforma product business plan, reducing the development cycle saved the company at least $1.3M in engineering expense for this new product, compared to the old way of doing business. Not only did this savings improve the profitability of the new product family, it freed up the allocation of engineering resources for new, innovative product development.

17

USING PRODUCT DOCUMENTATION TO CONTROL AND ASSURE PRODUCT QUALITY

When development is completed and a new product is released from engineering to manufacturing, we don't truly release a physical product so much as we release the documentation required to produce, deliver, and support that product. Product documentation is the real, measurable result of product creation. Certainly we may build a number of engineering models and prototypes, in fact, it is necessary that we do so in order to routinely assess the growing accuracy and content of our product documentation. Prototypes are not turned over to manufacturing at the end of the development schedule. Instead, based on an agreement between engineering and manufacturing, and with the consent of product management, the product documentation is officially released to the factory.

In chapter 18, we'll examine how manufacturing uses product documentation as the quality basis for defining and measuring its manufacturing delivery system processes. Before we explore that relationship, let's discuss the necessary content of product documentation. Once we understand the content, we'll look at the process involved in creating quality product documentation.

How to Create Product Documentation

Product documentation comprises the first real "product" of our quality delivery system. Based on accurate, well-defined product specification and definition, we approved an acceptable product business plan and initiated the development schedule. The success of product development is measured by regularly answering three questions:

1. Does the product perform as defined in the product specification and definition?
2. Is the product completely and accurately described in the product documentation?
3. Does the product documentation completely reflect the requirements defined in the product specification and definition?

Our goal is to be able to demonstrate 100 percent compliance for all three of these measurements at the point of first product delivery. Some portions of the documentation will need to be completed during the development process, because they serve as prerequisites for and drive the creation of manufacturing processes, schedules, and the remaining additional documentation.

Product engineers need to understand very clearly the importance of product documentation. Product development isn't complete until the documentation is complete. Periodic design reviews must include an assessment of product documentation including content quality and milestone achievement as required by the Development Schedule.

Product documentation (PD) is the definitive body of work describing our products, services or both. Consisting of various documents, as shown below in Figure 17.1, PD has two general characteristics. First, it includes the product specification and product definition, the baseline standards from which all other included documents are ultimately derived. Second, all documents comprising PD require strict control consisting of formal change control, regular audit and measurement against the baseline documents, and defined distribution control. The necessity for this level of control is the fact that all documents included in PD serve as working standards, describing our product or particular characteristics of our product. Not only do we measure our produced quality against these documents, but our market establishes and maintains its expectations based on our product documentation.

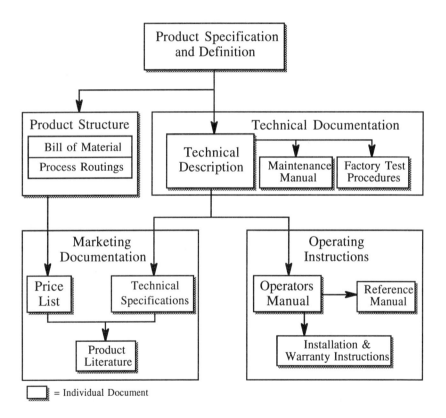

Figure 17.1 Product documentation hierarchy

The Four Categories of Documents Needed in Product Documentation

In addition to the product specification and product definition, PD consists of four categories of documents: product structure, technical documentation, marketing documentation and operating instructions. Although this discussion uses terminology from manufacturing, any organization with a defined product or service can adapt these basic concepts when creating their quality delivery system.

Product Structure

Product structure will serve as the basis for refining the manufacturing schedules and processes of the quality delivery system. Consisting of two files that have traditionally been viewed separately, the *bills of material* and the *process routings*, the product structure describes precisely what raw materials are required, what process steps are necessary, and in what sequence, in order to produce the defined product. In *The Haystack Syndrome*, Dr. E.M. Goldratt makes a convincing case for combining the two files into a single product structure file, in order to gain efficiencies afforded by today's computer systems and to establish the ability to routinely and rapidly conduct "what if" exercises.[6]

Their current separation contributes to the unwieldy, expensive, and time-consuming simulation capabilities of today's planning and scheduling software. As a result, few management teams avail themselves of simulation as a routine management tool. Simulation contributes to good decision making and we should look for advances in business system software that make it both affordable and timely. Even in our current environment, we will view our product structure as including the combined features of both bills of materials and process routings. As one of the first documents to result from starting the product development process, the product structure must be complete and totally accurate prior to releasing the new product to the factory. In a logical, hierarchical structure, it describes the precise relationship of all defined materials and processes needed to produce a finished product.

[6]Goldratt, Eliyahu M., *The Haystack Syndrome*, North River Press, 1990, Chapter 27.

Technical Documentation

Technical documentation is the final category of PD which is the responsibility of engineering. The fundamental document is the *technical description* of the product, which is fairly self-explanatory. In precise engineering language, the technical description narratively describes the form, fit, and function of the product. All applicable elements identified within the product specification and product definition must be included and readily discernible. Because they're derived from the technical description, engineering is also responsible for the product maintenance manual and any required factory test procedures.

Marketing Documentation

Marketing documentation is generally the responsibility of product management or product marketing, and includes the *price list, technical specifications,* and *product literature.* The price list is framed around the product structure. Engineering's technical description drives creation of the published technical specifications, which, together with information from the price list and customer benefits from the product specification, serve as input for product literature. Though these documents are not required to produce the product, they are part of the sales and marketing segment of the quality delivery system. A high degree of accuracy is required for marketing documentation, since these are the documents that most End-users see first.

Operating Instructions

Product management is also normally responsible for the final category of documentation, operating instructions, which include the *operator's manual, installation and warranty instructions,* and *reference manual.* The operator's manual is derived from the technical description and is written to be easily understood by the End-user. Derived from the operator's manual, installation and warranty instructions are necessary to assist the End-users immediately after product delivery. A reference manual is optional product documentation, that gives the End-user operational guidance beyond the scope and detail of the operator's manual.

HOW TO BEGIN THE PRODUCT DOCUMENTATION PROCESS

The hierarchical relationship of the documents within product documentation creates a predisposed documentation process during and immediately following product development. Product structure and the technical description need to be initiated first. All documents must be completed, approved, and released prior to the first delivery of product. Within this hierarchical structure, all document preparation must freely consult the baseline standards, the product specification and product definition. Figure 17.2 shows the general timing necessary for document development across typical stages of product development. Grouped by major category, a horizontal bar represents each defined document. The beginning, or leftmost edge, of each bar indicates the preferred time to begin creating the document during product development. The end, or rightmost edge, of each bar indicates when the document must be complete and accurate in order to support initial and ongoing product delivery.

Initiating Product Structure Documentation

As we mentioned in the last chapter, the product specification must be complete, along with the product definition, prior to beginning product development. Serving as the foundation for product documentation, the product specification and definition form the nucleus of our product structure and technical description. The product structure requires the participation of experts from engineering, product management, purchasing, planning, and production. It will grow and evolve throughout product development, becoming ever more complete and accurate as the product release date approaches. Intermediate milestones such as prerelease planning need to be carefully defined, so we can assess our level of decision-making risk, given the present level of product structure accuracy. For example, early in development we may want to focus on long-lead material, instead of complete bills of material. As development progresses, we may selectively add single-source items, proprietary purchases, then the complete product structure followed by the first MRP (material requirements planning) run. In addition to driving the entire planning process, the product structure directly drives other key manufacturing files. Inventory records, purchasing source file, and all work order files are derived exclusively from the product structure.

Initiating the Technical Description

The technical description can also be started at the beginning of product development. Completed almost exclusively by engineering, it serves as a technical working document during the develop-

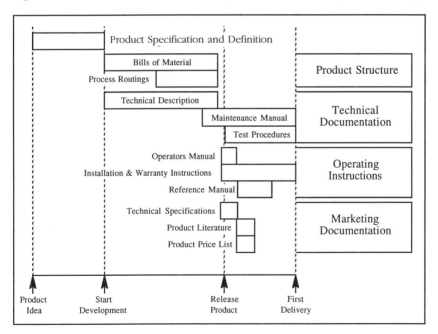

Figure 17.2 Timing for preparation of product documentation.

ment process. Expect to have a rough draft completed at the release milestone, and require a finished document sometime prior to first product delivery. The technical description should include a detailed analysis of product construction, functionality and operation, theory of operation, assembly drawings, schematics, proof of performance, and proof of product certification to the specified standards and regulations. This document will drive all remaining documents that are traditionally considered product documentation, including all documents within the operating instructions and marketing documentation categories. In addition, engineering derives the product maintenance manual and approves all required product test procedures. The initial issue and distribution of the maintenance manual and test procedures must coincide with first delivery of the product. Working copies of these documents are made available during product development to allow evolution and improvement of their content and accuracy, and to allow refinement of related production and repair processes.

Preparing the Operator's Manual

Upon completion of the rough draft of the technical description, work can begin on the operator's manual. Usually requiring rapid completion so it can be polished and printed prior to product deliveries, the operator's manual can be written by a professional technical writer with assistance from one or more End-users. Utilizing a functional product model during the writing, End-users will ensure, and communicate in user language, all specified operating parameters. An optional reference manual may also be required to define some product operations in more detail and to explain seldom-used capabilities such as expansion, networking, reconfiguration, or interface requirements. The installation and warranty instructions are sometimes included as a section within the operator's manual. More often seen as a separate document, it describes product warranty, servicing the product, and any required installation, commissioning, or setup. All documents within the operating instructions category must be complete and accurate for first product deliveries.

Preparing Marketing Documentation

Marketing documentation must be available at a defined point prior to delivering the product, and as soon after product release to manufacturing as possible. Marketing documentation is defined and planned within the marketing strategy section of the product definition. Marketing documentation is the foundation for accurate and consistent advertising and sales promotion. Technical specifications are taken directly from engineering's technical description and rewritten in a format acceptable to the market and the End-user. Features and options defined within the product structure form the framework for the price list. Pricing strategies vary widely from one industry to another. Final list prices should be evaluated against the product business plan to verify an acceptable average margin. Although list prices are sometimes printed directly in product literature, you may find that a price list insert for your brochures is more cost effective. With an insert, prices can be changed periodically without the expense of reprinting what is often full-color, costly literature. Product literature is the front-line product document. Often the first glimpse an End-user has of your product is in product literature. Literature must be visually appealing, excruciatingly accurate, and consistently high quality. Best realized through the services of a professional advertising department or agency, product literature extols your product's features and options, operating characteristics, and customer benefits, and may draw from any or all available product documentation.

EFFECTIVELY CONTROLLING PRODUCT DOCUMENTATION

The second general characteristic of product documentation is the requirement for strict document control. In chapter 7 we determined that basic control of quality documentation includes document approval, defined distribution, and ensuring that only current revision documents are in use. Control of product documentation, due to its overwhelming impact on product quality and business performance, must go beyond basic document control.

It's common to think of controlling product configuration through engineering change control. More appropriately called *product change control*, we can apply our definition of product, and change our paradigm to think in terms of *product documentation change control*. Your physical products and services are an accurate reflection of your documentation. Any change to the product must be preceded by an approved change to the documentation. Similar to the traditional paradigm of controlling engineering changes, product documentation change control has the following general characteristics:

1. All change requests are made in writing.
2. Engineering and product management review all change requests against the product specification and product definition.
3. Product management has final approval for all changes.
4. The incorporation timing for approved changes is jointly determined by engineering, product management, and manufacturing in order to assess and minimize the impact on the quality delivery system.
5. Approved changes to the product documentation are made and distributed before any actual changes in products or processes occur.
6. Revision control, configuration control, or both are employed to ensure that all past, present, and future products can be accurately traced through the product documentation.
7. Product documentation history is maintained by product management and is made available for customer service and support.
8. Expedient measures are taken to ensure that only the most current documentation is in use throughout the quality delivery system.

Thorough control of product documentation means that every single defined document must fall under the control system. While you're accustomed to controlling product structures and technical manuals, you must be committed to exercising the same control over price lists, product literature, operator's manuals, and all other defined product documentation. An assurance of product and process quality will be the result of your commitment.

A recurrent theme in this book is the creation of Circle-4 Customer satisfaction through consistent process definition, implementation, execution, and improvement. No where else in your quality system is this more important than in your product documentation. If the product specification and definition establish the achievable limits of product quality, then your overall product documentation establishes the achievable limits of process quality. Heavily dependent on data from product documentation, your process performance cannot exceed the defined boundaries set by its content and accuracy. We'll examine process definition and integration in some detail in the next chapter.

SUMMARY

1. The success of product development is measured by the answers to the following questions:
    a. Does the product perform as defined in the product specification and product definition?
    b. Is the product completely and accurately described in the product documentation?
    c. Does the product documentation completely reflect the requirements defined in the product specification and product Definition?
2. Product documentation has two general characteristics:
    a. It includes the product specification and product definition, from which all other documents are derived.
    b. All included documents require strict document control.
3. In addition to the baseline standards of product specification and product definition, product documentation is comprised of four document categories:

    a. Product structure
      —bills of material
      —process routings
    b. Technical documentation
      —technical description
      —maintenance manual
      —factory test procedures
    c. Operating instructions
      —operator's manual
      —installation and warranty instructions
      —reference manual
    d. Marketing documentation
      —technical specifications
      —price list
      —product Literature

4. All product documentation must be complete, accurate, and available prior to first product delivery.
5. The control structure required for product documentation is equivalent to a traditional engineering change control system.

Quality Applications

1. Make a detailed list of all of your product related documentation. Categorize each item according the documentation categories outlined in item 3 of the Summary. Can you confirm that each listed document accurately reflects your product specification and product definition?
2. Discuss converting your existing engineering change control system to product documentation change control. Which documents will be the most difficult to control? Which will be the easiest? Discuss the benefits of controlling product documentation.

Quality Benefits

1. The real products of the your business are product documentation, and product and process quality is ensured through the

accuracy, completeness, and control of product documentation.

2. Understanding and accepting this principle will save your company far more than the relatively small cost of compliance.

Many years ago I had dealt with a situation that proved to me that the product really is the documentation. During group discussions for a new product, several product features were discussed and discarded for technical and cost reasons. As we neared first deliveries, the product literature was prepared and distributed to the sales force. It wasn't a controlled document at the time, and we didn't discover that it touted one of our discarded features until we heard from one of the first customers, irately demanding to know what happened to "feature X"! The Product Literature, which was derived in part from handwritten notes, was prepared with the best of intentions. Our commitment to customer satisfaction, in addition to finding ourselves in a legal grey area, resulted in redesign of the product to match the literature. Due to competitive pressure we were also forced to maintain the initial list price, which significantly reduced our margin. This single failure to adequately control a product document cost us around $80K in redesign, rework, and retooling. This control failure, plus the creation of an expectation in the mind of the End-user, combined to clarify for me and my managers that the product is, indeed, the documentation.

18

HOW PROCESS DEFINITION AND INTEGRATION ENABLES CONSISTENT PRODUCTION QUALITY

We're now beginning to establish a Circle-4 Quality foundation for our delivery system. The complete and thorough work we did in creating the product specification and product definition established the limits of product quality and defined the product creation process. The product documentation resulting from product creation added required detail to our defined product quality plus established the limits of process quality for the remainder of the delivery system. We must now add the requisite level of detail to our process quality so our manufacturing and sales and marketing disciplines have a clear and unambiguous roadmap for producing, delivering, and supporting products. This exercise has two major components, *process definition* and *process integration*. In this chapter we'll examine process definition and we'll introduce process integration. Integration is a crucial element in our quality delivery system, and will be covered in greater depth in chapter 19.

It's important to keep in mind the interrelationships which exist between the quality delivery system documents identified to this point. Each new document adds to the detail of the overall product documentation in specifically defined areas, and no new document can be created without prerequisite documents being in place, validated and approved by the Company. Only in recognizing and following this relationship can you ensure that product quality in all its aspects is tied back to the original reference document, the product specification.

Figure 18.1 depicts both the interrelationships that must exist between our QDS documentation and the information evolution for products and processes. Referring to the product and the processes required to create and produce that product, and progressing from the general to the specific, and from the specific to the detail, the product specification provides a general product description, concentrating on thoroughly defining product functionality. Product definition results in specific product description, general description of production processes and costs, and specific definition of the product creation process. Product structure provides specific information for production processes and detail information for the product. The operating procedures that result from process definition and integration provide detail information for manufacturing

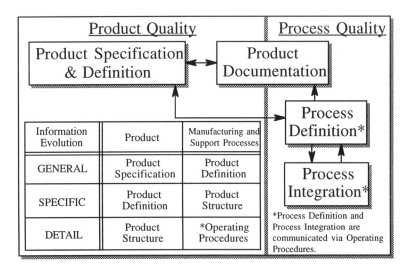

Figure 18.1 QDS document interrelationships and information evolution.

and support processes. Operating procedures within the engineering department provide the same level of detail for product creation processes. Engineering operating procedures are derived from the product definition, and manufacturing or support operating procedures are derived from the product structure. These entwined and complex relationships require the directed participation of responsible players from the point of creating the specification onward. Looking at manufacturing involvement, they contribute to the general definition of manufacturing processes during product definition. During product documentation, manufacturing input is required to evolve specific process information, and during process definition and integration, they are solely responsible for creating their operating procedures, based on all previous work.

Let's separate the discussion into two parts, first taking the evolution of process definition all the way back to our product definition process. Then we'll look at process integration as a crucial element in creating your quality delivery system.

A MODEL FOR ESTABLISHING PROCESS DEFINITION

When Dr. Rogers and her management team began analyzing the delivery system requirements for EWC, Inc. they had a desire to create a system that was rapid, flexible, and consistent in creating, producing, delivering, and supporting their products. They knew from experience that they could not survive with long product-development cycles, and they realized from their own total quality training that the key to short development cycles was comprehensive communications and involvement of key players early in the process. Using the structure of their operational network, EWC created an operational improvement team for new product analysis.

The team members assigned to the OIT were the director of product planning and support, as chair, the directors of marketing and sales, engineering, and manufacturing, plus several key engineers and product managers. The team was given the objective of creating new-product business through the rapid and timely analysis of proposed new-product business plans. Meeting weekly, the team accepted new product ideas from anyone in the organization. The submitted ideas were screened against general company objectives and for complementary fit with current products, markets, and plans.

Acceptable new product ideas were assigned to special corrective action teams called new product review boards (NPRB). NPRB membership included sales, product management, engineering, purchasing, and production staff. Each NPRB considered specific objectives for an assigned new-product idea using a defined evaluation process. Working against calendar milestones, the first result of their effort was the product specification, which was submitted to the OIT for review and approval. Following approval, the NPRB then looked at product definition and worked toward submitting a proforma product business plan as their final definition milestone. The product business plan followed an established format, requiring standard business plan elements in a condensed form. A risk analysis was submitted with each business plan, summarizing the risk assessments distributed throughout the text of the product definition. Early and continuous involvement of all operational disciplines in the new-product process prepared them to address process definition and integration from an informed point of view.

ESTABLISHING YOUR PROCESS DEFINITION

Early involvement in Product Specification and Definition by *all* operational disciplines is crucial to the realization of rapid product development and delivery. Equally crucial is the role of each player involved in the process. As discussed in chapter 16, product management and engineering play key roles in defining the substance of the product specification. Defining the important manufacturing, delivery, and support processes within the product definition requires the concentration of additional disciplines. This document will be the basis for predicting product business over time, therefore it must include informed estimates for product, quantity, cost, and time through the quality delivery system processes. The responsibilities for providing these estimates must be well defined and understood. At the onset of product definition, a number of key decisions are made that serve to chart future action in specifying and detailing all necessary delivery system processes.

Considering the Make-or-Buy Decision

Once the product is described, the team identifies the required major product components. Players from development, production, and support determine whether the components will be *made* or *bought*. The make-versus-buy decision depends, in part, on whether current processes can be used to make the component and on the projected loading of those processes. Projected investment costs of new or modified processes must also be considered when applicable. A thorough analysis of each of these three alternatives, loading current processes, modifying current processes, or adding new processes, must be made in consideration of the product life and product profitability before the final make-versus-buy decision is reached for each major product component.

Following the make-versus-buy decisions, the team can estimate the time and cost involved to create and produce the defined components, based on their knowledge and experience in dealing with similar product components. These estimates will take their place in the manufacturing strategy, product cost estimates, and in the pro-forma product business plan. Taken collectively, the make-versus-buy decisions establish a general delivery system model for manufacturing, by directing which major product components will be purchased and which will be produced internally. The delivery system model also helps characterize the emerging roles of engineering and the product support groups. Engineering tasks will be slightly different for a purchased component versus a manufactured component. The product support groups, such as customer service, will approach service and repair differently for purchased and manufactured components.

How the Team Functions in Process Definition

Once the team understands the general model to be used for realizing the product business, each member can focus on creating more precise models for their areas of responsibility. As engineering begins product creation and starts establishing the product structure, the manufacturing and product support disciplines must add their process expertise in order for the resulting structure to be considered complete. For example, as components and raw materials are added to the structure, purchasing needs to supply the necessary detail for leadtime, cost, and approved source of supply. For production operations, the production experts need to provide detail for workcenters, process times, labor rates, tooling, and other elements that characterize the defined manufacturing processes.

As the product structure is completed and additional product documentation defined, concentrated expertise from the product creation team members continues to supply the requisite detail. For example, delivery details for acceptable packaging and delivery and product support detail for warranty, spares, and repair logistics must all be supplied to the product documentation by the corresponding experts. The dynamics that make the product documentation process timely and comprehensive take place in a team environment. All of the experts on the team make their contributions in parallel, instead of in serial, fashion. As engineering adds end items, assemblies and components to the product structure, team members contribute cost estimates, leadtimes, sources of supply, and process steps to fully characterize the product. Similarly, the technical description, also written by engineering, provides the basis for factory test procedures, technical specifications, operator's manuals, and additional product documentation. This parallel teamwork approach allows the fastest possible creation of the most accurate and complete product documentation. The framework established and reflected in the product documentation sets the limits for all subsequent process definition.

THE IMPACT OF PROCESS DEFINITION ON COMPANY POLICIES

As the product creation team builds the product documentation, and as engineering creates the product, team members need to galvanize additional activity within their areas of responsibility. As product processes are clarified, those that reflect new investment and those that are modifications of current processes must be duly reflected in company policies. Reviewing and updating your policies will ensure that the quality information system continues to dovetail with actual activity in the company. Once your policies reflect the reality you envision for your new product, the processes themselves must be precisely defined via operating procedures. Operating procedures represent the most extensive effort required for process definition. Even if all prior analysis indicates that current procedures accurately reflect the processes necessary to produce, deliver, and support your new product, conduct a detailed conference room review, at a minimum, to ensure that you don't encounter any exceptions or surprises.

All operating procedures created for process definition have certain common characteristics. Each defined procedure must have specifically identified conditions, actions, and results.

Defining Conditions

Conditions are the input to the process; they identify the prerequisites in terms of material, documentation, tooling, and equipment in order for the process to be executed as defined. Often simply a list at the beginning of an operating procedure, conditions must be complete and specifically worded. For example, if the factory workmanship standards are referenced, the specific sections or pages that apply to the operating procedure should be noted. Conditions should also reference the enabling policies which direct the operating procedure. This reference will provide positive linkage for the documentation and will clearly establish the Shareholder for the process being documented through the operating procedure.

Defining Actions

Actions are the heart of the process and detail the sequence of steps required to convert the defined input to the required output. Actions also indicate responsibility for process execution and must reflect the decision-making authority granted to the process owner. In other words, there must be a clear indication of required action and decision making when nonconformities occur. One of the best methods for documenting the actions required in an operating procedure is through the use of flowcharting. Initially developed to assist computer programmers, flowcharting employs standard symbols with specific meaning. There are symbols for input/output, process steps, documents, decisions, auxiliary operations, and manual operations, to name a few. The appropriate symbols are arranged in the proper order, specifically labeled with the process step information, and are interconnected by arrowed lines showing the direction of activity. Anyone in your company with a programming background can help you define a simple, straightforward library of flowcharting symbols and conventions to be used in preparing the action sections of your operating procedures. Flowcharts are not only easier to follow than written procedures, but they also use less paper and are much easier to update.

Defining Results

Execution of the actions defined for an operating procedure will create a predictable output. Whether or not the output of the process conforms to requirements is determined by measuring actual output against the defined results. Results define the process "product" in sufficient detail to allow this measurement and analysis. Results for manufacturing processes should be stated in terms of product characteristics plus any supplied information that will accompany the product to both identify its status and provide evidence of conformance to requirements. Process owners are responsible for achieving the quality required by the defined results.

Defining Operating Procedures

Operating procedures are defined for every repeatable process within the quality delivery system. Operating procedures specific to product production will carry a unique identity within the product structure. This identity will allow the scheduling algorithms access to characteristics of the process that impact production scheduling, such as leadtimes, run times, setup times, available capacity for the process, and so on. Accurate representation of process characteristics within the product structure is essential for realistic production planning and scheduling. Each process may also have a requirement to report actual performance against the schedule, which along with their product performance, constitutes the complete measurement of the process as defined by the operating procedure. All such schedule reporting requirements are defined within the results section of the operating procedure.

Once process definition is well under way, consideration of process integration is the next priority. As depicted in chapter 15, our processes must be integrated into an efficient, functional whole in order to achieve the optimum quality delivery system.

INTEGRATING DEFINED PROCESSES

Integration of all delivery system processes occurs both vertically and horizontally. Integration is communicated through the operating procedure and follows the Circle-4 Customer paradigm discussed in chapter 14 for enabling information and decision timing (refer to Figure 14.2).

Every delivery system process defined through an operating procedure has a Circle-4 Customer. The process Shareholder is comprised of the enabling company policies that created the need for the process, as well as any specific product documentation required to support the process objectives. The Shareholder also includes the organizational supervisor of the process, who will enable and support process ownership through employee training, teamwork, and proactive management. The Shareholder's effect on any given process is to establish vertical integration by defining the operating framework for the process, including required product results, information requirements, available resources, and workmanship expectations. This operating framework empowers the Employee within the process by defining their parameters for process execution. In complex quality delivery systems, which may have nested process levels, the Employee may also act as a component of the Shareholder for subordinate processes. For example, an operating procedure may be defined for the automatic loading and soldering of electronic circuit boards. The procedure covers actions including component preparation, component magazine loading, soldering masking, component placement, reflow soldering, and board cleaning. Subordinate to this overall process may be an operating procedure for the preparation of new or replacement solder masks. The owner of the board assembly process also acts in a Shareholder capacity for the solder mask preparation process.

Horizontal integration is accomplished through recognition of the process End-user and Supplier. End-user and Supplier requirements are defined within the operating procedure as the results and conditions we discussed earlier. In a typical manufacturing delivery system, End-user requirements may be stated in general terms, such as "supply product in accordance with the factory schedule." While this is an excellent starting point, it may not be sufficient to ensure complete satisfaction of the End-user. The relationship between a process owner and the End-user must be one which supports and nurtures communications, innovation, teamwork, and continuous improvement.

The process owner has an obligation to understand the business of his or her End-user and, through that understanding, to create an ongoing win/win relationship. Blindly following the factory schedule and defined procedures often results in delivery system inefficiencies and unnecessary costs. For example, our factory had a production line which manufactured power supplies, one of which was used in several different products. The power supplies were fully assembled, tested, environmentally conditioned, and well documented when they left the production line. After we established our quality improvement teams, it was quickly discovered that all of the End-users for this power supply were partially disassembling each supply in order to change the voltage settings as required by their particular product. Our initial improvement was to begin providing the power supplies fully tested, but partially assembled, allowing the End-user to set the voltages and finish the assembly. The follow-on, quality improvement was a design change which externalized the voltage settings, precluding the need to disassemble the supply. The interesting point is that we built the supply for several years before making these changes, and during that time each process owner operated only within their own universe, obediently following their procedures and their schedules. By the way, the cost of the design change was recovered in three months through labor savings, which means after three months of producing the new design, we were not only satisfying the process End-user, but we also were doing it at a lower product cost.

A similar relationship needs to exist between the process owner and the Supplier. Process owners have an obligation to ensure that the Supplier fully understands their requirements. They must also understand the capabilities of the Supplier in order to foster win/win relationships. As illustrated in the previous example, horizontal process interconnection points present some of the greatest opportunities for realizing delivery system efficiencies and improvements.

HOW TO USE CIRCLE-4 QUALITY DYNAMICS FOR PROCESS INTEGRATION

The relationships that will result in full vertical and horizontal integration of quality delivery system processes can be facilitated with three of the Circle-4 Quality dynamics we've discussed previously. First, as the operating procedure for a process is defined, you should affirmatively answer the same four questions asked when defining your business unit objectives:

1. Can we meet Shareholder requirements and support Shareholder goals?
2. Can we produce a product that meets the needs of the End-user?
3. Have we created an operation that allows the Employee to be successful, enabling End-user satisfaction?
4. Have we created a partnership that satisfies our needs and allows the Supplier to be successful?

Second, the creation of win/win relationships between process owners and their Circle-4 Customer is enabled through the operational network established as part of your quality organization. This network will ensure that effective horizontal communications take place regularly throughout the quality delivery system, fostering teamwork and a mindset toward improvement. Third, as real customer requirements are identified and understood, they must be accurately reflected within the operating procedures, which are part of your controlled quality documentation.

In our company model, EWC, Inc., the department managers are responsible for documenting and controlling operational procedures for their assigned functional responsibilities. They designed a simple control mechanism to ensure that the vital Circle-4 Customer interrelationship is understood and supported. The control sheet for every procedure must be signed by the process owner and by the process End-user before the procedure is authorized by the department manager. This dual acceptance of responsibility ensures that End-user expectations are explicitly understood, committed to and documented prior to finalizing the characteristics of a given process.

You would do well, as the Company, to visualize your delivery system processes graphically to ensure that all the necessary Circle-4 Customer relationships have been identified and considered. You may need two, three, or four end-user signatures to approve a given process. You'll probably find that processes with a single customer are the exception rather than the rule. In most manufacturing environments, for example, you not only need to consider the immediate downstream process, you also must consider the needs of the factory scheduling or shop floor control system in constructing your processes. Defined results include all required process output, including any administrative or tracking reports and information. When these are included as part of the defined results for the process, whoever is responsible for the tracking and control elements of your factory will want to approve the process procedure as one of its End-users. As you probably know from experience, actual quality delivery systems can be very complex. Creating a detailed QDS flowchart or diagram will help you visualize that complexity and visualize the necessary customer relationships required for profitable system operation.

Provided that you've established the foundation through product specification and product definition, and provided that you're creating complete and consistent product documentation, the tasks of process definition and process integration are relatively logical and straightforward. This being the case, you should not ignore the need to address this part of your quality delivery system. Failure to properly document both the processes and their Circle-4 Customer interrelationships will cause inconsistent performance of your delivery system and result in an ultimate inability to satisfy your End-user.

In addition to being well on our way toward the completion of a working framework for the quality delivery system, we've also added to the body of total quality documentation. Process definition contributes to the evidence that we do what we say we're going to do. Process definition is traceable back to the product specification and definition, supporting the objective of supplying a customer-driven product. We now need to execute the defined and documented processes, measure the resulting product characteristics, and determine how effective the QDS is at achieving expected results. In the next chapter we'll look at additional integration requirements as we examine process execution and control, from the Company point of view.

SUMMARY

1. Within quality documentation, there is a structured interrelationship that allows definition of product and process quality from the general to the specific.
2. Process definition and process integration are detailed through operating procedures created for each process within the quality delivery system.
3. Accurate process definition is realized when process experts have the opportunity to make focused contributions to the general documentation that must logically precede operating procedures.
4. All operating procedures are characterized by conditions, actions, and results.
5. Process integration takes place vertically and horizontally and is accomplished through the consideration of the process Circle-4 Customer.

Quality Applications

1. Have each Company manager flowchart or diagram the links connecting their delivery system processes. Discuss how a Circle-4 Customer awareness within each process can lead to additional improvements in your delivery system.
2. Review your company policy and procedure for creating and maintaining operating procedures. Is there a mechanism in place to allow process Customer review and approval of your operating procedures? Would such a mechanism improve your operating procedures?

Quality Benefits

1. The Company realizes that the Circle-4 Customer dynamic applies not only to the definition of business unit objectives, but also applies to each process within the quality delivery system. This realization will lead to a Circle-4 Quality paradigm throughout the business.

2. A real improvement opportunity, made possible by the creation of customer-supplier relationships between processes, is ensuring that only fit-for-use materials and product flow through the delivery system.

     For example, although engineering is responsible for defining the raw material used to produce the defined product, they don't usually address the physical characteristics the material needs to have as it moves from one process to the next. A transistor is specified for use in a printed circuit assembly. Before the board assembly process takes place, the transistor leads must be cut and formed into a pattern that allows insertion into the circuit board. The preparation of components or raw material is routinely done by the process and is normally disguised as a setup operation for the process. In this example, the Supplier of the transistor will truly satisfy the process requirement if the transistor is supplied in a form that allows immediate insertion into the circuit board with no additional preparation. By establishing the requirement that all products and materials presented to any process must be fit for use, you can create the potential for major improvement and cost reduction within your delivery system. Over the years, I have used this approach to help companies save thousands of dollars by eliminating setup and material preparation. It can help save you money provided you create Circle-4 Customer relationships in all your delivery system processes, and provided your process owners strive to maintain win/win relationships with their Customer.

19

CONTINUOUS QUALITY IMPROVEMENT THROUGH EFFECTIVE PROCESS EXECUTION AND CONTROL

We've talked about defining your processes and we've talked about ensuring their integration with each other and with the quality information system. As we look at execution and control of those processes, you need to make sure you keep your perspective. You need to see your processes as the Company, you need to consider them within the context of your business objectives, and you need to be aware of the requirements of your Circle-4 Customer. From this perspective, we want to focus on the management direction you need to provide and the empowerment you want to create to sustain consistent and high-quality process execution and control. Therefore, we'll address the responsibilities of the owners of any given process or group of processes, regardless of where in your quality delivery system that process exists.

In the last chapter we talked extensively about defining and integrating various processes into a cohesive delivery system through the recognition of a Circle-4 Customer for each distinct process. Inside the boundaries of each process or group of processes there exists an additional need for integration, in addition to pure execution and control of process actions. By first ensuring the internal integration of process operations, the process owner creates the environment for effective execution and control. Internal process integration is achieved by balancing *material flow*. Once material flow is optimized for your product, execution is conducted through *resource management*, and control is assured through *defect prevention*. Material flow, resource management, and defect prevention represent the primary internal management responsibilities of any process owner. Let's examine each one in detail. We want to not only understand the concept of each of these responsibilities, but we also want to predict their effect on process performance and on your overall quality system.

We need to examine these responsibilities in the order given. Unless Material Flow is optimized between the Schedule and process operations, process owners will spend their time rescheduling and trying to juggle changing priorities. Consistent and efficient flow of materials will allow them to focus on optimizing the conversion of raw materials to products, through Resource Management. Control is then maintained and quality assured by creating an umbrella of Defect Prevention over the entire process. Let's begin by looking at Material Flow from the process owners point of view.

MANAGING MATERIAL FLOW
TO MINIMIZE INVENTORY
BY SHORTENING LEADTIMES

The flow of material is influenced greatly by the product structure and by the characteristics of our schedule. As process owners, we find ourselves the recipient of the results of the product creation and the scheduling processes, making us the End-user for a great deal of the provided information. We have a responsibility as an End-user to ensure that our expectations are clearly communicated and understood. Product structures should support our objectives, schedules must realistically model our operations, and we must be proactive in pursuing improvements in both areas.

Using Material Requirements Planning

Let's look at the influence of material requirements planning (MRP) on material flow. As a scheduling and inventory-control technique, it is in use in one form or another in most manufacturing companies today. It remains an excellent business tool, but you should acknowledge its limitations and its ability to influence your operation.

MRP, in an ideal environment, rewards the creation and management of commonality in planning the production of the company's products. The use of common assemblies in different product models, the inception of design standards that encourage use of currently active components and assemblies for new models, and the trend toward factories organized to group common processes are all evidence of the positive influence of material requirements planning. If you're not careful, however, you may find yourself influenced to the point of overly structuring bills of material, process routings, and the factory floor in order to maximize available commonality. Creating commonality within your products and processes is a good thing, if done for the right reasons. One of the reasons MRP first stressed the creation and management of material commonality was to improve software execution time in order to approach real-time processing. While this issue still exists to some extent, it is a relatively minor one in today's high-speed processing environment. The most important reason to promote commonality today is for maximizing resources. Commonality that fully utilizes your proprietary manufacturing or testing equipment, or that makes your employees their most efficient should be encouraged. Even at the expense of slowing down MRP regeneration, avoid commonality that does not contribute to resource maximization. If you approach commonality with the goal of maximizing your resources you may see a very different effect on material flow than if you approach commonality to maximize software execution time.

In order to support business objectives, material flow must minimize inventory by shortening leadtimes. Leadtime management, throughout the QDS, is the only successful means of controlling and reducing inventory. Optimum material flow seeks to minimize the time a component spends in the delivery system before it's delivered as part of a product.

There are two types of material flow, process flow and product flow. Most delivery systems exhibit a mix of both types. Process owners can analyze and model material flow to find the most efficient, profitable mix for your factory. In a model that begins with structuring the product to identify commonality for MRP planning purposes, material flow will be weighted in favor of process flow. Only comparisons against equivalent product flow models will allow you to find the most efficient middle ground.

In addressing material flow, your intent is to reduce the amount of chronological time inventory spends in the factory while becoming product, or in other words, minimize factory leadtime. As material proceeds through the factory it flows through process stages that can be grouped into the general categories of issue, queue, setup, run and test. A focused effort to minimize issue and queue times will have the greatest impact on optimizing material flow.

Defining the Role of Process Flow

Process flow directs raw material through process stages which turn the components gradually into finished product. For example, in a sheet metal fabrication shop, the computer network controlled (CNC) punch-press may be the most expensive capital asset of the company. In order to maximize its use, a workcenter is formed around the machine and all necessary material is routed to the machine for the conversion process. Complete product structures clearly identify the processes required to produce the product. Many companies mirror these processes in creating their factory workcenters, thus defining their material flow as predominately process flow.

The main advantage of process flow is maximizing the use of an expensive resource. As we approach a pure process flow environment, there are disadvantages in the form of additional cost. Because product quality must be assured before it's passed along to the next downstream process workcenter, it is commonplace to find costly duplication in inspection, testing, and measuring resources within the process flow delivery system. Quite often, more available, less costly resources are allowed to flourish and multiply in support of the expensive, critical resources. Pure process flow also complicates throughput and scheduling. It becomes extremely difficult for a product to be "pulled" through the factory, since products readily lose their identity as they all vie for a share of "common" resources. Queue times increase, causing unreliable completions and necessitating rescheduling. Rescheduling in turn, creates a pervasive nervousness throughout the delivery system, because any given process has the potential for affecting the schedule of all products, each to a different degree.

Defining the Role of Product Flow

Product flow, at its extreme, locates all the required material and resources in an area defined for a product family or group, where the material stays until fully converted into deliverable product. In lot sizes of one, demand for the end product pulls components into the front end of the pipeline, where operations are executed in their most efficient manner to build the defined product. The goal is to move the material required to build one product through the product build process with no queue time; wait time, move time, transit time, etc. In order for this focused teamwork to be successful, the production staff must be very knowledgeable and multiskilled. The most efficient manifestation of pure product flow is a small number of multiskilled talented workers who operate the machinery and tools required to build the product. Alternately picking up the slack for a worker who's been scheduled for a heavier workload, these workers *own* their delivery system, and they run it like a micro-business within the company. Working to "business plan" objectives approved by the Company, these flexible, talented professionals are rewarded for profitability and are expected to recover any operational losses.

A structured product flow delivery system is the ultimate goal for any manufacturing operation. Each product, product family, or product group is formed into a micro-business which contains all the constituent parts of a quality delivery system: engineering, manufacturing, and sales and marketing. Micro-businesses share a common quality organization and quality information system.

The transition from process to product material flow has already started in many companies. It's realistic to expect a total transition period spanning several years, as older products with problems too difficult to mention are phased out or replaced. Let's consider an example demonstrating a realistic mix of product and process flow: first a model with a deliberate process flow emphasis, progression toward a product emphasis, followed by a look at expected results.

REDUCING FACTORY LEADTIME

Our company model, EWC, Inc. markets two high resolution computer monitors, 12-inch and 17-inch. Initially convinced that maximum commonality and process flow would result in the most efficient operation, their original product structures are shown in Diagrams 1 and 2 of Appendix 5. It seemed logical to them to organize their workcenters along the lines of the product structure, creating commonality of processes as well as material. From historical data provided by EWC, we know that their manufacturing cycle time, the time it takes to build one unit, is 17 hours without burn-in and 86 hours including burn-in time. Burn-in time is the clock time required to environmentally stress an electronic product while it's operating in order to uncover weak and marginal components. We also know that total factory leadtime to build one unit is 54.5 hours without burn-in and 198.5 hours including burn-in. Within the 54.5 hour leadtime, 45 percent is queue time, consisting of wait and move time. Setup, run, and test times combine for 25.6 percent of the total, and issue (work order kitting) time accounts for the remaining 29.4 percent. Given these ratios, EWC has done a reasonable job in optimizing their operation within the constraints of their process flow paradigm.

The goal for optimizing material flow is to reduce the amount of time that inventory spends in the factory by reducing or eliminating issue time and queue time. In creating a recommendation for EWC, we may also want to look at product burn-in time. There are inconsistencies within the current process flow: all assemblies receive at least 48 hours burn-in, although some receive as much as 72 hours. It's an obvious way to potentially reduce the factory leadtime and the manufacturing cycle time.

Diagrams 3 and 4 of Appendix 5 represent a product flow orientation for the 12-inch and 17-inch monitors. The original product structure has been preserved. All the previous process workcenters have been replaced with a single product-oriented manufacturing cell. The owners of this product cell are responsible for optimizing their ability to build a lot size of one, allowing them to eliminate all wait and move times except for those entering and exiting the cell. All setup, run and issue times are exactly the same as in the process flow model, since it's not the function of optimizing material flow to improve these characteristics. Resource management will consider optimizing setup for a lot size of one, as well as look at run times and test times. Finally, in our product flow model, all tooling and fixtures remain the same, but are relocated.

By investigating burn-in time, EWC demonstrated evidence that a 24-hour burn-in cycle, with power and temperature cycling, would uncover all infant component failures. The new product flow structure consolidates burn-in for the entire product once assembly is completed.

The resulting manufacturing cycle time, without burn-in, actually increases from 17 hours to 22.5 hours, as a result of sequencing some operations which were done in parallel under process flow. Including the required burn-in time, we can see a 48 percent reduction in overall manufacturing cycle time, down to 46.5 hours from 89 hours. Even more significant is the decrease in factory leadtime per product unit. Without burn-in, total factory leadtime decreased from 54.5 hours to 31.95 hours, a 41 percent reduction. Including burn-in, the reduction leaps to 72 percent, going from 198.5 hours to 55.95 hours. Not a bad result, considering all we really did was change the factory operating paradigm from process to product, eliminating unnecessary, wasteful queue time and minimizing issue time.

The result of reducing leadtimes and improving material flow is a direct reduction in required inventory. If M represents the average daily amount of material required to produce product, and L is equal to the factory leadtime in days then $M(2L)$ represents the average necessary onhand inventory. Without changing any other variables, if L decreases by 48 percent, average inventory expressed as $M(2L)$ also decreases by 48 percent. Realizing that inventory control and reduction involve other variables and processes, you can conclude that by reducing factory leadtime, you've improved the potential for significant inventory reduction—in this case, by almost 50 percent. Inventory reduction drops right to the bottom line of the business, immediately improving profitability.

You can also reduce the complexity of scheduling and schedule maintenance with a product flow paradigm. In our example, the schedule now looks at one product cell instead of at eight work-centers. Demand for the product, either from customer orders or sales forecasts, will pull components through the product cell. This focus allows realistic and consistent priorities, which are not possible when you try to service demand from multiple products in a process flow environment.

MANAGING RESOURCES TO ELIMINATE TRADITIONAL SETUP TIME

Having established a direction emphasizing product material flow, as process owners we can now begin to look at resource management. Resources are those assets available for use in producing the product. Machinery, people, facilities, and tools are all resources which must be managed and coordinated. Given a typical, traditional manufacturing process, resource management strives to optimize setup, run, and test times. In addition, we also want to look at overall asset management, in terms of maximizing the *production capacity* of each resource.

Keeping product material flow in mind, let's deal first with the issue of setup time. When I previously mentioned that product material flow is optimized for a lot size of one, I could almost see you shudder at the thought of all the setup involved for multiple lots of one. Let's put process setup in perspective within product material flow.

It's difficult to imagine any delivery system that is completely process flow or completely product flow. The optimum for satisfying your Circle-4 Customer is to get as close to total product material flow as possible. Within the quality delivery system, some processes, such as purchasing and material control, may not lend themselves to efficient product flow. Generally speaking, manufacturing logistics processes must support a variety of company products, including engineering models for new product. There are clear economies of scale in managing purchasing and stores on a commodity, rather than a product basis.

Within your delivery system, you need to pay special attention to the interfaces between process and product material flow. Unless there is a well-understood customer partnership at each transition point, there is a real risk of creating delivery system constraints. A common area for such a constraint to surface is between the storeroom and the factory floor as material is issued to satisfy the schedule. The storeroom deals with inventory as a commodity: pounds of sheet metal, reams of paper, reels of electronic components, and so on. The factory is only concerned with material in the context of the product: In order to build one product we need 100 transistors with their leads formed in a specific pattern to allow insertion in the circuit board. The historical lack of a Circle-4 Customer relationship between the storeroom and factory has contributed to the waste of time and money categorized as setup time.

The concept and use of setup time evolved for two reasons. First, setup time is used to *prepare* the raw material received for use in the production process. In other words, deliberate steps are taken to change the inventory from a commodity orientation to a product orientation. Second, setup time is used to *configure* people and machinery so they can produce the product demanded by the schedule. By utilizing product material flow, you can eliminate this second reason. You have created a product cell that deals with a single product or a group of related products, and once the people and machinery are properly configured, no setup changes are required. As soon as you establish the ability to efficiently produce a single product, you also have the ability to repeat this single unit cycle as many times as required by the schedule. Your product focus does not change, nor does the configuration of your resources.

The remaining reason for setup time, preparing the raw material for production use, is an issue that should be dealt with while establishing the process interface between the storeroom and the factory. Given your goal for Circle-4 Customer satisfaction, the storeroom has an obligation to supply the raw material in a form immediately usable by production. Some of the requirements may be passed all the way back to the raw material Supplier, or they may be satisfied during the material issue process itself. There should also be a mutual recognition that material cannot economically be continuously issued for single products. Further, an agreement should be reached to periodically issue the material required for a block of the schedule. For example, it's effective to consider issuing one days worth of production material based on the forecast driving the schedule. Once issued, actual order demand will consume material by pulling units through the production process.

Given the Supplier requirement to issue material which is fit for use, and given the fact that your people and machinery are in a stable, product-oriented configuration, you should be able to completely eliminate traditional setup time. Now let's look at resource management aimed at optimizing run times and test times, or in other words, execution time. Process execution includes all the process or operation steps wherein the conversion of raw material inventory to product takes place. In a factory setting, execution time is commonly expressed as standard run hours. Achieving the goal of reduced execution times will result in additional inventory savings as well as a lower total product cost.

How to Enhance Employee Effectiveness in Your Quality System

Resource management for optimizing execution time is centered around each individual employee. The primary catalyst for this aspect of resource management is training. Training, with the intention of developing multiskilled employees, is a cornerstone for every aspect of the quality system. Compensation for all employees should reward the acquisition and demonstration of additional skills, and the training program should require a training plan for each individual. If your human resources are multiskilled, the complexity of managing throughput is greatly reduced.

Each employee should be fully responsible for their own world. The person who operates the machine should also perform the preventative and corrective maintenance, and he or she should also define the improvements required and benefits to be attained by enhancing or replacing the machine. Employee talents must include teamwork dynamics and self-management, which will empower them to manage their own throughput and work to successfully with upstream and downstream processes. Thoroughly knowledgeable of overall business performance and objectives, your employees must continually expand their comprehension and understanding of business operations and constantly improve and evolve their role within the quality system.

Success and compensation for employees are measured by their demonstrated value to the company, not by any organizational or longevity basis. How exciting to think of a company where all the employees not only execute their roles with consistency, but also with the complete knowledge and perspective of a seasoned, trained manager. As the Company, you must establish as an objective the realization of *complete* employees, each with authority and accountability for his or her role in the operation and participation as a partner in creating a successful business. You, as the Company, are the conductors of an orchestra which must write, rehearse, and perform original music satisfying to your Circle-4 Customer, and it must all be done with complete musicians who perform in harmony and with anticipation for the next movement of the baton.

The realization of complete employees will allow process owners to exercise empowered resource management. By further segmenting the process, individual employees can be given responsibility and authority for discrete operations or groups of operations. Supporting a defined role on the team, each employee contributes to successful, interdependent resource management.

Given the goal of optimizing run and test times, every employee will have the opportunity to mix creativity with experience toward developing improvements in the methods and techniques reflected in manufacturing execution times. The amount of improvement in execution time through resource management will vary from business to business. The most important result you can achieve is the establishment of an improvement trend. Once your employee actions create and sustain this trend, the financial reward is incvitablc.

DEFECT PREVENTION FOR CUSTOMER SATISFACTION

With an optimized material flow, and having begun the process of managing your resources by nurturing complete employees, we can now address defect prevention. Defect prevention is the natural consequence of commitment to Circle-4 Customer satisfaction. You know the cost of doing something right the second time. We've talked at length about defining requirements, setting objectives, and controlling your documentation. You've ensured a 100 percent accurate translation of your Circle-4 Customer requirements through your policies, procedures, and schedules. Your employees know with explicit detail what they need to do to achieve the defined result. They will reap the reward if their roles are executed right the first time, every time, and in harmony with the efforts of their colleagues. The urgency for improvement leads them logically to experiment with anticipating and preventing defects in both their product and in the processes that produce the product. Your role is to support and reward creativity and innovation aimed at defect prevention. The attitude and mindset necessary for effective defect prevention will arise naturally in your complete employees, as they seek to further improve their worth to the business. The outcome will be consistent, constantly improving process execution, with automatic controls as a result of the improvement process established as the pathway to personal and professional success.

We've come to the end of Part 3, where we've defined a quality delivery system that will assure real product quality and achieve the throughput required for Circle-4 Customer satisfaction. In the first two parts of the book we established the Company, defined and sought to understand the Circle-4 Customer, established a quality organization to support customer requirements, and built a quality information system to supply accurate communications and feedback throughout our universe. We've defined Circle-4 Quality as the result of satisfying the prioritized requirements of the Customer, the consideration of the needs of the Customer in all business activities and decisions, and the commitment to work in cooperation with the Circle-4 Customer in pursuit of a profitable business. We've also demonstrated that the paradigm of Circle-4 Quality applies to every individual in our employ and that our quality system will function only through the ministrations of each dedicated, complete employee. Employees, that special influence group within our Circle-4 Customer, deserve our commitment to their satisfaction as well as our commitment to satisfy our Shareholder, End-user, and Supplier.

SUMMARY

1. Material flow, resource management, and defect prevention represent the primary internal management responsibilities of any process owner.
2. Material flow is optimized by emphasizing product versus process material flow in as many delivery system processes as possible.

3. Optimizing material flow will reduce factory leadtimes, which will reduce inventory, which will increase profits.

4. The realization of complete employees will allow process owners to exercise empowered resource management, which will maximize production capacity.

5. Defect prevention is the natural consequence of employee commitment to Circle-4 Quality and Circle-4 Customer satisfaction.

PART 4

HOW TO EVOLVE YOUR BUSINESS TO ACHIEVE CIRCLE-4 QUALITY

In the final part of *The Quality-Empowered Business*, we're going to examine the application of Circle-4 Quality with the goal of realizing a functional quality system within today's typical business operation. The nucleus of our defined transition will be our employees and the necessary tasks to educate and empower them to create a quality system.

We will approach the application of the concepts discussed in the first three parts of the book. We will look at the timing and the activities necessary to evolve an existing business operation into a complete, responsive quality system.

It's necessary for us to define a baseline from which we can grow and evolve as we approach Circle-4 Quality. Our discussions will be based on the assumption that an operating business exists. Start-up operations require a different approach, with a different sequence and emphasis of activities, and won't be the focus of this discussion. Any operating business, regardless of current performance, will benefit from the methodical, coordinated approach to operations improvement that we'll undertake shortly. Business size and current business performance will affect the amount of time it takes to restructure operations and realize the benefits of Circle-4 Quality. Those businesses that have made a conscientious effort in the past to create a total quality business will progress faster than those still operating with a more traditional mindset.

It's extremely important to stress once again that the diagnosis and prescription you create for your own business, based on the quality system concepts we've defined, do not constitute an improvement *program* for your business. Instead, they represent a totally different means of managing the operation. Especially during the last decade, management has been obsessed with short-term results, quite often in order to survive. Other well-founded and beneficial improvement concepts have unfortunately been approached as being the latest fix for the company, the quality "program of the month" if you will.

If you're running a typical business, one for which total quality has been tried but just hasn't seemed to "take," one for which consistent, improving performance trends have been difficult to establish and maintain, or one where resources seem so overloaded that basic business issues don't receive proper attention, then you're part of the mainstream of American business. For your operation to truly benefit from Circle-4 Quality, you, the Company, must be committed to changing your basic business paradigm and approach. This is not a program, and for most businesses, real results will not be seen for two to five years. Your expectations and your business planning need to accept this timeframe, and your commitment and involvement must be renewed on a daily basis if you expect the rewards of running a long-term, profitable venture.

As I've stated previously, 95 percent of all problems that exist in any given company are management caused. Failure to achieve advertised benefits from previous business and quality improvement concepts rests squarely on management resistance to change. Management is necessary, will always be necessary for successful, profitable business operations. Management must be approached with a different perspective and with different objectives if you're to be successful throughout the 1990s and beyond. As we look at the dynamics of creating Circle-4 Quality, we will also address the shift in focus and direction that you're required to make as managers.

Although manufacturing companies have been the focus of our examples thus far, and will continue to be, the principles of Circle-4 Quality can be applied to any business interested in long-term profitability, stability, and improvement. Every business in existence has a "product" and every business must have the means to create, produce, market, and support that product.

Part 4 chapters will be organized and presented in a manner slightly different from previous chapters. Chapter titles indicate the general area of emphasis, and chapters are presented in the chronological order they should be addressed by your business. Within each chapter, subheadings are replaced by specific, sequentially numbered recommended improvement activities. Where appropriate, a checklist is provided within a described improvement activity. As in previous chapters, a Summary, Quality Applications, and Quality Benefits will conclude each chapter. The Quality Applications section will consist of enumerating the improvement activities discussed in depth within the chapter.

Trying to evolve and improve the basic operations of a business is a difficult task. There are no shortcuts, and there are no easy fixes. The improvement activities recommended represent business subsystems that must be established as ongoing operations if you truly desire Circle-4 Quality, the total ongoing satisfaction of your Circle-4 Customer. These subsystems require user ownership if they're to become part of your business culture, which means your employees must be involved in their definition, implementation, ongoing operation, and improvement. All business improvement activities must be enthusiastically supported by the Company, through your commitment, involvement, continuous participation, and leadership.

20

ASSESSING CURRENT BUSINESS OPERATIONS

Before you can effectively prescribe improvements and corrective action for your company business systems, you have to do an equally effective job of diagnosing the problems. Many companies that begin the implementation of total quality concepts start with the best of intentions, only to slide back into old habits and routines. A shortage of resources and immediate business priorities are often cited as reasons for turning away from total quality. While many causes underlie these failures, one of the most pervasive is the failure to properly diagnose and prioritize quality system problems.

Quite often a company will make an excellent beginning towards total quality. They may educate all their employees, establish an improvement organization, and begin the improvement process. Unless improvements are prioritized and directed by the Company, each improvement team will create its own priorities and improvement projects. The results can be devastating to morale and to the total quality process. Some teams may find that they've taken on too great a task and may watch it mushroom until they're overwhelmed and overburdened. Other teams may successfully complete their improvement activity only to realize no discernible improvement in process performance. Still others make recommendations for supporting improvements in other processes, only to be ignored by the management team, which is overloaded by recommendations from all other quality teams. When these problems occur, the improvement process fails to be responsive to the employees, who become disillusioned with total quality and retreat to their old habits. It's sad to see these kinds of problems scuttle a total quality effort, because they're so easy to prevent by diagnosing and prioritizing the problem areas in the beginning.

20.1 ESTABLISH AN INTERNAL AUDIT SYSTEM.

An internal audit system should be in place and functioning before you consider organizing a quality improvement process. An audit allows you to compare your practices and systems with either your own definition or with an external standard. The objective of every audit must be to evaluate the *intent,* the *implementation,* and the *effectiveness* of the process or system being audited. For example, if you decide to audit the receiving inspection process, the audit will consist of three parts. First, does a receiving inspection procedure exist and if so, does it satisfy the requirements of its directing policy? By examining the process documentation, you will be able to determine the defined intent of the receiving inspection process. Second, are the employees responsible for receiving inspection following the procedure? In other words, has the defined procedure really been implemented? And third, is receiving inspection effective in achieving what the procedure is designed to achieve? How is their measured performance compared to expected results? For instance, if the procedure states that one of the activities of receiving inspection is to physically isolate nonconforming material and report it to purchasing for expedient disposition, you can evaluate actual practice to see if nonconforming material is indeed being segregated and purchasing notified.

The term *audit* has taken on somewhat of a negative connotation over time. Often employees view an operational or quality audit with the same distaste they view an upcoming root canal. Incompetent auditors, management overreaction to audit results, and incorrect management prescriptions for audit results have all given the term *audit* a bad name. Even in the best of circumstances, employees are inconvenienced by audits, since they are usually obliged to get their normal work done in addition to suffering the intrusions of an audit team. The idea of conducting internal audits must be presented as a tool for your employees to use in assessing their areas of responsibility.

Your internal audit system must carry the weight of management support and must therefore be directed through a company policy. The policy will require regular audits to assess the intent, implementation, and effectiveness of every aspect of your quality system on a regular basis, in accordance with a defined and maintained audit schedule. A sample policy for quality management audits is included in Appendix 2. You should realistically recognize that an audit system cannot assess every single aspect of your business and should be viewed as a tool to confirm system integrity and direct improvement efforts. An internal audit system is not a replacement for, or even an addition to, your quality information system, or the performance feedback loop within the QIS. Internal quality audits will allow the Company to effectively steer the direction of improvement activity within the operation, by means of defined audit priorities.

Audits are conducted against specific requirements, which may be the defined policies and procedures of the company, a recognized standard, such as ISO-9000, or a specific customer contract. As you begin the process of creating your Quality System, you may encounter operational areas that are not covered by existing company policies and procedures. An audit and subsequent audit report for these instances should only address this lack of documentation and control. The first improvement activity in such a case would be for responsible employees to properly document the policies and/or procedures for the process or system audited. In fact, you will see when we address defining audit priorities that you will specifically target quality documentation first. It is impossible to audit a system or process if it is not formally defined.

Audits should avoid allowing the individual opinions of the auditors to influence the audit conclusions and should therefore be based only on objective evidence. Objective evidence can take many forms, all of which must be uninfluenced by emotion or prejudice. Evidence that exists, that can be documented, and that can be verified either through documented records or observation constitutes objective evidence. Objective evidence can be quantitative, or countable, or it can be qualitative, measured by degree. During the course of an audit, one of the primary means to ensure that an auditor focuses on collecting objective evidence is by framing audit questions along the lines of "Show me evidence" or "Demonstrate to me."

Audits follow a specific, repeatable, and understood format. You will want to construct a format that meets the needs of your specific business. A general sequence of repeatable audit steps may include the following:

1. Define the scope and objective of the audit.
2. Determine the scale of the audit and the required resources.
3. Collect past audit history, current problems, and management concerns.
4. Establish the audit date.
5. Prepare audit checklists.
6. Review the planned audit with the responsible employees or manager.
7. Conduct the audit.
8. Review the findings with the responsible employees or manager.
9. Prepare an internal audit report and submit to the Company.

An audit checklist basically defines the sample to be taken during the audit. The checklist should be prepared in light of the documented requirement being audited and should consist of a series of questions devised around thinking of "what to look at" and "what to look for."

Generally speaking, internal audits are conducted by a single qualified individual. As you look at the creation and building of a quality system, it is in your best interest to begin the process of internal auditing by including not only an expert auditor, but a responsible employee from the area being audited, in order to begin fostering user ownership in the audit process. Initially, you should identify at least one individual, preferably someone from the Company, to be your internal auditor. This person must have a good understanding of the business systems and operations of the company, should possess excellent communications skills, and should be viewed with respect by the organization.

Once identified, your internal auditor should participate in an external program of auditor training and education. There are a number of training programs available, one of the best of which is offered by the British Standards Institution. Once trained, your internal auditor should participate in creating an internal audit policy, procedure and audit schedule. As audits are conducted, time should be taken during initial audits to familiarize audit participants from each area audited with the concepts and procedures defined for internal auditing. As time progresses and your system improves, you will establish a group of recognized, qualified auditors who can jointly share the ongoing task of internal auditing. Under normal circumstances, it is more difficult for an auditor to be completely objective if he or she is auditing areas of own responsibility, though it is permissible to do so. In an ideal quality system, all employees would become qualified internal auditors, and the system would be tailored so that these employees would audit those processes for which they are either the End-user or the Shareholder.

20.2 DEFINE AUDIT PRIORITIES.

The audit schedule that is defined as part of your internal audit policy will ensure routine audits of every aspect of your quality system. Audit priorities, on the other hand, are necessary for the Company to establish the control and direction required for creating the quality system. Your quality system is a complex entity and you must ensure that you're "chasing the right rabbits at the right time" in order for improvement activities to effectively contribute to improved business performance.

The purpose of defining audit priorities is to direct your initial internal audits so that the results can be used to create a quality action plan. The quality action plan defines the tasks required to establish the proper foundation for the quality system.

There are three control systems that constitute the initial priorities for a quality system foundation. They are an internal audit system, which was just discussed, a document control system, and an employee training system.

One of the shortcomings of many businesses is the failure to adequately define and control company documentation. If you desire consistent business performance, your processes must be directed by consistent and controlled documentation. In order for you to accurately assess past performance, records of that performance must also be defined, collected, and maintained in a controlled manner. The documentation that should be controlled through a formal system includes policies, procedures, work instructions, workmanship standards, product documentation, quality records, customer records, and the business database. Appendix 2 includes a sample policy for quality documentation.

An employee education and training system is necessary to ensure proper planning, administration, and record keeping for employee training and education. This control system requires elements that identify the present qualifications of each employee, either upon hiring or at inception of the system, that record employee education and training as it occurs and that require the establishment of a training plan for each employee, which is reviewed and updated at least annually. You will only achieve the goal of realizing complete, self-managed employees through a consistent and coordinated training effort.

20.3 BEGIN INTERNAL AUDITING.

As the next step in assessing current operations, you need to begin auditing those priorities we've established above. Following your defined audit process, audit results will identify necessary improvements for the internal audit, document control, and employee training systems. As mentioned previously, your audits must assess the intent, implementation, and effectiveness of each system. Identified nonconformities and recommended improvements will be the basis for your quality action plan.

20.4 ESTABLISH A QUALITY ACTION PLAN.

The quality action plan is the precursor to an operating quality system, with its built-in assessment and improvement processes. Based on your audit results, tasks, task ownership, and completion dates for the activities necessary to establish functioning control systems form the basis of your action plan. Because these systems are so crucial to your initial and ongoing success, audits should be repeated at the conclusion of the identified tasks and either additional improvements defined or assurance received from the auditor that you have effective systems for internal audits, document control, and employee training.

Once you have assessed the foundation of your current operations, and ensured the establishment of basic system controls, you can address the important issue of creating the proper cultural foundation for your quality system.

SUMMARY

1. The business must be diagnosed before improvements or corrective action can be prescribed.
2. An ongoing internal audit system will allow you to diagnose the business.
3. The objective of every audit must be to evaluate the *intent*, the *implementation*, and the *effectiveness* of the process or system being audited.

4. Audits must be presented as a tool for your employees to use.
5. The internal audit system must be directed through company policy.
6. Audits are conducted only against specific requirements and results should be based only on objective evidence.

Quality Applications

20.1 Establish an internal audit system.
20.2 Define audit priorities.
20.3 Begin internal auditing.
20.4 Establish a quality action plan.

Quality Benefits

1. At the conclusion of these activities, the business will have the ability to routinely assess any or all business operations and processes.
2. Through the established quality action plan, the business will be able to build functioning control systems to support a quality system.

21

ESTABLISHING
A CULTURAL
FOUNDATION

The creation of a company culture that will allow your business to continuously address the satisfaction of your Shareholder, End-user, Employee, and Supplier is perhaps the most difficult, but most essential, task you will ever encounter.

Culture can be defined as an integrated pattern of human behavior and interaction. This behavior is all encompassing, and includes thought, speech, action, and those objects created as a result of our actions. Culture endures and evolves through our capacity for learning and subsequently passing along acquired knowledge to succeeding generations. In fact, behavior only becomes part of the culture through learning and through validation as acceptable and desirable by the majority of society. Learning is predicated on the availability of a learning delivery system and upon the willingness of people to avail themselves of that system. It is your responsibility as the Company to provide a learning environment, to encourage your employees to actively participate in the learning process, and to reward their demonstration of newly learned behavior and utilization of new-found knowledge.

Culture is also predicated on a given pattern of acceptable behavior accompanied by socially uplifting rewards and the disconfirmation, through socially negative reinforcement, of behavior that violates the established cultural norm. Your company culture will have as its foundation the policies, procedures, and objectives that you cause to be established for the business. Every action taken in creating your Quality System, every concept covered in this book, provides substance to your company culture. The foundation of your culture, however, must be the creation of a learning system that fosters and promotes the ideals and principles of Circle-4 Quality, and does so in a manner that results in the combined, ongoing success of your Circle-4 Customer.

One of the most important maxims for management that I've ever heard, and that I've taken as a personal goal is to "treat every employee as you would like them to treat your best customer." The learning process which leads to a cultural foundation must begin with your Employee before it can be extended to include your End-user, Supplier, and Shareholder. The learning process includes an educational delivery system, but it goes beyond the mere acquisition of knowledge. The learning process also includes the daily application of acquired knowledge and the observation of fellow employees in that application. You cannot establish a culture of complete Circle-4 Customer satisfaction if you, as the Company, do not actively demonstrate the principles of Customer satisfaction in the way you manage and direct your business.

What is your motivation for establishing a cultural foundation, a learning process, and an educational delivery system? If you can accept the basic definition of Circle-4 Quality, the consideration of the needs of the Circle-4 Customer in all business activities and decisions, you have taken the first successful step in motivating a new company culture. Such a definition of quality, and its ramifications for your management approach, can make you very uncomfortable and uneasy in the face of traditional management beliefs and practices. While no business can be run as a democracy, an aspiration toward Circle-4 Quality requires a significant paradigm shift wherein you view your employees not as dispensable cogs within a machine, but as proactive participants in the management and decision-making processes. While we will continue to develop a new definition of the Company throughout this part of the book and summarize your new business role in chapter 25, if you can embrace the idea of all your employees being active participants in company management, you can begin to establish a cultural foundation with the correct paradigm and focus.

21.1 ESTABLISH AN EMPLOYEE EDUCATION AND TRAINING SYSTEM.

In chapter 20 we discussed and established the need for control and record keeping for employee education and training. In this section, we're going to begin to explore the necessary content, as well as the delivery itself, of an education and training system.

It has often been said that the half-life of a typical college education is about four years. That is to say, the applicability, usefulness, and retained capability of a college education decreases by 50 percent within four years of graduation. Successful medical doctors, lawyers, and engineers have long recognized this occurrence and routinely avail themselves of supplementary education and training in their field of expertise. Postgraduate courses, seminars, trade journals and professional organizations help these professionals to keep their knowledge and skills current and applicable for today's challenges. On the other hand, we routinely hear of displaced or laid-off workers with outdated skills and capabilities who require retraining before they can become productive employees for another company. We don't stop to think that the reason those layoffs had to occur was because the involved companies allowed their operations to become as outdated and obsolete as the employees they laid off and therefore could no longer successfully satisfy current Customer requirements in their chosen marketplace. Many of these types of companies reorganize and hire new employees with up-to-date skills and capabilities in order to try and regain their competitiveness. This *modus operandi* is very expensive, and the chances for real, lasting success are low. A senior manager once told me that he felt all middle managers and supervisors should be replaced every three or four years in order to get new blood and fresh ideas into the organization. If the real professionals in society recognize the need to constantly improve their knowledge and hone their skills, wouldn't a company be more successful if the same rule were applied to all its employees? And if this were the case, should you, as the Company, be responsible for your employees' ongoing education and training?

If we wish to *continue* satisfying the Customer, we must compete within our marketplace, and we must employ the latest, state-of-the-art thinking in all aspects of our operation or we're going to get run over by the competition. Why do we always point out the little upstart, entrepreneurial companies as our greatest threat? We say they're flexible, responsive, and don't have the historical baggage to carry around with them that we do. We forget that they're generally formed with bright, eager minds right out of college, armed with the latest thinking for product creation, production and delivery. The baggage we have to carry around with us is not our historical product line or our historical performance; instead it's our antiquated thinking and outdated methods. We can be every bit as flexible, responsive, and innovative as start-up companies if we keep our employees trained, educated and up-to-date.

Replacing current employees with ones who have the skills the Customer requires is an expensive proposition. The average cost of hiring a new employee and making him or her a productive part of the operation is about a half year's salary. That means if I'm running a company without an education and training program, and my payroll is $20M annually, over time I'm going to have to spend at least $10M to bring in new employees with the skills that will allow me to remain competitive. It would be so much more cost effective for me to spend 5 percent to 10 percent of my annual payroll on employee education and training. Given the half-life of an employee's knowledge and skills, four years, to remain truly competitive it would cost me $25M over a 10-year period to keep all my employee skills current through replacement. On the other hand, if I have a program that mandates that 5 percent of the payroll budget be spent toward employee education and training, I will spend $1M per year to keep my employees current and innovative, or $10M over that same 10-year period. I've just saved $15M in added cost to my company—in my mind, certainly enough justification by itself for employee education and training.

Finally, besides the cost involved in replacing employees, and besides the risk to our success if we don't keep our employees current, we cannot ignore the benefits and wisdom brought to the operation by experienced employees. Employees who grow and evolve as the company grows and evolves are truly the people who establish the cultural standard for the company. The experience gained and the relationships created over time with the Customer cannot be replaced and cannot be educated into an employee. The ideal we can hope to achieve in an employee is one who has a depth of experience, and solid relationships with the Customer and who eagerly seeks continuous improvement through the application of the latest thinking and skills. It truly is your responsibility to educate and train your employees if you have a real commitment to satisfying the Customer.

The exact structure of your education and training system will depend on the nature of your business, your market, and your community. There are specific goals, however, that you can adopt as a common framework for your system.

1. In accordance with established policy, maintain current and accurate training records for all employees and maintain a current training plan for each employee.
2. Spend a minimum (5 to 10 percent) of your annual payroll budget on employee education and training. This does not include so-called on-the-job training.
3. Commit to the realization of complete employees who are self-managed, current in their assigned skills and responsibilities, and competent contributors to the management and decision making required for your business success.
4. Commit to the regular renewal and improvement of the knowledge, skills, and capabilities of all your employees.

Additionally, there are a wide variety of methods and tools you can employ to ensure the success of your education and training system. Some of the ones which I've utilized or am familiar with include the following:

1. Establish employee tuition reimbursement program that allows employees to pursue company approved degree programs. Reimbursement is based on actual performance in completed courses. For example, an *A* grade would be rewarded with 100 percent tuition reimbursement, a *B* with 75 percent, and a *C* with 50 percent.
2. Encourage or mandate attendance at on-site or external professional seminars.
3. Train key employees as instructors, giving them the ability to educate their peers on newly acquired skills and knowledge.
4. Arrange with a local college to teach an applicable course on-site for a group of employees.
5. Permit sabbaticals or leaves of absence to allow employees to pursue specialized education or research.

21.2 Define the complete employee.

In order for you to thoroughly ascertain the education and training needs of your employees, you need to characterize your complete employee in specific terms. The general definition presented here should be supplemented with specific details taken from the characteristics of your own business and community.

1. Complete employees are self-managers. They are in control of their lives and actively pursue win/win relationships with their Circle-4 Customer. They understand the meaning of interdependence: the necessity to work as a team toward common goals and objectives. They have high self-esteem, see success in personal terms, and are supportive of others' efforts to succeed. They make positive contributions to the operation and expect to be fairly rewarded for their efforts. They understand the value of continu-

ously improving their own capabilities and encourage similar improvement in others.

2.   Complete employees have a thorough and complete understanding of their assigned job function. They compete with themselves to improve their competence and performance and they're always trying new techniques and methods.

3.   Complete employees understand the business. They are familiar with the Customer served by the business and they understand their own impact on profitability. They understand the various operations of the business and the interrelationship of those operations. They're eager to measure and report the performance of their operation and are always looking for the means to improve their performance and become better company citizens. They understand the basics of business finances and contribute to business planning within their defined role in the operation. At their level of operations, they understand the value of relationships and constantly strive to improve their relationship with their Shareholder, End-user, Employee, and Supplier.

4.   Complete employees have a vision of the future for themselves and for their role in the business. They actively establish and pursue goals that are beneficial to both themselves and the business. The goals they set are designed to promote their personal success, their standing in the company, and their role within the community.

5.   Complete employees have excellent communications skills, including the ability to listen effectively. They freely share their knowledge and expertise with others, realizing that knowledge is power only when it's shared and utilized. They are decision makers who base their decisions on analysis of the pertinent facts and the potential business risks. They will not rush into a decision and insist on having the appropriate information available for analysis. Though their decisions may not always be "right," they take responsibility for all the decisions they make and do not try and blame

another for a bad call. They are not afraid to make mistakes and understand that often the greatest learning and personal growth occur as the result of making mistakes.

6.   Complete employees always show respect and consideration for others. They realize that to be respected, one must first show respect. They value the differences they see in their friends, family, and colleagues and constantly try and exploit those differences to the benefit of the operation. In a very real sense, they exhibit leadership for both themselves and the people around them.

We've created quite an ideal definition for a complete employee. Imagine the power and synergy you can bring to bear in running your business if all your employees have these characteristics. The fact that I've included leadership as a characteristic of a complete employee is not a contradiction. You can have a company full of leaders. All excellent leaders recognize that the first and most important quality of a good leader is to be a good follower. Also keep in mind that it is your responsibility to create a quality system that allows complete employees to exist. You must seek these same qualities in yourselves if you're to ensure a successful, satisfied Customer.

21.3 CONDUCT EMPLOYEE SELF-MANAGEMENT EDUCATION

To establish a cultural foundation that is both beneficial and that promotes the realization of complete employees (and therefore, successful Customers) requires that you provide guidelines for consistent acceptable behavior. Respect for others, interdependence and teamwork, ethical and moral behavior are all concepts that must be discussed, agreed to, and assimilated into your company environment in order to stimulate an atmosphere conducive to success. Only through personal effectiveness can you establish corporate effectiveness. Only through proactive self-management can you establish proactive business management.

Self-management education must be provided to all employees from the CEO down through and including the janitor. The establishment of a common set of values and a consistent approach to individual, group, and corporate behavior are indispensable prerequisites to an effective quality system.

One of the best programs in self-management that I've encountered is *The Seven Habits of Highly Effective People* conceived by Dr. Stephen R. Covey. The program is administered through a variety of means and media by the Covey Leadership Center, which has as its mission to "empower people and organizations to significantly increase their performance capability in order to achieve worthwhile purposes through understanding and living principle-centered leadership." The seven habits serve to move an individual from dependence, through independence, finally realizing true interdependence. The seven habits include:

1. Be proactive.
2. Begin with the end in mind.
3. Put first things first.
4. Think win/win.
5. Seek first to understand, then to be understood.
6. Synergize.
7. Sharpen the saw.[7]

In 1990, our company presented the "seven habits" to all of our employees as a prelude to establishing a total quality operation. The results of the training were tangible and long lasting. Dr. Covey's terminology became a part of our company vocabulary and his concepts infused their way into our thinking and our actions. If we hadn't begun with such a comprehensive program for self-management and principle-centered leadership, our total quality effort would not have succeeded or even progressed beyond the first discussions.

[7] Covey, Stephen R., *The Seven Habits of Highly Effective People,* Simon and Schuster, 1989, Part One.

There are other programs available to encourage self-management and interdependence. As the Company, you have a responsibility to identify and adopt a program that fits within your culture and that contributes to your realization of complete employees.

21.4 CONDUCT TOTAL QUALITY MANAGEMENT EDUCATION.

The desire to build a quality system that continuously satisfies the requirements of your Customer is not divorced from the main body of knowledge on total quality management. In fact, more than anything, your defined quality system is a natural extension and a practical application of that knowledge.

Once your employees understand the personal and corporate behavioral standards established through self-management education and training, ensure that you also establish a common understanding of the principles and terminology of total quality management (TQM). Primarily concerned with continuous improvement and total customer satisfaction, a TQM education program should also cover other quality principles such as organizing for total quality, teamwork, problem-solving techniques, and employee involvement concepts. There are a wide variety of sources for TQM education, and since it has become a relatively widespread phenomenon during the past several years, I won't provide any specific references. However, I would recommend, following the initial generic TQM education, that you define and discuss the fundamentals of creating a quality system as we've defined within these pages. A conceptual and classroom understanding serves to enhance and accelerate the implementation process.

21.5 FORM THE QUALITY ORGANIZATION.

Once your employees understand and can apply principles of self-management and total quality management, it's time to create an organization for them to operate within. The time and effort required to establish a quality organization will vary depending on the current state of your company operation. It may be useful for you to review chapter 7 before continuing with this section.

You're now getting into the real mechanics of creating a quality system. Since every company will begin with a different starting point, the best approach will be to offer you a checklist, in the form of successive questions, which will allow you to gauge the progress, and therefore the remaining needs of your business toward realizing a functional quality organization.

As you approach the definition of job responsibilities, company policies, and the like, there is often a tendency to try and define the company as it should be rather than how it is. In order for you to make real and beneficial improvements to your operation, you must have a clear and unambiguous starting point. Remember that governing policies, such as a quality policy, should define how things should be, whereas operating policies should reflect the current reality of the business. It is not wasted effort to thoroughly define the operation that exists today. Such activity provides an invaluable stake in the ground from which you can move forward with your improvement activities. It also allows you to approach continuous improvement in a logical and controlled manner. I've always told my quality improvement teams that they cannot recommend any process or product improvements without first demonstrating the current state of affairs through the internal audit of a published policy, procedure, or product document.

1. Is there a published organization chart for your business that shows the position of each employee?
2. Do all employees have a written description of their functional job responsibilities, extracted from and referring to company policies and procedures?
3. Is there a formal, documented process for creating, maintaining, and disseminating company policies and procedures?
4. Are major business objectives and business processes defined and communicated through company policies?
5. Do all employees recognize their specific Circle-4 Customer

and do they understand their own quality responsibilities?

6. Has an operational network been created which allows employees to discuss quality issues and suggest process and product improvements?

7. Does the operational network allow for directing, monitoring, and communicating quality improvement activities?

8. Do employees meet regularly in defined groups to discuss quality improvement?

9. Are the overall details of quality improvement efforts regularly communicated to all employees?

10. Is the established operational network used to routinely run the business?

21.6 CONDUCT BUSINESS OPERATIONS TRAINING.

As soon as you have the basic elements of your quality organization in place and operating, you can begin training all employees on your business operation. This activity will further support the creation of realistic quality improvements and will give your employees additional competence toward becoming complete business managers in their own right. Through an understanding of current business operations and through a perception of their own role within the operation, your employees will begin to make valuable and informed decisions concerning how and where to improve their performance.

It makes sense during this process to employ the experts in each functional area in giving an overview of their operation to the rest of the organization. If your company is very large, you may want to video tape the overview and have the expert join the group at the end of the video to answer questions.

The process of establishing and evolving a company culture never ends. The steps we've identified for laying a foundation for that culture may take anywhere from six months to three years depending upon the size and the current effectiveness of your operation. Don't shortcut the process. Keep all your employees involved and begin to create a style of open and honest communication that will foster and support the company culture required to sustain an effective quality system.

SUMMARY

1. Culture is an integrated pattern of human behavior and interaction that is acquired and passed on through education, training, and experience.
2. Creating a company culture must revolve around the ongoing education of your employees.
3. It cost more to replace an employee than it does to keep one educated.
4. An employee education program must be based on a defined standard you wish your employees to reach; that standard is the complete employee.

Quality Applications

21.1 Establish an employee education and training system.
21.2 Define the complete employee.
21.3 Conduct employee self-management education.
21.4 Conduct total quality management education.
21.5 Form the Quality Organization.
21.6 Conduct business operations training.

Quality Benefits

1. The Company has created the ability to direct the culture of the organization through ongoing employee education and training.
2. The quality organization has defined horizontal and vertical communications throughout the business, allowing all employ-

ees to participate in quality forums, discussions, and improvement activities.

As your quality organization becomes established, your employees will want to begin working on improvement activities. Until you can establish priorities for improving your quality information system and quality delivery system, give them some improvement experience by challenging your teams to find ways to permanently reduce operating expenses. If this is your first venture into total quality management, they'll easily come up with activities that will reduce total operating expenses by 15 percent to 20 percent. This savings to the operation will offset, or perhaps pay for the initial expense of establishing employee education and training, documenting all business operations, and setting up an internal audit system.

22

CREATING AN INFORMATION NETWORK

Second only to establishing the foundation for your quality culture, the most important aspect of your quality system is the quality information system (QIS). The volume and pace of information in today's global economy is staggering. If you have any hope of successfully satisfying your Customer, you must be able to disseminate information in an accurate and rapid fashion, leading to informed decisions that will allow your business to flex and flow in response to changing needs.

As described in Part 2, the quality information system consists of four major communications paths: *objectives*, which are measurable and translated throughout the operation: *performance feedback; recognition* and the request for *simulation*; and *customer feedback*, which is used to validate and update your objectives.

22.1 DEFINE THE QUALITY POLICY, PHILOSOPHY AND OBJECTIVES.

The basis for translating your objectives throughout the operation is the establishment of company policies that reflect your mission, direction, and the major responsibilities of your defined organization. The quality policy is the cornerstone of your governing documentation. It should reflect the mission of the company, which is essentially the long-term requirements of the Shareholder. Additionally, the quality policy must reflect your commitment to satisfy the understood requirements of the entire Circle-4 Customer.

There are practitioners who advocate allowing the employees to develop the quality policy for the company. While it is certainly necessary for everyone in the operation to understand and lend their support to your quality policy, only the Company is in the right position to perceive and understand potential synergies with the Circle-4 Customer, which must be succinctly expressed in your quality policy. Therefore, it is the Company's responsibility to create and disseminate the Quality Policy, and following that, the quality philosophy and quality objectives.

The quality philosophy expresses the values and ethics you espouse in managing your business. It is an essential part of the cultural business climate and is necessary for assessing your continuously improving behavior in both a moral and ethical sense. Certainly you desire to be honest and forthright in all your business dealings. This desire must be expressed through your philosophy so that no ambiguity exists in the minds of your Customer. Your quality philosophy will serve as a cultural benchmark for the business, to both assess past performance and plan future behavior.

Quality objectives state the macro-intentions of your quality system, and provide the overall goals for the continuous improvement of your products and processes.

Once established and approved, the quality policy, philosophy, and objectives will change very slowly over time. They must be in place to serve as your anchor, your foundation, your constancy of purpose in a world deluged with transition and change. Appendix 2 presents an example of each type of policy for your guidance and for stimulating your thought processes.

The following brief checklist may be beneficial in establishing these all-important policies:

1. Does a quality policy exist which expresses the company

intent to satisfy the long-term requirements of the Circle-4 Customer?

2. Has a quality philosophy been created which clearly defines the behavior expected in conducting business operations and which can serve as a model in developing a quality culture?
3. Have quality objectives been identified which clearly state the intended course of the quality system in pursuing Circle-4 Customer satisfaction?
4. Have forums and discussions taken place with all the employees to ensure that they understand and are committed to the realization of the quality policy, philosophy, and objectives? Have all employees been willing to express their commitment in writing?

22.2 DEFINE QUALITY DOCUMENTATION.

In an overall sense, quality documentation consists of the set of policies, procedures, and other documents that define and direct your business operations. Quality documentation must also include the document control system established in Chapter 21 so that all company policies are controlled in terms of content, approval, and dissemination. Equally important, document control must allow for the expedient updating of policies, including the requisite approvals and distribution. The policy control system of the company must ensure that all employees have access to the most recent versions of all company policies.

Appendix 2 presents an example of a policy for quality documentation. Your document control system should take full advantage of today's computing power and computer networks to minimize the required overhead. For example, in my last company we created an on-line policy system where all company policies were available in an on-line, networked database available to all employees. One approval copy of each policy was maintained in the human resources department in order to create audit and historical trails. Policies under revision were taken off-line until the revised version was completed and approved. All policies "expired" following 12 months with no revisions so an operational audit could confirm that they were still current and valid, after which they were reissued.

Your policy must identify all the operational documentation of the business and direct its control and retention for audit and historical purposes. Retention times for various documents within the business system will depend on Customer and legal requirements, which should be well understood before establishing the policy. Governing policies, such as our quality policy, should reflect how we want the business to become. By doing so, they will serve as the attainable standard for the operation. Operational policies and procedures, such as material control, should reflect the actual operations currently in place. By thoroughly understanding and documenting existing operations, you create the knowledge base that can institute improvements toward the conditions described in your governing policies. Improvements will be reflected through revisions or updates to your documentation. Though it may seem like wasted effort to accurately document a poorly functioning process, the resulting visibility will give you the capability to make rapid, precise, and controlled process improvements.

The following checklist may provide you with some guidance for specifying your quality documentation:

1. Has a policy defining quality document control been written and approved? Does this policy define quality documentation and records and specify the required responsibility, retention and control for each document?

2. Are policies in place defining the responsibility, control, and distribution required for company policies and procedures? Has this policy been implemented and the requisite employees trained in its use?

3. Have the company organization and business responsibilities been communicated via approved policies?

4. Have the governing policies of the operation been established, approved and communicated?

5. Have the responsible managers documented their existing processes through approved, operational policies, procedures, and instructions?

6. Do all the employees understand the quality documentation system and all the currently released quality documentation?

22.3 DEFINE THE CIRCLE-4 CUSTOMER AND IDENTIFY CUSTOMER REQUIREMENTS.

While it is certainly necessary, in a traditional sense, to understand the requirements of the Shareholder and End-user in order for your business to function, your continuing success will depend upon your detailed understanding of the Circle-4 Customer. If your goal as the Company is to orchestrate the mutual success of the Shareholder, End-user, Employee, and Supplier, thus ensuring your own success, you must understand each of them completely from their perspective. It's not enough for you to only understand your role in their world; you must understand their total world so you can proactively reassess your position and your contribution to their success. This understanding has to take place, and has to be demonstrated to your Customer, before you can synergistically communicate your own requirements.

Understanding the Customer is a time-consuming, continuous process for which most of you have little real experience beyond the End-user. A thorough understanding means that for each major influence group within your Circle-4 Customer, you must understand their relationship to their Supplier, End-user, Shareholder and Employee. Although a variety of techniques may be employed, none is more accurate and effective than face-to-face communication and discussion. The following outline may provide a framework that you can expand and tailor to encompass the unique characteristics of your Customer. It may be necessary for you to segment each group into smaller divisions depending upon your business requirements. For example, among the Suppliers, you may have major suppliers from a number of different markets or technologies which will need to be considered separately from one another. Once you understand each major segment, you can look for common ground as well as for unique requirements that must be satisfied within the segments.

1. Characterize your End-user:
   a. Who are their customers (End-users)?
   b. How does their operation make money?
   c. How does your product or service fit into their operation? What problems are you solving for them?
   d. Do their employees understand and accept your products and services as part of their operation?
   e. What unique requirements do your End-users have from their employees, such as union membership, culture, etc.?
   f. Who are the owners and what mission have they established for your End-user?
   g. What do they see as the market forces directing their business?
   h. How will these market forces affect their requirements for your products and services?
2. Characterize your Supplier:
   a. What markets do they serve (End-users) and what is your relative position within their markets?
   b. Who are their suppliers and what is their relationship to those suppliers?
   c. Who are their Shareholders and what mission has been established for their operation?
   d. What are the characteristics and constraints of the processes they use to produce and deliver your required material?
   e. Do their employees understand and accept your requirements?
   f. What unique employee issues do they have to deal with?
   g. If you require a unique product or service from your Supplier, what makes your requirement different from their standard offering?
   h. What market forces do they see as directing and evolving their business, and what is the potential impact on your relationship?

3. Characterize your Shareholder:
    a. Do you thoroughly understand the mission given you by your Shareholder?
    b. To what extent do you contribute to the overall success of your Shareholder?
    c. What is the motivating or directing force behind your Shareholder?
    d. Do you understand the detailed, short-term results and reporting requirements of your Shareholder?
    e. Does your Shareholder have a good understanding your End-user, Supplier, and Employee?
4. Characterize your Employee:
    a. What are the unique demographics that segment your employees?
    b. What are the educational achievements and goals of your employees?
    c. What are the career achievements and goals of your employees?
    d. What are the financial achievements and goals of your employees?
    e. Where does your employee compensation fit within local, national, and industry parameters?
    f. Do your employees understand personal money management? What percentage of their salary do they save?
    g. How do your employee benefits compare with local and national norms? Do employees pay a fair share of those benefits?
    h. Are there any unique benefits or programs which would make your employees more valuable and productive?

22.4 ESTABLISH THE BUSINESS PLANNING POLICY.

One of the important governing policies you must establish is for business planning. The business planning policy should tie together long-term strategic planning with medium- and short-term tactical planning. Provisions should be made to ensure the integration of long-term and short-term plans.

As is the case with most business management issues, there are opposing opinions concerning the relative merits of long-term strategic planning. At one end of the spectrum, we have the example of a number of Japanese companies, such as Matsushita, who reportedly have 250-year plans. At the other end, we have the practitioners that advocate little or no long-term planning in the face of retaining ultimate flexibility in the marketplace. I would like to suggest a pragmatic and progressive middle ground.

In Figure 10.2 we suggested that a business plan should span five or more years. This timeframe allows you to plan for the realistic leadtimes involved in acquiring additional resources, capital equipment, facilities, and employees. Starting with a five-year minimum planning horizon, you can establish milestones or decision points within the plan that redirect your actions based on the relative direction of your Customer. Later, in chapter 25, we'll discuss some valid reasons for expanding your business planning horizon in order to not only anticipate, but to influence the future course of your business.

Your business planning policy must identify and direct the creation and interrelationship of the various plans and schedules required to operate your business. Figure 10.2 is a reasonable starting point from which to construct your own unique business planning diagram. For additional assistance, the following checklist is provided:

1. Has a multiyear business plan or master plan been established?
2. Have the contents of the business plan, along the lines of products, processes, markets, customers, suppliers, and systems been defined?
3. Has the annual process of validating and updating the business plan been implemented?
4. Does the business plan policy direct the creation and maintenance of subordinate, shorter-term plans, such as a production plan, development plan, marketing plan, support plan, and operating budget?

5. Have the contents of the subordinate plans been clearly specified?
6. Have processes been defined for regularly validating and updating the subordinate plans?
7. Do the subordinate plans direct the creation and maintenance of the various schedules required to enable plan execution?
8. Have the contents and process requirements been clearly defined for each of the required schedules?
9. Do the appropriate tools exist to manage the creation, maintenance, coordination, communication, and execution of the defined plans and schedules?
10. Do the employees understand the planning process, the interrelationships of the plans and schedules, and their role in plan and schedule preparation, measurement, and execution?

22.5 REDEFINE BUSINESS UNIT OBJECTIVES.

Now that you have a more thorough understanding of your Customer, and now that you've clarified your business planning process, you need to reexamine your business unit objectives.

1. Do your long-term business goals, including your quality objectives, satisfy and support the requirements of your Circle-4 Customer?
2. Do your medium- and short-term business objectives support your long-term goals?
3. Have you maintained Circle-4 Customer priorities in establishing business unit objectives? (Refer to chapter 4.)
4. Are all business unit objectives complementary?
5. Are all business unit objectives accurately reflected in both your governing policies and your business plans?
6. Do your employees understand your business unit objectives and their relationship to your business plans and to the requirements of your Circle-4 Customer?

22.6 TRANSLATE OBJECTIVES THROUGHOUT THE OPERATION.

For business unit objectives to be useful, they must be translated into measurable objectives for every individual in the operation. This translation is done using constraint analysis, as defined in chapter 9.

1. At the Company level:
   a. Have expected results been defined for the business unit objectives?
   b. Have measurements been defined for these results?
   c. Have the operational constraints for realizing the objectives been identified?
   d. Have the constraints been assigned to specific managers within the Company?
   e. Have the constraints been restated as department manager objectives?
   f. Have the expected results been defined for the department manager objectives?
2. At the Department Manager level:
   a. Have measurements been defined for own Department Manager Objectives?
   b. Have process constraints been identified?
   c. Have the process constraints been assigned to employees or work teams?
   d. Have the process constraints been restated as employee or work-team objectives?
   e. Have expected results been defined for employee or work-team objectives?
3. At the employee or work-team level:
   a. Have measurements been defined for employee or work-team objectives?
4. At the Company level:
   a. Have all objectives and their associated measurements been collated, reviewed and approved by the Company?

b. Have all approved objectives and their associated measurements been communicated to all employees?

22.7 ESTABLISH THE SCHEDULE.

The end result of translating objectives throughout the organization is the Schedule and specific requirements to execute the Schedule. The Schedule is the complete group of operational plans and schedules, development, factory, support, etc., necessary to conduct daily operations, meet the requirements of the business plan, and satisfy translated business objectives. Within this improvement activity, you need to fully implement the planning, scheduling and execution process you defined under 22.4.

Where scheduling is already done on a routine, accurate basis, this may be a fairly straightforward implementation step toward creating your quality information system. Where no accurate schedule or schedule methodology exists, this step may take 12 to 18 months to complete.

A manually created and maintained schedule is not a schedule. The complexities of today's business world require the speed and complexity-management capabilities available only through computer processing. As we mentioned in chapter 10, although material requirements planning and manufacturing resources planning (MRP and MRPII) do present some scheduling limitations, they remain the best overall, comprehensive tool for factory scheduling. For development planning, there are good project planning and tracking systems available, including packages that will run on mainframes or personal computers. The availability of good software tools for marketing information systems and customer support is somewhat limited and tends to be specialized by market. Even if you create some of your own software tools, such an investment is less risky than trying to manage data, information, and operational schedules manually.

Planning and scheduling systems represent the central nervous system of your business. If not defined and implemented com-

292 CREATING AN INFORMATION NETWORK

pletely and accurately, you'll end up with open circuits where the "hands" won't even hear the "brain," much less carry out the transmitted orders. Hundreds of books, videotapes, seminars, and classes have been brought to bear to define the best methods for creating and maintaining scheduling systems. We can't do justice to the complexity of the problem or the requisite prescription for your particular company with a short, generalized checklist. Neither can we take all the time and space necessary to thoroughly address the issue of establishing the Schedule. We will present a short checklist that will allow you to test the completeness and validity of your current scheduling system. Beyond that, if you do so for no other aspect of your quality system, get some outside assistance to audit and improve your planning and scheduling system. You'll save money in the long run, and you'll ensure that you create a complete and accurate connection between the quality information system and the quality delivery system.

1. Do the policies for your various business plans direct the creation and maintenance of the schedules required to run the business?
2. Are the data supplied by the various business plans sufficient in content and accuracy to serve as valid schedule input?
3. Have the users defined the data and information required from each schedule in order to ensure timely production of the specified products or services?
4. Have the necessary software tools been defined and implemented which allow the regular, accurate, and consistent presentation of defined scheduling information to the users?
5. Are the data used for all business plans and schedules maintained in a common, controlled database?
6. Have individual users been assigned responsibility for the completeness and accuracy of all data elements?
7. Is data accuracy measured and reported on a regular basis, and is overall schedule accuracy regularly assessed and reported as the algebraic sum of the various data accuracies?
8. Is schedule accuracy regularly assessed against the directing plan?

9. Is schedule accuracy maintained and managed based on actual factory or department execution?
10. Are all schedule changes assessed and approved against the directing plan before being implemented?
11. Are the employees committed to faithful schedule execution, maintaining schedule accuracy, and reporting performance against schedule requirements?

22.8 CREATE A PERFORMANCE FEEDBACK SYSTEM.

Quantitative, timely, and accurate performance feedback is a must if you wish to make valid business decisions. Performance feedback should follow the path established by the translation of objectives—but this time in reverse, up through the operation until it reaches the Company.

The timing and frequency of performance feedback is particularly crucial. Performance measurement should be at its most frequent directly at the processes which create, produce, deliver, and support your products and services, your quality delivery system. Measurements made hourly or even more frequently provide the necessary feedback to assure product quality, process quality, and schedule execution. Measurements at this local level often employ statistical process control techniques in order to monitor and control highly repetitive processes. As measurements get farther away from the quality delivery system, reporting frequency is less critical and usually decreases. For example, schedule performance may be reported daily to the production manager and only weekly or monthly to the general manager.

Performance is always reported against specific objectives, the ones created in support of our business unit objectives. Performance reports should be simple, concise, and easy to understand. Computer-generated measurements are acceptable, provided they're validated and accepted by the individual or team responsible for the objective being measured. Lower-level performance reports can and should be used as input and supporting evidence for measurement of more general, higher-level objectives.

Performance feedback is incomplete without the inclusion of local improvement decisions which strive to bring actual performance closer to the objective. Status of previous decisions and the rationale used to reach the reported improvement decisions should also be mentioned. The following guidelines may be useful in creating meaningful performance feedback:

1. Does a company policy exist which directs regular performance feedback against objectives?
2. Do local policies and procedures exist which support and implement the company policy on performance feedback?
3. Is performance measured routinely at the local level and are the measurements used to make decisions supporting local objectives and responsibilities?
4. Are the inputs for measured performance, including data, information, and lower-level measurements, assessed for accuracy prior to their use?
5. Are performance feedback reports simple and straightforward to prepare and easy to read and understand?
6. Is performance feedback always evaluated against given objectives?
7. Do the reports include local decisions made to improve performance against objectives?
8. Is all performance feedback finally summarized as performance against your published business unit objectives?

22.9 CLARIFY THE MANAGEMENT DECISION-MAKING PROCESS.

The onset of regular performance measurement and the requirement to immediately follow measured performance with improvement decisions creates a heightened awareness for the accuracy and totality of the decision-making process itself. Just as you need accurate and timely performance measurement to precede all business decisions, you also need an accurate and timely decision-making process to precede your improvement activity. If your analysis is flawed and inconsistent, the resulting decisions will be flawed and inconsistent. Such decisions may have a greater negative impact on your business than those made with inaccurate and untimely data, since the availability of accurate and timely information may give rise to a premature confidence in the validity of any subsequent decisions. Such confidence is only justified if you have an equal level of confidence in the consistency and accuracy of the decision-making process.

In the last chapter's discussion of educating employees, we talked about giving all employees a well-rounded exposure to the basics of business management, with emphasis on the particulars of your own operation. Some of you may have felt somewhat uncomfortable with this recommendation. One of the most important reasons for instilling this knowledge in your employees will soon become very clear.

Your *modus operandi* in managing your company toward complete customer satisfaction is the continuous consideration of the needs of your Circle-4 Customer. Your objectives, your decisions, and your results are based on that consideration. In order for consistent and accurate business decisions to be made at the local level, local decision makers must employ this same consideration: the needs of their Circle-4 Customer. In order for them to manage their "micro-business," they need the perspective brought about through knowledge of the total operation. From such knowledge they can more readily discern their role within the operation, their Circle-4 Customer relationships, and the impact of potential decisions made at their level. Only through this knowledge and perspective can you truly empower your employees and honestly give them the tools to make consistent, high-quality business decisions.

The following guidelines may be useful in assessing whether or not your operation has the ability to create consistent, accurate decisions at all levels of the operation (you may also wish to review chapters 8 and 14 at this point):

1. Do all employees understand business operations in general, and your business operation in specific detail?

2. Can all employees demonstrate competency in various problem-solving and analysis techniques?
3. Do all employees understand and utilize trend analysis for monitoring process and product improvement?
4. Do all employees know their Circle-4 Customer, and are they committed to the continuous satisfaction of that Customer?
5. Do your employees accept responsibility for their objectives, for the performance of their operation against those objectives, and for the decisions they make to improve that performance?
6. Do your employees consider the prioritized requirements of their Circle-4 Customer in all decisions?

22.10 ESTABLISH RECOGNITION AND REQUEST SIMULATION.

The flow of information provided through performance feedback will soon wither and die if not sustained and validated by recognition. We often get so caught up in the daily running of the business that we fail to recognize the results and achievements created by our team. Recognition will serve to create ownership, promote a sense of community in the operation, and reinforce acceptable behavior in the organization. Recognition must also be extended to your Circle-4 Customer for all those reasons and to instill within them a sense of partnership and real involvement with your business.

Recognition can take many forms, limited only by your imagination. It is important that you're honest and consistent. Though you must tailor your recognition to fit the company culture you're creating, the following ideas may be useful:

1. Recognition to your Employee:
   a. Monthly meeting held by the general manager with all employees to review actual business performance and expectations.
   b. Special recognition and reward for particularly creative and noteworthy decisions and improvement activities.

   c. Monthly quality newsletter that summarizes business performance, elaborates on business objectives and expectations, and highlights significant achievements.

   d. Regular informal discussions across organizational lines to share ideas and brainstorm future activity.

2. Recognition to your Supplier:

   a. Monthly report of supplier performance against objectives.

   b. Regular supplier newsletter summarizing business and supplier performance, identifying exceptional, certified suppliers, and sharing market trends and expectations.

   c. Annual supplier awards banquet to recognize productive supplier partnerships and review business performance and expectations.

3. Recognition to your End-user:

   a. Regular customer newsletter that shares industry trends, highlights significant end-user partnerships and discusses product applications and new product ideas.

   b. User groups which meet regularly as a forum to discuss product applications, new features and options for products, new product ideas, and the emerging business trends in the end-user marketplace.

4. Recognition to the Shareholder:

   a. Regular reports that go beyond financial results to include details of significant operational improvements, relationships with the Circle-4 Customer, and noteworthy employee achievements.

   b. Special meetings or forums where the Shareholder is invited to participate in planning strategy with key Customer partners.

The sense of involvement and ownership created through recognition establishes an environment suitable for you to request simulation from your Circle-4 Customer. That is, ask them to give their input on specific ideas you put before them for improving your products, processes, and performance. Without first performing to their expectations and recognizing that performance, including their contribution, you will not receive consistent and thoughtful replies to your requests for simulation. Such requests can, and should be a part of the total recognition package you establish for each element of the Customer. By asking for analysis and input on your ideas, you're drawing them into a closer relationship and partnership with your enterprise.

22.11 CREATE A CUSTOMER FEEDBACK SYSTEM

The customer feedback resulting from your simulation requests and arising from your recognition of customer involvement and performance will give you the opportunity to stimulate your business with diverse, creative input and ideas. Customer feedback may be presented in many forums—through an employee suggestion program, through user groups, at shareholder meetings, or by individual letters from end-users or suppliers.

To ensure that customer feedback is encouraged as well as used as valid change input to your business, there are several key characteristics to a functional customer feedback system:

1. The Company sees and reviews all customer feedback.
2. Every idea or suggestion is discussed and analyzed.
3. Each input is given a personal reply describing the analysis and the action to be taken.
4. Acceptable ideas are recognized and rewarded through the recognition system.
5. Applicable customer feedback is used to evolve and improve company business objectives.

The process of creating a harmonious and functional quality information system requires tremendous attention to detail and a commitment to involve all employees. Based on your starting point, it may take anywhere from 6 months to 24 months to see lasting results and consistent information flow. The effort will be justified as you begin to see higher-quality decision making, enthusiastic employee and Customer involvement, and as you in the Company feel a greater confidence in your visibility and control over the direction of your business.

SUMMARY

1. The quality information system consists of four paths of information flow: communicating objectives, performance feedback, recognition and simulation, and customer feedback.
2. The quality policy is the cornerstone of your governing policies.
3. The quality philosophy expresses your business values and ethics.
4. Quality objectives state the macro-intentions of your quality system.
5. The quality documentation system provides for the creation, approval, distribution, maintenance, and retention of defined business documents.
6. Defining Circle-4 Customer requirements must be done by the Company and should be done face-to-face.
7. Business unit objectives reflect the prioritized requirements of the Circle-4 Customer.
8. Objectives are translated and communicated throughout the operation through constraint analysis.
9. Decision making throughout the business must be done in consideration of the Circle-4 Customer.
10. Customer feedback must be validated and used to improve your business unit objectives.

Quality Applications

22.1 Define the quality policy, philosophy, and objectives.
22.2 Define quality documentation.
22.3 Define the customer and identify customer requirements.
22.4 Establish the business planning policy.

22.5 Redefine business unit objectives.
22.6 Translate objectives throughout the operation.
22.7 Establish the schedule.
22.8 Create a performance feedback system.
22.9 Clarify the management decision-making process.
22.10 Establish recognition and request simulation.
22.11 Create a customer feedback system.

Quality Benefits

1. A functioning quality information system will permit the realization of Circle-4 Quality within the business.
2. The QIS will result in higher-quality decision making throughout the business, enthusiastic customer involvement in the success of the business, and will give the Company confidence in their visibility, control, and management of the business.

23

STREAMLINING THE DELIVERY SYSTEM

Our goal in this chapter is not to describe the creation of a quality delivery system. Rather, given the existing operation of some collection of processes that create, produce, deliver, and support products and services, our goal is to maximize the effectiveness and integration of those processes. We will talk about generic characteristics of delivery systems, including those aspects that ensure integration with your information system, allow accurate process monitoring and control, optimize resources and material flow, and enable defect prevention, rather than detection.

Streamlining your delivery system must be approached with thought and deliberation; it's vital that you not degrade your ability to deliver products and services during the improvement process. The coordination and direction for improvement will eventually be self-sustaining by the process owners themselves. Initially ensure that the right priorities and direction are taken by including improvement objectives as part of the overall objectives given to delivery system process owners. This approach will have the added benefit of allowing you to monitor improvement progress through regular performance feedback, which should be provided for all objectives.

301

23.1 ESTABLISH DELIVERY SYSTEM RESPONSIBILITIES.

Every process within the delivery system must have a responsible owner. The following guidelines can be used to gauge the completeness of that assigned responsibility:

1. Is every process directed by an approved operating procedure?
2. Are operating procedures derived from approved operational policies?
3. Are operating procedures approved, maintained, and updated by a responsible individual?
4. Do all personnel within a given process understand and use an approved procedure for process execution?
5. Does the operating procedure identify the process Shareholder, End-user, Employee, and Supplier, in terms of required conditions, actions and expected results?
6. Are all process owners committed to satisfying their process customers?
7. Do all process owners accept responsibility for both the results of their process and for making decisions to improve process performance?

23.2 ESTABLISH A COMMON BUSINESS DATABASE.

This concept was established in the previous chapter when we discussed the creation of a quality information system. It is so fundamental to consistent process execution as well as accurate information flow and decision making that it is well worth reconfirming for your delivery system.

A common database gives you the ability to ensure the completeness, accuracy, and accessibility of all business data; it gives you control of your data. There are no justifiable arguments for multiple databases containing duplicate data. They will cease being the same data at the moment of separation, and you will have increased your control problem by a magnitude, to say nothing of dramatically increasing the risk of inaccurate data polluting your processes and decisions. For example, both engineering and manufacturing must utilize a product structure database to execute their respective schedules. Engineering builds the product structure as a result of executing the product development schedule. Manufacturing uses the product structure to purchase raw material and define the factory schedule. Why not give each department its own database, so each can work without fear of interfering with the other? My first response is that engineering and manufacturing *should* be working together through both the development and the production processes. More to the point, what mechanism will ensure that the data in both databases are the same? After all, you do want to work with a common product structure. You may offer me a mechanism to regularly look at both databases to ensure that they're identical. If there are differences, which one of the two is accurate? I could continue with this line of logic for some time. The bottom line is this—if you wish to create a unified quality system, wherein your employees work in concert toward Circle-4 Customer satisfaction, they must all sing the same song, in harmony with one another. The most cost-effective, accurate means of guaranteeing that you consistently sing the same song is through putting the music in a common database that is accessible to and usable by all.

A common database is beneficial only when accompanied by the necessary responsibilities and controls. The following steps may be useful to in assessing your business database:

1. Do all business processes, software, and operations utilize data from a common source?
2. Is the business database protected from unauthorized access and/or modification?
3. Have individual users been assigned responsibility for each data element within the database?
4. Does that assigned responsibility include timely entry and maintenance as well as periodic assessment of data completeness and accuracy?
5. Is a control procedure implemented which defines the require-

ments for defining database changes and obtaining approvals for those changes?
6. Is detailed database accuracy published to the organization on a regular basis?

23.3 DEFINE PRODUCT DOCUMENTATION.

Control and consistency of product documentation are crucial to establishing and sustaining the quality of your products and the efficiency of your operations.

Product documentation is any product-related document that is used to specify, define, develop, produce, sell, or support your products. This documentation should be controlled to ensure accuracy and to guarantee that only the most recent, approved version is in use. The sample policy on quality document control included in Appendix 2 contains a list of documents you may want to consider as part of your product documentation. The following checklist will help ensure definition and control of your product documentation:

1. Is there a governing policy defining the components of your product documentation?
2. Is there an implemented procedure for controlling changes to product documentation?
3. Does each product document have a control number and is the document revision evident?
4. Has each document been assigned to a responsible individual for management?
5. Are steps taken to ensure that superseded documents are taken out of circulation and no longer in use?
6. Is there a historical record for product documents that provides an audit trail and a record of changes?
7. Is there a defined relationship for all product documents so that completeness and accuracy can be traced back to the product specification and product definition?

23.4 CREATE A PARALLEL IMPROVEMENT PROCESS FOR THE QDS.

Once your basic data and documentation are under control, you can begin to address improvements in the processes themselves. Keeping in mind the need to coordinate process and subsystem interfaces, you can approach process improvement in a parallel fashion. For example, you can simultaneously begin process analysis and improvement within engineering and manufacturing. Or, within manufacturing, you can simultaneously pursue purchasing, logistics, and production improvements. A parallel improvement process is effective if you maintain a liaison between the improvement teams. In this way necessary linkages can be preserved and strengthened and potential conflicts can be ameliorated before they becomes crises.

The operational network created as part of your quality organization will evaluate and determine the most effective way to apply parallel improvement. Their decisions will be based on the logical arrangement of the operation as well as the resources available for improvement activities.

All of the remaining assessment elements included in this chapter may be applied to any process or group of processes taken as a parallel improvement activity.

23.5 EMPLOYEE EMPOWERMENT.

The issue of employee empowerment has a tendency to spark an emotional response in some managers, filling them with fear, uncertainty, and doubt. As a result, efforts to create and enable empowered employees may fall short of the requirement.

What is the requirement? Let's look at it first from a personal level. As senior managers, participants on the management team for the business, we have certain expectations for our operating environment. First, we want a clear and consistent operating framework, usually provided by our Shareholder and supplemented with

Customer requirements. Our framework starts with our mission and goals and usually extends to include the constraints for operating expense and investment levels as well as expected profitability. Second, within that given framework, we expect to be in control, exercising our management capabilities to bring about customer satisfaction and to meet or exceed the expected financial result. Nothing creates conflict faster between the Shareholder and the Company than a situation wherein the framework is established, then the Shareholder tries to direct and manage the business, encroaching in areas we believe to be our responsibility. Our first response is likely to be, "I'll do it, but I won't be responsible for the result." We accept accountability only through the exercise of our own control and authority. Third, we expect that a portion of our compensation will objectively reflect our performance. We try to negotiate rewards for meeting or exceeding our profitability goals or for improving productivity and throughput. In summary, we expect consistent marching orders, we expect to have the responsibility and authority to carry out those orders, we expect to be accountable for the result, and we expect to be rewarded for excellent performance. Any breach in this paradigm causes us frustration and dampens our motivation.

What makes us think that our employees expect anything less? We're quick to delegate responsibility, but we've been notoriously slow to confer the authority and rewards that would create a consistent, controllable environment for our employees. A typical scenario in business today is the delegation of responsibility and some authority, with the proviso, "I'll make the final decision," which is another way of saying to our people that we don't trust them to make the tough calls. We also have to be honest with one another and admit that giving up our authority makes us feel as if we're less in control of the operation. After all, why should I be judged on the decisions made by my subordinates? Have I touched a raw nerve? I hope so, because you need to understand your own psyche if you have any hope of moving beyond the traditional paradigm into a higher level of mature management thinking.

How can you truly empower your employees, and at the same time preserve your own management environment which we just described? We must define a new role for ourselves within the context of our quality system. Defining this new role will be the subject of Chapter 25, when we discuss the global issues of the empowered business. Let's focus for the moment on the issues involved in truly empowering your employees.

Based on the objectives you've translated throughout the operation, you've created small teams of employees who are working toward satisfying those objectives. For each of these teams, you must create the same type of working environment that you expect for yourselves. You've established their operating framework through the objectives and through governing and operational policies. The procedures required to execute their assigned processes are their responsibility to define, maintain, execute, and control. So far, no problems, right? This normal assignment of responsibility is routine and nonthreatening to your environment.

Each of these teams must also have an operating and investment budget. As operations progress and improve, they will play a role in establishing their budget for future fiscal periods, similar to the way you seek approval for your long-range business plan. Once the budget is approved, it's theirs to manage. Operating expenditures, capital investment, salary administration, and employee hiring, firing, and promotion must all be delegated to this local level. Don't forget that you've taken steps to give your employees the tools to handle this authority by educating them in business operations, management, and decision making. You will be able to see the decisions they make in executing their responsibilities through the regular performance feedback reports, which must identify improvement decisions. While you should offer advice when requested and should seek to understand the motivation behind the decisions your employees make, if you're committed to empowerment, always support and never override those decisions. Finally, each team must be rewarded for meeting or exceeding their objectives. As a general rule, 10 percent to 25 percent of annual compensation should be based on actual, demonstrated performance.

This is only a brief overview of true employee empowerment. It certainly doesn't address all the intricacies involved, nor does it address some of the unique conflicts which may arise at the onset of the program. One of your primary new tasks, which we'll discuss in depth in chapter 25, is managing the relationships between these empowered "micro-businesses." Your main tools in this management effort are employee education, to ensure that they have the tools necessary to carry out their assignment, and studious attention to your translated objectives, to ensure that they instill and promote a commitment to Circle-4 Quality and Circle-4 Customer satisfaction.

The principles of empowerment can be summarized in the following checklist:

1. Do your employees and teams understand the framework of responsibility established for their operation?
2. Have your teams been given the tools necessary for them to fully manage their operations?
3. Do your teams understand that they have complete authority to direct their operation?
4. Has a reward system been established that compensates your teams for meeting or exceeding their operational objectives?
5. Do you stress improvement trends over the long run, rather than short-term financial results, in empowering your employees?

23.6 GUARANTEE DATABASE ACCURACY.

Though we've discussed database accuracy at length previously, it plays a vital role in the improvement and streamlining of your delivery system. Each constituted element or team within your delivery system must be confident that the basic data governing their operational decisions are both timely and accurate.

The checklist defined in 23.2 won't be repeated here, though it does apply. Your employees and teams must be presented with regular visibility on database accuracy, and they must actively participate in achieving and maintaining that accuracy to the extent defined by their responsibilities. As an example, for a production work area there is a responsibility to maintain database accuracy on the status of inventory and work-in-process which resides in their area. This means that they are responsible for ensuring the accuracy of inventory quantities, order due dates, component shortages, and all other variables that affect record accuracy for their operation. Other areas may have more comprehensive database responsibilities. Purchasing, for example, has a major task in dynamically maintaining the purchasing database so that it reflects the reality of the moment. The need for this high level of accuracy and attention to detail cannot be overemphasized.

23.7 ASSURE DOCUMENTATION ACCURACY.

The need for documentation accuracy within the delivery system extends beyond ensuring the accuracy of product documentation, though it certainly is a major factor. Documentation accuracy is best assured by preventing errors through control procedures. Such controls need not be stifling, but they must ensure the completeness and currency of the process documents in use. Ambiguities or perceived errors must be corrected before process execution continues.

A common source of documentation error comes during the recording of actual process performance. Improper training, urgency to complete or continue the process, or a misdirected desire to exhibit perfection often results in the process End-user discovering and reporting defects introduced by their Supplier. Prevention is also the best solution for this category of documentation accuracy. Proper training and real accountability for customer-reported defects will establish the proper employee attitude and attention to detail. Human error can be minimized by using computer measurement of process performance wherever possible. When computer measurement is not possible, each critical process parameter should be monitored by at least two individuals on the team.

The following guidelines will help ensure proper documentation accuracy:

1. Are all required process documents identified and linked through the approved operating procedure?
2. Can all process documents be validated for currency prior to process execution?
3. Is there a mechanism to expediently evaluate and correct perceived errors in process documentation?
4. Does the operating procedure require the validation of produced products and services against the requirement?
5. Are documents indicating actual product performance and characteristics controlled through computer measurement and/or team validation?

23.8 OPTIMIZE MATERIAL FLOW.

As discussed in chapter 19, optimizing material flow is an effective means of streamlining the delivery system, reducing overhead costs and leadtimes. Your basic intent is to move the inventory as few times as possible during the conversion of raw material to finished product. This is best approached by taking a product-oriented view of the conversion process rather than a process-oriented view.

Optimizing material flow is best addressed by a group of related teams. For example, the owners of all the production processes may want to meet periodically to review and analyze material flow through the factory. The owners of the logistics processes, purchasing, receiving, receiving inspection, and inventory control may want to meet periodically to discuss material flow through the logistics operations. The two groups may even want to meet together occasionally to ensure an optimum transition of material between logistics and production. An opportune time for these meetings is during the new product development process. Time can be taken to envision material flow for the new product, and conference room or pilot tests can be conducted prior to product release to test the efficiency of various alternatives.

Your employees should expect and even anticipate the continuous restructuring of the delivery system as they periodically seek optimum material flow. This means that work assignments and teams will change from time to time. If you've done your job in nurturing complete, multiskilled, proactive employees they will see these changes as challenging rather than threatening.

Although we can't really create a checklist to assess the results of your efforts to optimize material flow, we can establish some general goals you should keep in mind as your teams address this issue on a periodic basis:

1. Product orientation rather than process orientation.
2. Material flow established for a lot size of one.
3. Factory leadtime as short as possible.
4. Throughput as high as possible.
5. Minimized or eliminated queue time.

23.9 MANAGE RESOURCES EFFECTIVELY.

Resource management is also an area where the expression of general goals is more useful than an assessment checklist. Within the confines of managing process execution and performance, resource management is the single most important task of the team and the team leader. The entire team must be aware of resource management goals and intentions so they can contribute to their realization in a positive and proactive manner.

Resource management seeks to maximize the application of available resources while eliminating waste and inefficiency. The general resources at the disposal of your process teams include time, employees, tools, capital equipment, budget, and facilities. All of these must be considered within the context of the following resource management goals:

1. Multi-skilled employees who are rewarded for their demonstrated abilities.
2. Proactive employees who train and support one another.
3. Availability of the right, high-quality tools to do the job.

4. Regular evaluation of available capital equipment that will support improved schedule performance and enhance the quality
of the product.
5. Efficient use of the physical facility.
6. Avoidance and elimination of hazards and protection of the
environment and employees.
7. The continuous reduction or elimination of wasted time and
resources.

23.10 PREVENT DEFECTS.

Once you've addressed, at least on an initial basis, the delivery
system improvement areas defined thus far, you're positioned for
real quality improvement. Although we've discussed the creation of
proactive elements within your delivery system, the majority of our
prescriptions have been aimed at the detection and elimination of
system defects. Now that you eliminated at least the first layer of this
chaff that's been hogging your resources and your management
time, let's look at the fundamental goal of your quality delivery system, *preventing* defects while producing products that meet the
requirements of your Circle-4 Customer.

Defect prevention cannot be mandated or even established as a
defined objective. If you try to do so, employees will look at you
with disbelief. What do you mean, prevent defects? We can't anticipate all possible failures in our products and systems! In fact, they
can—they just don't know it yet.

Defect prevention will begin to occur as the natural result of the
establishment of your quality delivery system. By focusing your
complete employees on customer satisfaction and by having them
continuously improve their effort to realize well-defined business
objectives, they will embark on defect prevention as a matter of
course. During your start-up and clean-up phases, everyone will be
focused on eliminating the inherent waste, inefficiency, and defects
built in to your traditional operation. As they move beyond this
effort, a concerted focus on realizing objectives, improving perfor-

mance, and satisfying the Customer will result in further improvements to products and processes. You see, instead of chasing around to correct known problems, everyone will begin proactively seeking their goals. Instead of trying to fix a broken machine, you reach the point of trying to get additional horsepower out of a functioning machine. This is the essence of defect prevention. The attitude of seeking the goal, and once achieved, setting it higher, the attitude of never being satisfied with less than perfection, and the pride of knowing the appreciation of a fulfilled Customer; these are the true measures of a successful quality delivery system.

SUMMARY

1. Improvements to the quality delivery system must not degrade your ability to deliver your products and services.
2. Prioritized improvements must be given to process owners as objectives within their overall set of objectives, allowing priority, control, and regular measurement of improvement progress.
3. Delivery system responsibilities must be clear, unambiguous, and documented within the operating policies and process procedures.
4. A common business database ensures the completeness, accuracy, and accessibility of your business data.
5. Improvements to processes within the QDS can be done in parallel. Quality application steps 23.5 through 23.10 can be accomplished within any process or group of processes identified for improvement activity.

Quality Applications

23.1 Establish delivery system responsibilities.
23.2 Establish a common business database.
23.3 Define product documentation.

23.4 Create a parallel improvement process for the QDS.

23.5 Enable employee empowerment.

23.6 Guarantee database accuracy.

23.7 Assure documentation accuracy.

23.8 Optimize material flow.

23.9 Mange resources effectively.

23.10 Prevent defects.

Quality Benefits

1. You have improved your quality delivery system by easing the constraints to Circle-4 Customer satisfaction.
2. Your quality delivery system has the ability to improve itself and to continuously pursue the satisfaction of the Circle-4 Customer.

What kind of return can you expect from such a concentrated, comprehensive improvement effort? If I were to relate even a dozen examples, I would grossly understate the potential for improving business profitability. The real key is the idea of consistently improving trends over the long term. Just to prove it to yourself, extrapolate your business profitability out for 10 years in annual increments. Now calculate a profit improvement of just 5 percent per year, compounded across the 10-year period. Perhaps you've arrived at a respectable number, but probably nothing to really shout about. Where can you generate a 5 percent profit improvement every year? Increase sales by 5 percent? Reduce inventory by 5 percent? Reduce operating expenses by 5 percent? Improve productivity by 5 percent? Increase throughput by 5 percent? Reduce raw material costs by 5 percent? These areas, and others, have a measurable impact on the bottom line. With a continuously improving quality delivery system, you will see profitability improve steadily as a result of improving performance trends in all these areas— and more!

24

BUILDING PARTNERSHIPS WITH THE CIRCLE-4 CUSTOMER

In the months since you began restructuring your business into a quality system, you've seen a more concerted, harmonious operation. Your employees clearly understand your business objectives and their role in realizing them. They make local decisions with confidence and approach change with alacrity and enthusiasm, always striving to improve their Circle-4 Customer satisfaction. Your Customer is also seeing the fruits of your labors. Though you're not always perfect, they see in your efforts a commitment and a consistency that gives them confidence in your ability to fulfill your promises and contracts. They have a new insight into your business, and they're beginning to feel as if their participation will really make a difference in your results.

This new and refreshing confidence must be nurtured and cultivated into real and lasting partnerships. When you began the process of total quality improvement, your Circle-4 Customer kept you at arm's length, unwilling to invest time and energy in supporting your operation until you first demonstrated an ability to meet your commitments and satisfy requirements. Your consistent performance has withstood the test of time as you've demonstrated improvements,

315

even by small degrees, in your products, services, prices, and support. Your Customer now has a degree of certainty that you stand committed to their success and that you will listen to and understand the issues and constraints that stand in their way.

The actual timing to begin involving your Shareholder, End-user, Employee, and Supplier in true partnerships with the Company will vary with each business, and may be different for each of the influence groups affecting the business. You'll know when the time is right based on the level and consistency of business performance and based on the willingness of your Circle-4 Customer to discuss substantive and meaningful issues.

Establishing Customer partnerships doesn't happen with a wave of the hand or with the definitive statement "I want to be your partner." Just as the process of defect prevention arises from the sum total of a unified, functional quality delivery system, Circle-4 Customer partnerships will arise naturally from the sum total of the fundamental relationships created with your Customer. Throughout this chapter we will explore those interfaces and relationships. A note of caution, however: Any generic structure and presentation must be influenced and molded by the unique blend of characteristics brought about by the intersection of *your own* Circle-4 Customer with *your own* business.

24.1 ESTABLISH AN EXTERNAL AUDIT SYSTEM.

There's that "a" word again! It certainly isn't your desire to force your way into the premises of Suppliers and End-users in order to root out waste, inefficiency, and incompetence. Instead, an external audit system must be designed to consistently and uniformly capture the needs and requirements of Suppliers and End-users, when you're invited to visit them. You should certainly request regular visits, and when they're granted, an established format will guide your inquiries and discussions.

Whether visiting a Supplier or an End-user, an external audit system will have the same goal, namely "to seek a thorough understanding of the Customer." The process is very similar to the one described in chapter 3, when we first sought to really understand the Circle-4 Customer, and it is also congruent with the process identified in section 22.3 during the creation of your quality information system. At this point, ensure that your communications with your Supplier and End-user are formalized to a point that allows consistent collection, collation, and analysis of customer information. To this end, create a policy for external audits that defines the feedback required as the result of visits to End-users and Suppliers.

During normal business conduct, sales personnel will be responsible for visits to End-users, and purchasing personnel will be responsible for visiting Suppliers. On those occasions where it is important for Company managers to be involved, carefully follow the same guidelines established for sales and purchasing, and always be accompanied by the responsible salesperson or purchasing agent. Finally, concerning visits made by the Company, always keep in mind the empowered decision making established in your business. Sales personnel are empowered to book customer orders, to work within the system, and to decide whether a given End-user's requirements truly constitute an order for your products and services. Purchasing agents are empowered to provide the best raw material for your products and services, in terms of material quality, delivery, cost, and any other identified parameters. During visits to Suppliers or End-users, even though you represent the total business and the total Circle-4 Customer, never short circuit the decision-making authority of your responsible employees. In fact, for all intents and purposes, the primary reason you should make such visits is at the *request* of sales or purchasing personnel, and with the purpose of following a script which you've defined and rehearsed with them.

In a traditional business environment, sales personnel are interested in pushing product and booking orders. Within the quality system, they're interested primarily in solving problems for the End-user. In a traditional business environment, purchasing agents are interested in coercing the lowest price and fastest delivery from suppliers. Today, they're interested in establishing and maintaining consistent, long-term sources of quality raw material. Both groups of employees will want to actively participate in framing the context of the external audit system. Before you and your employees visit a given Supplier or End-user, everyone must be well-versed in the current state of the relationship and prepared with specific status on any pending business and/or specifically defined actions for any unresolved issues. In generic terms, you seek to understand the following through regular Company manager visits to End-users and Suppliers:

1. How are they organized and who are the players with responsibility and authority?
2. Who are their customers (End-users) and what unique requirements do they have?
3. How does their operation make money, and what role does your business play in the process?
4. What unique problems must they address to be successful?
5. Who is their Shareholder (owner), and to what extent does the Shareholder depend on their success?
6. How do they view their business in the future, and what market forces do they feel must be addressed to continue their success?
7. How do they view their relationship with your business, now and in the future?
8. What expectations do they have from you?

Information derived from Customer visits is presented, in a uniform format, to the sales and marketing department for End-users, and to the purchasing department for Suppliers. Since external audits will usually be conducted by one or two Company managers, summarized results are also shared with the complete management team. (External Audits, conducted by Company managers, do not replace supplier quality audits, conducted by purchasing in the pursuit of supplier certification. Refer to improvement activity 24.3.)

24.2 CREATE A CUSTOMER-BASED DECISION-MAKING MODEL.

In section 22.9 (Clarify the management decision-making process) we talked about clarifying the decision-making process so that all decisions reflected a sensitivity to Circle-4 Customer requirements. You have been encouraging your employees to not only make decisions, but to also consider the needs of, and the impact to the Circle-4 Customer in those decisions. Now that you've established a new decision-making paradigm, it's time to formalize the concept within a company policy.

A company policy will allow you to establish and communicate the content and consistency required in all business decisions. While again, the exact construction of the decision parameters will depend upon your business and your unique blend of Customer by virtue of the four defined influence groups themselves, it's possible to recommend the general considerations which must be given to each as alternatives are analyzed and decisions made. The general considerations to consistently follow in making any Customer-based decision include:

1. Considering the Shareholder, will the decision:
   a. reduce operating and/or product cost?
   b. improve profitability?
   c. cause reporting requirements to change?
   d. improve your ability to meet your given objectives?
2. Considering the End-user, will the decision:
   a. improve the product?
   b. improve delivery?
   c. satisfy an End-user requirement?
3. Considering the Employee:
   a. Do your employees understand the need for and the rationale behind the decision?
   b. Do your employees have the tools necessary to implement the decision?
   c. Will the decision improve job performance and satisfaction?
   d. Does the decision complement the direction and objectives of your assigned responsibilities?
4. Considering the Supplier:
   a. Will the decision cause your Supplier requirements to change?
   b. If so, does your Supplier have the ability, willingness, and incentive to make the necessary changes?

c. Will Supplier quality (material quality, delivery, price) improve as a result of the decision?

The considerations are given in order of priority for Customer satisfaction. As alternative actions are considered, each should be evaluated against these prioritized Circle-4 Customer considerations. Local Circle-4 Customers should be consulted during the evaluation as necessary to clarify potential decision impacts. As a general rule, involving them in the decision-making process can take less time and yield more positive results than assuming you know the impact of the potential decision, based only on history. Quite often, satisfying a consideration can be accomplished as part of the actual decision. As a Customer-based decision-making model is constructed and formalized, it must be clearly understood that you are not empowering "group" decision making. Carefully considering local Customer requirements and consulting local Customers during deliberations does not change or dilute the specific decision-making responsibility and authority conferred on your employees through the quality system. Once all employees form the habit of considering their complete environment in making business decisions, you'll find them actually spending less time in the process than they did when decisions were made on the fly and were frequently followed by lengthy clean-up and corrective action. Finally, your decision-making model should ensure that all actions resulting from business decisions are accurately reflected in your quality documentation.

24.3 ESTABLISH SUPPLIER CERTIFICATION AND PARTNERSHIPS.

In cultivating business relationships with your Circle-4 Customer, you strive to identify and nurture the most proactive and responsive partners. One means of recognizing the special and important relationships you've created with your Suppliers is through a Supplier certification program. To receive certification, a Supplier must consistently demonstrate the behavior and performance you deem necessary to an ongoing, successful, and profitable relationship.

One of the most widespread and recognized certification programs today is ISO-9000. Established as an international standard, ISO-9000 is the quality cornerstone of the European Economic Community, and is validated by recognized, third-party audits. Certification to the standard must be renewed every three years and carries with it a recognized completeness, consistency, and commitment to continuous improvement for the certified business. Requiring your key Suppliers to be ISO-9000 certified will allow you to create cost-effective Supplier certification, in that you won't have to formulate the requirements.

Whether you choose to adopt ISO-9000 for Supplier certification or whether you choose to create your own certification framework, there are some characteristics you must recognize. First, you cannot ask anything of your Suppliers that is not also demonstrated in your own operation. The characteristics of a certified Supplier must be extracted from the characteristics of your internal operation. From an ISO perspective, if you establish a quality system as defined within this book, you should have little trouble achieving ISO-9000 certification for your own business. Second, you need to recognize and communicate to your Suppliers, that you are certifying the quality and consistency of their operation, not the quality and consistency of their product. Within the framework of your relationship and your requirements, product quality must be demonstrated on an ongoing, order-by-order basis. Certainly, you may treat incoming product from certified Suppliers differently than you do for uncertified Suppliers, but the quality of received product must repeatedly stand on its own merits. Last, your Suppliers must understand that certification constitutes the prerequisite to a true partnership. If a Supplier is unwilling to commit themselves to the standard you establish, be it ISO-9000 or an internally created certification program, you will not be willing to pursue a more comprehensive and interdependent relationship.

The requisite characteristics of a Supplier certification program are straightforward:

1. The program must specifically define required operational and performance characteristics.
2. The program must be consistently applied to all Suppliers.
3. Certification must be renewed on a regularly defined basis.
4. Certification must be done through a specifically defined audit program either administered by purchasing or through a third party. Suppliers cannot certify themselves.
5. The certification audit program must require quantitative, objective evidence of conformance to the requirements you've defined.
6. When requested, you must be willing and able to provide guidance and advice to Suppliers who wish to become certified.
7. Certified Suppliers must be given visible recognition of their accomplishment and must receive preferential treatment which is not available to uncertified Suppliers.

One of the most visible forms of preferential treatment given as a reward for Supplier certification is the opportunity for a Supplier to become a partner in your business operation. Your willingness to create such a partnership demonstrates your commitment to a long-term, mutually beneficial arrangement.

The programs initiated for your Supplier partners must be synergistic, enhancing the success of each partner beyond the bounds of a normal customer-supplier business relationship. Though your unique Suppliers will steer the direction of your partnership programs, some ideas that are worth considering include:

1. An electronic interchange of schedule requirements and purchase orders, thus mutually reducing logistics overhead, and consequently reducing prices and leadtimes.
2. An electronic interchange of raw material parameters and specifications.
3. Supplier participation on new product development teams, assuring them business for future product production.
4. Your participation in Supplier marketing efforts to new customers and markets.

5. Joint quality improvement teams, where the resulting cost savings are shared equally by the participants.
6. Location of representatives of some of your Supplier partners within your facility, or location of one of your purchasing agents at the Supplier facility.

24.4 DEFINE END-USER FORUMS.

Strive to have the same relationship with your End-user that your Supplier strives to have with you. As you see a benefit to your long-term success, be willing to proactively participate in any certification and partnership programs offered by your End-users. You may also become members in professional organizations that represent their business and their marketplace.

Beyond these obvious relationships, and beyond the Customer feedback established in chapter 22, you must seek to create an ongoing forum with your End-users that allows you to demonstrate a responsiveness and a commitment to their success. Though again, specific solutions will be unique to your business and your marketplace, some ideas you may wish to consider include:

1. Technical roundtable discussions, where key End-users are invited to discuss pertinent technology and product evolution with your principal engineers. You should pay travel expenses for such discussions.
2. Similar technical discussions, but in this case you assemble key End-users, key engineers and key Supplier engineers, to discuss the direction and evolution of the basic technology that drives your products.
3. Participation with End-users to promote and support their business, possibly by lending of equipment and personnel.
4. Periodic, frank discussions with key End-users concerning product pricing and the cost drivers steering your pricing.
5. Direct involvement of End-users on new product development teams.

24.5 ESTABLISH A SHAREHOLDER ROUNDTABLE.

Your Shareholder also needs a perspective of your business which goes beyond the financial results or the quarterly reports. You have a responsibility to expose your Shareholder to the excellent operation and the long-term business relationships you're developing. Such an exposure will give you the opportunity to more fully understand the long-term motivation and expectations of your Shareholder.

Who your Shareholders actually are is as wide and diverse as your companies themselves. Regardless of who they are, a traditional Shareholder relationship has been an arm's-length, formal one, perhaps consisting of regular trips to the boardroom, interspersed occasionally with a carefully orchestrated on-site "dog and pony" show. While you need to maintain the respect your business relationship demands, and you don't want to engage in frivolous and time-wasting discussions, you should try and encourage a modicum of additional insight into your business on the part of your Shareholder.

One of the most proactive ways to involve your Shareholder is through an annual business roundtable. Chaired by your general manager, and limited to key and principal players from your End-users, Suppliers and Employees, the roundtable would be a full-day discussion following a specific agenda. Limited to two dozen or fewer participants, the roundtable would begin with a "state of the world" presentation from each of your attending groups, the Company, the Shareholder, the Supplier, the End-user, and the Employee. Based on the nature and temperament of the participants, there may be more than one point of view or presentation per group. The goal of the roundtable is not to make any business decisions, strategic or otherwise, but to share concerns and perspectives on what has happened, and why, and what this collection of experts expects will happen in the future. The day will promote a greater understanding between your major Customer constituents and should end only with a renewed commitment to continue working together toward mutual future success. The insight each participant takes away from the roundtable will be a positive influence in upcoming business decisions and will sustain and support existing relationships.

24.6 PROMOTE THE COMPLETE EMPLOYEE.

You've taken tremendous strides in improving the expertise and participation of your employees in proactively running the business. You've given them a solid business education, you've made sure they have an ever-increasing set of skills to support the business operation, you've empowered them with responsibility, authority, and accountability, and you've established a reward system that allows them to share in the fruits of their labors. Through your commitment, and their effort, they have become your single most valuable asset.

You will continue to renew your human asset through continuing education and training programs. Those who desire may pursue a post-secondary degree in a discipline beneficial to the business, which you will pay for based on individual performance. Your employees come to work excited and challenged, and they go home satisfied, anticipating the next day.

If you truly want to consider your Employee as part of your Circle-4 Customer, and if you're truly committed to Circle-4 Customer satisfaction, you must be prepared to support the total needs of your Employees. No, you certainly don't want to run their lives, nor do you even want to stick your nose into their private affairs. However, you do want to make sure they have every opportunity to be successful and responsible citizens. You can do your part through employee benefits. Not only those benefits which are looked upon as traditional, such as medical insurance, life insurance and a pension plan, but through other nontraditional benefits that truly allow your Employees to become responsible, contributing citizens without penalty from you.

I realize that this concept flies in the face of current trends in business, where employee benefits have really taken a nosedive.

Keep in mind for a moment the climate of growth and profitability you've created in your business and forget about what's happening "out there." You've created a truly empowered workforce. They make good business decisions. They don't always make the right decisions, but you've let them know it's OK to make mistakes. They do always consider the needs of their Circle-4 Customer, and as a result, you're managing a more efficient business than you ever thought was possible. Your Employees have earned the right to *define* their own benefits, and they have the wisdom and experience to make these decisions well.

By giving your Employees the responsibility for defining their benefits, you're promoting complete Employees by telling them, "You know what's best for yourself. You tell us what we can do to support your personal success." I think most of you will be surprised at the fair and equitable conclusions that result from this additional empowerment.

Of course, the Employees themselves will need to create a mechanism to arrive at their desired benefits. For your part, you should establish a "not to exceed" percentage of the payroll for the benefits package to fall within, you will provide resources to evaluate alternatives they're considering, you will offer advice and suggestions when requested, but for the most part you'll only act as participating employees in the process.

If you tell your Employees, for example, that beyond the legally mandated expenses such as worker's compensation, unemployment insurance, and social security, they have a benefits pool in the amount of 25 percent of payroll, they may come up with some very creative and pertinent benefits for themselves. While we can't hope to enumerate all the possibilities, your new benefits paradigm may possibly yield the following:

1. A commitment to after hours *pro bono* administration of some benefits, saving the company and the Employees overhead expense.
2. Individually tailored medical plans, where Employees can choose their coverage and can choose the percentage they pay from their wages and from their benefits pool.

3. Paid time off to participate in community affairs or volunteer social or environmental programs.
4. On-site preschool or daycare.
5. Employee fitness programs, which may include group membership in a local health club or on-site fitness facilities.
6. Accrual for Employee recreation.
7. Group purchase of a vacation condominium for an Employee-managed timeshare.
8. Special savings programs for children's college education or other defined purposes.

Involving your Circle-4 Customer will be your reward for creating consistent and profitable business operations through your quality system. The costs involved will be minor compared to the cost of the waste and inefficiency you've eliminated. The cost of detection and correction is always much higher than the cost of prevention. The cost of a satisfied, participating Circle-4 Customer is much lower than the cost of poor, inconsistent quality.

SUMMARY

1. You can begin to truly involve the Circle-4 Customer in your business success because you have demonstrated commitment to their requirements, consistent performance, and improvement in satisfying those requirements.
2. External audits serve as the means for the Company to regularly assess the needs and requirements of the End-user and Supplier.
3. A Customer-based decision-making model formalizes the process of considering the prioritized needs of the Circle-4 Customer in all business decisions, at all levels of the operation.

Quality Applications

24.1 Establish an external audit system.
24.2 Create a Customer-based decision making model.
24.3 Establish Supplier certification and partnerships.
24.4 Define End-user forums.
24.5 Establish a Shareholder roundtable.
24.6 Promote the complete Employee.

Quality Benefits

1. An involved, participating Circle-4 Customer is your reward for assuring Circle-4 Quality through a proactive, integrated Quality System.
2. Circle-4 Customer involvement will enable self-sustaining feedback into your business, ensuring that you understand and consider evolving Customer needs and requirements.

25

MANAGING AN
EMPOWERED BUSINESS

We've made significant progress in revitalizing and restructuring our businesses to be responsive to the evolving needs of our Circle-4 Customer. Our improvement process has integrated common-sense business management with the total quality principles necessary for Customer satisfaction. Our approach and perspective has been that of the Company, the management team responsible for the performance and the results of the business unit. Let's take a few minutes to describe the operation of a representative rejuvenated business, again from the Company point of view, and with the intent of understanding our new role of managing an empowered operation.

The business is characterized by a relatively flat organization structure. The Company team leader is the General Manager (or CEO, or president, or division manager, or managing director—take your pick). Senior management assignments represent the major functions critical for the success of the business. Management functions as a team: They individually work toward results defined through business unit objectives which are jointly established, and they understand that the entire team must be successful if they're to be individually successful and rewarded. Collectively with the

329

General Manager, they think of themselves as the Company; they establish the direction and enable their operation to work in that direction toward defined results.

At the most, there are four hierarchal levels in the business, including the GM. Below the Company level, organizational flexibility is used as a tool, allowing the operating structure to mold itself to meet the needs of the Circle-4 Customer and the requirements of the products. This dynamic structure is possible because multiskilled, talented employees who make good business decisions on a regular basis, make up the entire workforce. Organizational flexibility is managed and communicated through a Quality Organization, which includes all the governing and operational policies used to establish the business framework. All employees thoroughly understand the operational framework and their role within it. Quality system documentation is tightly controlled so that changes occur based on Company approval and timing.

The process of business planning has become a cumulative, as well as an iterative process. The master plan extends for at least five years, the current year being expressed in monthly increments, the second in quarters, and the remaining years expressed annually. The master plan is product oriented, with emphasis on the evolution of Circle-4 Customer requirements. The Company sees their Circle-4 Customer as the major influence groups which can affect the direction and results of the operation; the Shareholder, the End-user, the Employee, and the Supplier. The Company meets quarterly as a quality steering committee. Quarterly meetings last one to two days during which they test the validity and currency of all business objectives based on the most recent actual performance and the most recent Customer feedback. The quality steering committee always adjourns with a complete master plan in place. Sensitive to resource leadtimes and operating budget requirements when revising the plan, they aggressively anticipate driving business objectives through proactive execution of all plans and schedules, rather than being buffeted by the vagaries of the marketplace. The Company is in tune with, and sensitive to, the total marketplace, the universe of their Circle-4 Customer. They make incremental changes in business unit objectives rather than radical, wholesale changes. They have a high degree of confidence in the accuracy and validity of the information they're using as a basis for all decisions, and they always consider the impact on the requirements of their total Customer when evaluating and evolving those objectives.

Their high level of confidence is a result of the quality information system that functions within the business. Each manager has accepted the responsibility for achieving defined results against their agreed upon business objectives. At the Company level, objectives encompass all requirements that ensure the business can "make more money now and in the future": focusing on Customer requirements as they relate to products, markets, operating expenses and investment. As a team, they've translated these objectives throughout the operation so that they're expressed in increasing detail, in terms applicable to the local level and in consideration of the constraints which exist in the operation as a result of the defined organization and processes. The operation receives their objectives through participation on quality improvement teams which meet on a regular basis to assess their performance and decide on improvement actions to bring performance closer to the objective. Every employee understands their role in terms of expressed objectives and expected results. Each also understands, with a well-rounded knowledge of business operations, how their role affects the whole, and each accepts the responsibility of managing or operating within the "micro-businesses" constituted through the local objectives.

Employees meet in their quality improvement teams at least weekly. First ensuring that they're using accurate and timely information, each team assesses actual performance of their micro-business against expected results. In consideration of their local Circle-4 Customer, they determine improvement activities to ease the constraints on performance. The range of improvement activities reflect the extent of their empowerment and authority and cover the full business gamut from managing resources, including employees and equipment, through restructuring operations, to the application of additional or updated capital equipment. As is the case for the larger business, they submit regular reports to their local Shareholder, identifying achieved results and decisions made for improvement.

Local performance reports are consolidated upward through the organization until the management team reports against own business unit objectives to the general manager. This reporting takes place on a monthly basis during which they assess the direction of the business and confirm and support the decisions of their operation. When the Company encounters improvement decisions which they believe are counterproductive, they seek to understand the decision basis. If they realize that either the necessary information or the decision-making process was lacking in accuracy or completeness, they seek to correct the fundamental problem. They do not usurp the empowered authority of their employees; if through greater understanding an employee wishes to alter their decision, they may do so. The Company role in this respect is one of understanding, oversight, and education, not one of concurrence, modification, or dictation.

As business performance and improvement are evaluated monthly, they look for opportunities to increase the effectiveness of the operation. Company emphasis is to identify trends which may only be visible from their perspective and then communicate those trends, as well as overall performance, to the operation. The general manager meets with all employees monthly. A review of overall business results is given, followed by recognizing employees and teams which made significant decisions or contributions during the previous month. All employees receive a monthly "production incentive" based on business profitability and performance results. The employees singled out for special recognition may receive dinner certificates, savings bonds, show tickets, or some similar reward. Finally, the GM identifies business trends and expectations, knowing that all employees will keep these in mind as they steer their micro-businesses during the coming month.

Every two weeks, product development teams meet to review the progress of new product development as well as active product production. Organized by product family, team members represent their quality teams, which encompass the entire quality delivery system. With an eye toward satisfying the established product plans and schedules, each team anticipates potential upcoming constraints in schedule execution and takes appropriate action to minimize, eliminate or compensate for those constraints. The new product development teams also act as the oversight committees for the completeness and accuracy of all product documentation.

Education and training within the business is accepted as a normal part of the job. A full 10 percent of available time for each employee is spent in the classroom, including all senior management. Each year, everyone receives a refresher course covering the business quality system, which includes a review and analysis of all the most current business objectives. This overview is also used as a forum for the employees to review the quality policy and quality philosophy, to discuss how they've progressed as an entity, to debate possible changes and modifications, and to explore new concepts and thinking. Part of annual refresher training is an overview of business management and decision making. With an eye toward improving management capabilities, all employees are re-exposed to the concepts of self-management, creating win/win relationships, and understanding the requirements of the Circle-4 Customer on both a local and a business level. Time is spent validating and improving the Circle-4 Customer concept. Additional training time is spent expanding the skill base of all employees in accordance with individual training plans.

The business spends some amount of time auditing its own systems. Two internal auditors are busy full time and then some, as empowered employees vie for their attention and evaluation. Realizing that an objective, outside look at their micro-business is an important improvement tool, employees look forward to operational audits, which occur at least annually for every facet and process of the business. The results are handled by the employees in the same manner as performance feedback: What improvement decisions are required to ameliorate the audit findings? Audit results are kept as historical records; and employees work hard to ensure that negative findings only occur once within their audit history.

An outsider looking at the business would be hardpressed to distinguish between Employees, Suppliers, and End-users in some areas. Several key suppliers have offices in the material department. They participate on the improvement teams, have access to the scheduling database, and are linked directly to their factories or distribution networks. Key End-users are working side by side with development engineers, creating new applications for existing products, as well as molding emerging technology into new products. Other End-users work directly with product support personnel, identifying faster and more efficient means to support their products. Other forms of communication and Customer feedback have helped solidify relationships and have created a real interdependency between the business and the Customer.

The Company has come to realize that their greatest responsibility in their new environment is in establishing and nurturing the relationships that allow their business to be profitable and successful. They exercise leadership, manage by understanding all required internal and external relationships, and enable those relationships by creating mutually beneficial environments. Second only to this responsibility, the Company strives to keep in mind the big picture and to share with their Circle-4 Customer all emerging trends which allow them to direct a course for the future which further strengthens Customer relationships, business operation, and profitability.

So what's the bottom line here? Will this recipe we've presented allow each and every business which tries it to be successful and profitable? What will be the real level of success and profitability? The answer to these questions can be found within each of you. Yes, the recipe will work, if you have the commitment to establish the proper foundation and the patience to realize that results will not come overnight and if you have the resolve to truly empower your employees. We haven't presented any magic formulas or cure-alls within these pages. Simple and straightforward by design, the quality system is based on sound, consistent business management combined with the integration of total quality philosophy into a comprehensive and controlled operating environment. The level of success and profitability you can achieve will be limited only by the business objectives you establish.

We have tried to paint a picture of a living, vibrant company, one within the grasp of all who would dare to reach for it. Based on mutually beneficial relationships and founded on Circle-4 Customer satisfaction, you can create a quality system that lives and breathes to satisfy your Shareholder, End-user, Employee, and Supplier. Your achievement will be the continuous reduction of cost-added activities, the continuous improvement of product and process quality, the continuous evolution of business unit objectives, and the continuous increase of success and profits. Your achievement will be Circle-4 Quality, the commitment to work in cooperation with the Circle-4 Customer in the pursuit of a profitable business, the consideration of the needs of the Circle-4 Customer in all business activities and decisions, and the result of satisfying the prioritized requirements of the Circle-4 Customer.

EWC, INC. KEY DATA (COMPANY MODEL)

EWC Plan (constant $)	1993 Actuals	1994 Budget	1995 Budget	1996 Forecast	1997 Forecast
Sales, Avg. Sell Price	11,000	13,200	15,840	19,008	22,810
Selling Cost	990	1,188	1,426	1,711	2,053
Net Sales	10,010	12,012	14,414	17,297	20,757
Materials	6,006	7,087	8,216	9,686	11,209
Operating Expense	3,904	4,444	5,045	5,708	6,642
Components	1,001	1,181	1,369	1,614	1,868
Finished Goods	1,668	1,702	1,682	1,441	1,730
Capital Equip.	1,000	1,000	1,100	1,210	1,331
Receivables	1,375	1,650	1,980	2,376	2,851
PP&E	2,000	2,080	2,163	2,250	2,340
Total Inventory	7,044	7,613	8,294	8,892	10,120
Throughput	4,004	4,925	6,198	7,611	9,548
Net Profit	100	480	1,153	1,903	2,906
Net Profit (% Sales)	1.0%	4.0%	8.0%	11.0%	14.0%
ROA	1.4%	6.3%	13.9%	21.4%	28.7%

APPENDIX **2**

SAMPLE POLICIES FOR EWC, INC.

QUALITY POLICY

I. Purpose: To provide clear, concise quality direction for EWC, Inc.

II. Policy:

    A. Circle-4 Quality is considered the highest priority in all business operations and decisions.

    B. Circle-4 Quality constitutes:

        1. the commitment to work in cooperation with the Circle-4 Customer in the pursuit of a profitable business;

        2. the consideration of the needs of the Circle-4 Customer in all business activities and decisions; and

        3. the result of satisfying the prioritized requirements of the Circle-4 Customer.

    C. Our Circle-4 Customers, the Shareholder, End-user, Employee, and Supplier are the only valid source of specification for our products and processes.

    D. In addition to the principles of total quality management, we are committed to utilizing the ISO-9000 standard as the framework for our quality system.

III. Scope: It is the responsibility of all EWC employees to understand and support the quality policy. Employees are responsible for incorporating the spirit and intent of this policy in all other company policies, procedures, and business operations.

QUALITY PHILOSOPHY

   I. Purpose: This quality philosophy is intended to describe the ideal behavior of our organization. It is intended as a behavioral benchmark, realizing that it will take hard work and continuous improvement to fully achieve these traits.
  II. Policy: The following characteristics describe the desired behavior of our organization:
      A. We take as our basic personal and operational goal the understanding, and subsequent satisfaction, of the needs of our internal and external customers.
      B. All our employees understand how their work contributes to and influences business results.
      C. All our employees know who their customers are and have developed a partnership with those customers.
      D. All our employees accept personal responsibility for rapid and relentless performance improvement.
      E. The leaders of the organization encourage all employees to take an active role in key issues that affect them.
      F. Our leaders continually reinforce the core mission of EWC, Inc.
      G. The cross-functional quality improvement team structure of the organization encourages the interfaces required to make the business successful.
      H. The organization is flexible and product driven versus department or territory driven.
      I. All our employees are involved in problem solving, decision making, planning, and implementation within their circle of influence.
      J. The values of our organization are well defined, frequently discussed, and widely understood by all employees.
      K. Key values include:

1. The primary indicator of success is customer satisfaction.
2. Decisions will be made closest to the source of the issue.
3. There will be no unnecessary barriers that limit anyone's ability to make a contribution to the organization.
4. Constructive disagreement will be encouraged.
5. People will be rewarded for appropriate risk taking.
6. The customer will always be provided with the best value.
7. Information will be freely shared.

L. Our employees are rewarded based on the skills and the work-related knowledge they possess and on their initiative to apply them to the improvement of the business.

M.Our employees have and use a variety of skills and work effectively in multiple team functions within the organization. They focus on the "work to be done" as opposed to "their job."

N. Openness, honesty, respect, and constructive feedback are highly regarded and are demonstrated by all supply center employees.

III. Scope: It is the responsibility of all employees to understand, promote, and contribute to the realization of the ideal behavior described. The EWC management team, operating as the quality steering committee, is responsible for assessing the behavior of the company on a semiannual basis and recommending improvements that will promote the quality philosophy.

QUALITY OBJECTIVES

I. Purpose: Specific quality objectives are described in order to provide guidance for continuous improvement activities.

II. Policy: In accordance with the quality policy, and aspiring toward our quality philosophy, the employees of EWC, Inc. seek to achieve:

A. a customer-minded, "determined-to-win" culture, through aggressive employee development and communication;

B. continuing competitiveness in the market, through continuous efficiency improvement and cost reduction, as measured against the best in the world;

C. improved flexibility, time to market, and customer response time through improvements to the quality system;

D. world-class customer support by becoming a proactive provider of services to our End-users; and

E. the highest levels of success for our customers through the quality and reliability of our products, systems, and services.

III. Scope: It is the responsibility of all employees to understand, promote, and adopt these objectives as they seek to improve their products and processes.

QUALITY ORGANIZATION

I. Purpose: To describe the organization employed within EWC, Inc. to assure quality operations and to support the quality policy, promote the quality philosophy, and realize the quality objectives.

II. Policy: The quality organization of EWC, Inc. is identical to the functional organization in that all managers are assigned specific functional quality responsibilities within the framework of ISO-9000 and with the intent of creating total quality management.

III. Scope: All employees are responsible for understanding the quality organization. They are further responsible for understanding their role and its relationship to the activities of their colleagues in achieving a total quality operation.

IV. Program Elements

A. Definitions

1. *quality steering committee* (QSC): The management team of EWC, Inc.

2. *management team:* The General Manager of EWC, Inc. and those managers reporting directly to the GM.

3. *quality improvement team* (QIT): The teams that take direction from the QSC. Quality improvement teams direct

the quality improvement activities of EWC. Each QIT consists of designated members of the management team and other key managers, supervisors, and employees of EWC as designated by their functional responsibility. Each QIT member will have a designated alternate from within his/her functional department. Any reference to a QIT includes both the team members and their alternates.

4. *operational improvement team* (OIT): A standing functional, or cross-functional team chaired by a QIT member. An OIT has a specifically assigned responsibility within the improvement process, related to functional operations; for example, an OIT may be formed to address material control issues.

5. Corrective Action Team (CAT): A temporary team, directed from either the QSC, a QIT, or an OIT, formed for the express purpose of satisfying a specifically defined objective within a given period of time. The CAT is the primary vehicle for defining specific quality improvements and for involving the majority of EWC employees in the total quality process.

6. *ISO-9000*: A certifiable standard, issued by the International Standards Organization, that identifies the operational elements required to achieve a controlled and consistent quality operation.

7. *total quality management* (TQM): The philosophy of involving all employees in the continuous improvement of products and processes with the intent of achieving complete customer satisfaction.

B. The quality objectives of EWC will be carried out by the management team through their role as the quality steering committee and through their participation on the established quality improvement teams.

C. The QSC members will be specifically responsible for the elements of the ISO-9000 standard as outlined in Exhibit 1, below. The job responsibilities for each manager will further specify accountability for product and process quality.

D. The QIT's will meet weekly to discuss EWC quality issues.

Each QIT will be chaired by a designated member, to serve in that capacity for 6 to 12 months. Current QIT membership and responsibilities are available from the office of the GM.

E. Each QIT will cause the establishment of operational improvement teams that represent the critical functions delegated by the QSC to the QIT. Each OIT will be chaired by a QIT member or alternate. Currently established OITs are available from the office of the GM.

F. Based on recommendations approved by the QIT, various corrective action teams (CATs) will be created to deal with specific improvement issues. CATs will operate against defined objectives for a length of time authorized by their directing team. An employee may serve on no more than two CATs concurrently, in order to promote widespread participation in the quality improvement process.

G. The quality steering committee (QSC) will meet on a quarterly basis to assess the progress and performance of the quality improvement process against the quality objectives. Any changes in direction or priority will be communicated to all employees.

H. On a regular basis, at least quarterly but preferably monthly, the QITs will report status of their efforts to improve the quality system to all employees. This status will include, but not be limited to, a description of active, authorized improvement projects, projected/actual costs, and projected savings. The results of completed projects will be monitored and actual cost savings will be reported. Significant improvements by teams or individuals will also be recognized and reported.

EXHIBIT: ISO-9000 RESPONSIBILITIES

ISO-9000 Element	*Responsibility*
1. Management Responsibility	General Manager
2. Quality System	General Manager

3. Contract Review	Director, Marketing and Sales
4. Design Control	Director, Engineering
5. Document Control	Director, Product Planning and Support
6. Purchasing	Director, Manufacturing
7. Purchaser Supplied Product	Director, Manufacturing
8. Product I.D. and Traceability	Director, Manufacturing
9. Process Control	Director, Manufacturing
10. Inspection and Testing	Director, Manufacturing
11. Inspection, Measuring, and Testing Equipment	Director, Engineering
12. Inspection and Test Status	Director, Manufacturing
13. Control of Nonconforming Product	Director, Manufacturing
14. Corrective Action	General Manager
15. Handling, Storage,and Delivery	Director, Manufacturing
16. Quality Records	General Manager
17. Internal Quality Audits	General Manager
18. Training	Director, Administration
19. Servicing	Director, Customer Service
20. Statistical Techniques	Director, Administration

QUALITY MANAGEMENT AUDITS

I. Purpose: To provide clear and consistent guidelines for the regular auditing of the quality system.

II. Policy: On a regular, scheduled basis, internal quality management audits will be conducted to assess the intent, implementation, and effectiveness of the quality system.

III. Scope: This policy applies to all EWC employees who may be involved in preparing, conducting, or supporting an internal quality management audit.

IV.   Program Elements
   A. Definitions
       1. *quality:* The totality of features and characteristics of a product or service that bear on its ability to satisfy a given need.
       2. *quality system:* The organization, structure, responsibilities, activities, resources, and events that together provide organized procedures and methods of implementation to ensure the operation can meet quality requirements.
       3. *quality management audit:* A systematic investigation of the intent, the implementation, and the effectiveness of selected aspects of the quality system.
   B. In order of importance, all audits will be conducted against the following specific requirements:
       1. Specific customer contract(s).
       2. The EWC Quality Manual.
       3. The ISO-9000 Standard.
   C. Audits will be conducted in accordance with a published audit schedule. Though additional emphasis and more frequent audits may be conducted in some areas, the audit schedule will ensure that the following major areas of the quality system are audited at least annually:
       1. product planning and support
       2. engineering
       3. administration (includes quality policy, management review, training, etc.)
       4. planning and scheduling
       5. material control (includes inventory control, receiving, receiving inspection, shipping and shop floor control)
       6. purchasing
       7. sales and marketing
       8. production
       9. calibration
   D. An internal auditor will be designated by the general manager. It is recommended that the auditor have some formal

education and training in auditing quality systems. In general, the internal auditor must have a thorough grasp of the operating quality system, must be able to communicate well, and must be objective. An ability to offer improvement suggestions is highly desirable. The internal auditor will be responsible for:

1. creating and maintaining an internal audit procedure;
2. creating the audit schedule for the approval of the QSC;
3. conducting internal audits in accordance with the approved audit schedule and the internal audit procedure;
4. assisting with supplier audits as requested by the materials manager; and
5. assisting with coordinating third-party certification audits as requested by the general manager.

E. The general steps that will be undertaken by the internal auditor for each internal audit are as follows:

1. Define objective and scope of the audit.
2. Determine the scale of the audit and identify any additional resource requirements.
3. For the area to be audited, collect any past audit history, identify any current problems, and ascertain any management concerns or priorities.
4. Confirm the audit date and set the agenda.
5. Prepare audit checklists.
6. Review the planned audit with the responsible manager.
7. Conduct the audit.
8. Review the audit findings with the responsible manager.
9. Prepare an internal audit report and submit it to the quality steering committee and quality improvement teams.

F. Following receipt of an internal audit report, the responsible department manager will present a plan for any required corrective action at the next meeting of his/her quality improvement team. Based on the nature of the findings, the quality Steering committee may elevate the priority for the corrective action.

G. Internal audit records, including the audit checklists, the

auditor's notes, and the internal audit report will be retained
for not less than two years from the date of the audit.

QUALITY DOCUMENT CONTROL

I. Purpose: To provide clear and consistent guidelines for the
documentation and record keeping required to effectively
operate the EWC quality system.
II. Policy: As defined in this policy, operational documentation
and historical performance records will be managed and controlled in order to ensure consistent business operations.
III. Scope: This policy applies to the management team as they
construct, manage, and improve the quality system of EWC,
Inc.
IV. Program Elements
A. Definitions
1. *policy:* An approved philosophy, objective or direction
followed by EWC in conducting business.
2. *procedure:* A complete description of a process, defining
how a policy is to be carried out on a repetitive basis.
Procedures must contain sufficient detail so that reaching
the desired result is straightforward and unambiguous.
3. *work instruction:* A product-specific document, utilized
by a procedure, that defines the detailed steps required to
manufacture and test the product. Work instructions are
part of the overall product documentation.
4. *workmanship standard:* A process-specific document, utilized by a procedure, that identifies normal practices and
acceptable quality criteria for all elements within the
process. Workmanship standards may be internally created or they may be external, recognized standards.
5. *product documentation:* The complete set of documentation required to develop, manufacture, market, sell, and
service a specific product. Product documentation
includes, but is not limited to:

    a. product specifications

    b. product definition

    c. product drawings and schematics

    d. operator, technical, and user manuals

    e. work instructions

    f. test procedures

    g. certification records and test results

    h. product structures

    i. product software and firmware; source and object code

    j. engineering change orders and field engineering bulletins

    k. product sales literature and application notes

    l. product sales guides and price lists

6. *quality records:* Those records relating to the specific performance of products, processes and audits. Quality records include, but are not limited to:

    a. product test data and results

    b. inspection reports

    c. audit reports

    d. material review reports

    e. calibration and repair history

    f. cost of quality reports

    g. process performance measurements

    h. quality manual

    i. supplier handbook

7. *customer records:* A specific type of quality record, customer records relate to customer orders. Customer records include, but are not limited to:

    a. customer purchase order or contract

    b. customer sales order

    c. systems diagrams, if required

    d. customer quality requirements

    e. system configuration data and test results, if required

    f. customer acceptance form

8. *business database:* The business database is defined as

the set of data elements available to the employees through the business system network, wherein said data elements are used to manage, direct, and define business operations.

B. All EWC operations will be governed via authorized company policies. Policies will be controlled documents and history will be kept for a minimum of two years.

C. Authorized procedures will define the appropriate application of company policies. Procedures will be controlled on a local, departmental level and history will be maintained for a minimum of two years.

D. Work standards will support approved procedures and will be defined and controlled on a local level, by the originating manager. History will be kept for two years. In the case of external standards, the system will ensure that the most recent version of the external standard is approved, specified, and made available to the appropriate employees.

E. All product documentation will be controlled by the director of engineering via the engineering change order policy and procedure. Product documentation history will be maintained for a four-year period. Product documentation will be retained for a minimum of seven years following the completion of the final scheduled production run of the product. The responsibility for defining product documentation is as follows:

1. Product Planning and Support
   a. product specifications
   b. operator, technical, and user manuals
   c. product structures
   d. field engineering bulletins

2. Engineering
   a. product definition
   b. product drawings and schematics
   c. test procedures
   d. certification records and test results
   e. product software and firmware; source and object code

      f. engineering change orders

   3. Manufacturing

      a. work instructions

   4. Sales and Marketing

      a. product sales literature and application notes

      b. product sales guides and price lists

F. Quality records will be controlled on a local level and will be retained for a period of two years.

G. Customer records will be controlled by the director of customer service and will be retained for a period of seven years following expiration of the period of the order.

H. The business database will be managed and controlled locally. Backup and retention of data will be in accordance with MIS/EDP policy. Employees will be assigned responsibility for specific data elements and will be assessed regularly to ensure the completeness and accuracy of those elements.

PROCESS
CONSTRAINT MODEL

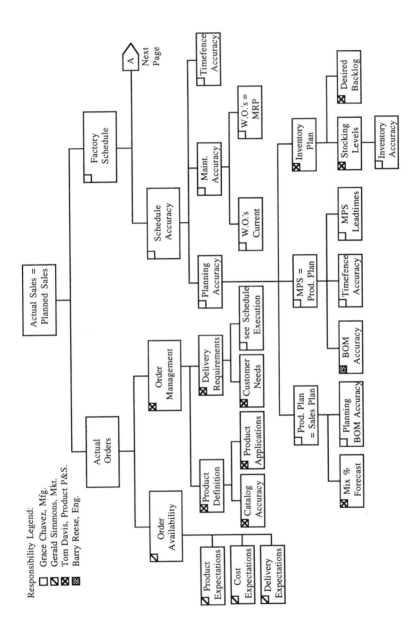

Appendix 3 Process Constraint Model

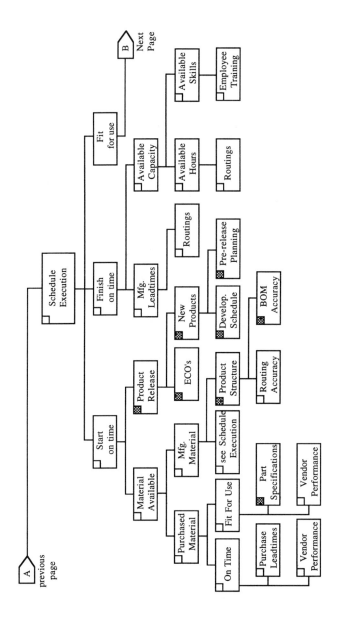

Appendix 3 Process Constraint Model, Page 2 of 3

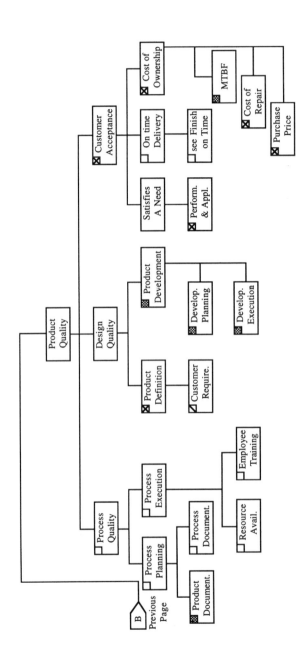

Appendix 3 Process Constraint Model, Page 3 of 3

BUSINESS PLANNING
SYNOPSIS

(Refer to Figure 10.2 for relationships.)

I. Business Plan

A. *Description*: The business plan encompasses and includes all the plans and schedules of the business operation.

B. *Input:* All the plans and schedules defined for the business via the Quality Organization; company policies.

C. *Process:* Collate all plan data into a summary performance result for the business.

D. *Output:* Planned profitability, ROI, ROA, balance sheet, and income statement as defined by the Company. First year expressed in months, second year in quarters, following years annually.

E. *Horizon:* Five or more years.

F. *Update Frequency:* Annually.

II. Product Plan

A. *Description:* The product plan is a comprehensive compilation of the product direction of the Company. Combining feedback from the Customer, this plan includes the projected life cycle of each product line or family. Actual performance displaces the plan as products are introduced into the marketplace, and the remaining plan for each product line is modified based on actual data and trend analysis. If a company deals with multiple product lines or plans to evolve single product line, the product life curves should be timed and overlapped so that the business can "ride the crest" of product maturities. The extensive information available from the product plan is the basis for all other plans and schedules

B. *Input:* Customer requirements pertaining to product specification, delivery, and cost of ownership. Market size and competitive information are also essential.

C. *Process:* Define product line lifecycles and correlate the lifecycles for different and evolutionary product lines. Based on customer requirements create product specifications. Collate all Customer and marketplace data.

D. *Output:* Life-cycle windows, product benefits and applications, market share, product specifications, competitive data, volume and price trends, demand cycles, product mix, product rollout, customer delivery, desired backlog, desired stocks, repair history, user base, support horizon, support inventory. Quite often, in addition to product specifications, the product plan is highlighted through the publication of quarterly product assumptions, which summarize current results and expectations for all product lines or families.

E. *Horizon:* Five or more years.

F. *Update Frequency:* Annually.

III.   Development Plan

A. *Description:* The development plan presents a time-phased allocation of engineering resources. Further out in the horizon, macro-blocks of engineering capacity are allocated to product lines, in accordance with the product plan, allowing for the projection of future development budgets. As the plan gets closer to reality, action is taken to define specific developments into the development schedule based on product plan specifications.

B. *Input:* Product line lifecycles from the product plan. Time-phased product specifications from the product plan, with cost and time targets.

C. *Process:* Maintain a macro long-range plan, allocating development resources. Create product definition and proposed development schedules for approval by product management.

D. *Output:* Long-range planned development. Proposed product definition and development schedules.

E. *Horizon:* Three to five years.

F. *Update Frequency:* Entire plan, annually. Creation of schedules and definitions, as required by the product plan.

IV. Development Schedule

A. *Description:* The development schedule defines and directs the actions of the engineering department for the creation and evolution of product. It specifically defines the resources and timing to be applied to each approved development project.

B. *Input:* Proposed product definitions and development schedule as approved by product management.

C. *Process:* Schedule execution for the timely creation of new and improved products.

D. *Output:* Complete product documentation, in accordance with development schedule, interim schedule performance measurements, product release schedule, prerelease planning information.

E. *Horizon:* One to three years.

F. *Update Frequency:* Monthly.

V. Engineering Change Order Schedule

A. *Description:* Often done in an unscheduled, uncontrolled manner, the ECO schedule must reflect control and management of product configuration. The incorporation of all required product design changes or improvements needs to be scheduled to conform to customer and production priorities and requirements.

B. *Input:* Engineering change requests identifying product problems and enhancements.

C. *Process:* Engineering evaluation of required product changes, with product management approval of all changes and priority of incorporation.

D. *Output:* An ECO incorporation schedule which defines the timed implementation of product changes.

E. *Horizon:* Four to six months.

F. *Update Frequency:* Weekly, or as required.

VI.   Revenue Plan

A. *Description:* The revenue plan reflects the planned shipment of goods or services to the End-user. Expressed in dollars by product line or family, the first year is monthly, the second year quarterly, and any additional years annually.

B. *Input:* The order intake plan for planned bookings and the product plan for product rollouts and assumptions.

C. *Process:* Create a timed shipping plan based on planned bookings and product availability.

D. *Output:* Rolling 12-month plan, by dollars, by product line.

E. *Horizon:* Three to five years.

F. *Update Frequency:* Preferably monthly, at least quarterly.

VII. Production Plan

A. *Description:* The production plan is a rolling 12-month plan that reflects the mix of end items to be produced on a monthly basis in order to satisfy the revenue plan.

B. *Input:* The revenue plan, the inventory plan, the mix percentage forecast for feature/option mix, any independent demand, and the development schedule for new product releases.

C. *Process:* Based on required customer delivery and factory delivery leadtimes, create a 12-month rolling plan that identifies the quantities of end items required each month to satisfy the revenue plan.

D. *Output:* Twelve-month product line forecast, by units, with a known predicted mix within each product line, expressed as a planning bill of material.

E. *Horizon:* Twelve-months, rolling.

F. *Update Frequency:* Monthly.

VIII. Master Production Schedule

A. *Description:* The MPS reflects the netted requirements for product line end items as forecasted by the production plan. The MPS represents the planning gateway into the factory schedule. In preparing the MPS, the master scheduler establishes firm planned orders which drive the material requirements plan. The timing and quantities for the FPOs take into account both the requirements of the production plan and the capabilities of the quality delivery system.

B. *Input:* The production plan, the ECO schedule, the product structure, inventory records.

C. *Process:* Gateway judgment on order quantities and timing for sellable end items, followed by explosion of requirements in order to create demand for MRP.

D. *Output:* A schedule of FPOs that drives the factory schedule through MRP.

E. *Horizon:* Twelve months, rolling.

F. *Update Frequency:* Weekly.

IX. Material Requirements Plan

A. *Description:* The material requirements plan nets all the component and assembly requirements demanded by the MPS.

B. *Input:* The MPS, inventory records, product structure, QDS process information.

C. *Process:* Computer-generated netting process that accounts for existing inventory and replenishment leadtimes for all required products and components.

D. *Output:* Time-phased order action and reschedule action reports for purchased and manufactured items.

E. *Horizon:* Six to twelve months, depending on leadtimes.

F. *Update Frequency:* At least weekly, preferably daily.

X. Purchase Schedule

A. *Description:* The purchase schedule is the compilation of open purchase orders placed on suppliers to satisfy MRP requirements. Generally reflected in daily or weekly deliveries, quantities and delivery dates must comply with MRP.

B. *Input:* Order action and reschedule action reports from MRP, component sourcing information, vendor information.

C. *Process:* Purchase orders are placed to satisfy MRP requirements in accordance with vendor constraints.

D. *Output:* Open purchase orders for material to satisfy MRP, purchase commitment report, other reports as required.

E. *Horizon:* Four to twelve months, depending on purchase

leadtimes.

F. *Update Frequency:* Daily.

XI. Factory Schedule

A. *Description:* The driving force for the quality delivery system, the factory schedule contains the detailed manufacturing requirements to satisfy the MPS. Specifying the four dimensions of product, quantity, cost, and time, the factory schedule is the basis for creating a consistent level of throughput in our business.

B. *Input:* Order action and reschedule action reports from MRP, product documentation, purchase schedule, and customer backlog.

C. *Process:* Creation of the required products from raw materials, in the time specified, at the required level of cost and quality.

D. *Output:* Finished products, ready to deliver on customer orders.

E. *Horizon:* One to four months, depending on factory leadtimes.

F. *Update Frequency:* Daily.

XII. Customer Delivery Schedule

A. *Description:* The customer delivery schedule is a focused subset of the factory schedule. It defines the time-phased execution of the process to fill and ship customer orders.

B. *Input:* Customer backlog, filtered through product availability from the factory schedule and inventory.

C. *Process:* Based on product availability, determine delivery dates for customer backlog. If factory order processing is required, consider and include process leadtimes and calculated start dates.

D. *Output:* Daily or weekly shipping schedule, by order, by ship date.

E. *Horizon:* Determined by the size of the backlog and by customer delivery requirements.

F. *Update Frequency:* Daily or hourly.

XIII. Order Intake Plan

A. *Description:* The order intake plan expresses desired dollar volume of bookings, by product line. Monthly for the first year, quarterly for the second year, and annually thereafter.

B. *Input:* From the product plan, expected volumes by product line, volume trends, price trends, planned product introductions and phase outs, and demand cycles.

C. *Process:* Determine monthly intake expectations, by product line, in dollars.

D. *Output:* Rolling 12-month plan, by dollars, by product line, using the time buckets described.

E. *Horizon:* Three to five years.

F. *Update Frequency:* Preferably monthly, at least quarterly.

XIV. Inventory Plan

A. *Description:* Inventory strategy based on the product plan.

B. *Input:* Demand cycles, customer delivery expectations, order intake plan.

C. *Process:* Determine average order delivery, desired backlog, and stock levels by product line or family.

D. *Output:* Inventory plan, by month, by product line, in dollars; annotated by process requirements.

E. *Horizon:* Twelve months, rolling.

F. *Update Frequency:* Monthly.

XV. Booking Schedule

A. *Description:* Short-term prognosis of potential customer orders.

B. *Input:* Order intake plan, sales leads, proposals and bids.

C. *Process:* Analyze potential orders in terms of close probability, time frame, order size, and expected delivery.

D. *Output:* Bookings schedule by sales region, by product line, by date, indicating order potential, status, and open issues.

E. *Horizon:* Three to six months.

F. *Update Frequency:* Daily or weekly.

XVI. Marketing Plan

A. *Description:* Based on the product plan, the marketing plan defines the major marketing goals for each product line for the next 12 months.

B. *Input:* Product documentation, applications, benefits, volume, and price trends and expectations, competitive information, planned product rollouts and phase outs, demand cycles, product assumptions, order intake plan.

C. *Process:* Create marketing strategies for realizing the business plan for each product line or family.

D. *Output:* Monthly plan for product pricing, promotions and advertising.

E. *Horizon:* Twelve months, rolling.

F. *Update Frequency:* Monthly or quarterly.

XVII. Marketing Schedule

A. *Description:* The marketing schedule translates the marketing plan into specific tasks and timeframes for all product promotional activities except advertising.

B. *Input:* Marketing plan.

C. *Process:* Quantify and schedule the requirements of the marketing plan.

D. *Output:* Time-phased schedule with task ownership and milestones for product promotions.

E. *Horizon:* Twelve months, rolling.

F. *Update Frequency:* Monthly.

XVIII. Advertising Schedule

A. *Description:* The advertising schedule converts the marketing plan for advertising into specific tasks and deadlines for product advertising.

B. *Input:* The marketing plan, information on available market media for advertising.

C. *Process:* Define the creation and placement of product advertising as required by the marketing plan.

D. *Output:* Time-phased plan for the creation and placement of product advertising.

E. *Horizon:* Twelve months.

F. *Update Frequency:* Monthly or as required.

XIX. Product Support Plan

A. *Description:* The product support plan is based on the product plan and defines the requirements and timeframes for support of products no longer in production.

B. *Input:* Product phase-out plans, customer expectations, legal support requirements.

C. *Process:* Create a general plan over the required support horizon that defines the extent of support services provided for each affected product line.

D. *Output:* See process.

E. *Horizon:* One to three years, or required product support horizon.

F. *Update Frequency:* Annually.

XX. Product Support Schedule

A. *Description:* The product support schedule defines any time critical support requirements driven by the product support plan.

B. *Input:* Product support plan, actual customer requirements.

C. *Process:* Evaluate customer requirements against defined support criteria, and if covered, schedule fulfillment of requirements.

D. *Output:* Specific schedule of support events to satisfy customer support requirements.

E. *Horizon:* Twelve months.

F. *Update Frequency:* Weekly or monthly as required.

MATERIAL FLOW
OPTIMIZATION

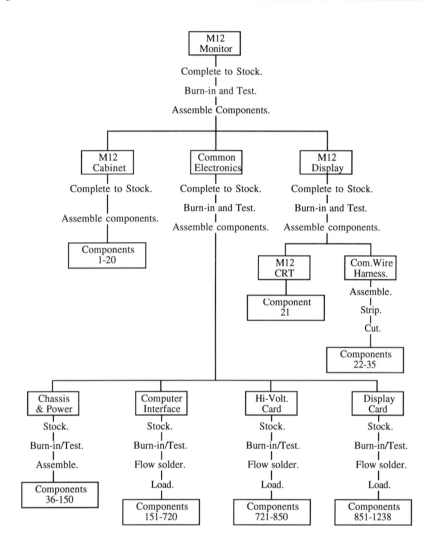

Diagram 1 Model 12 Product Structure

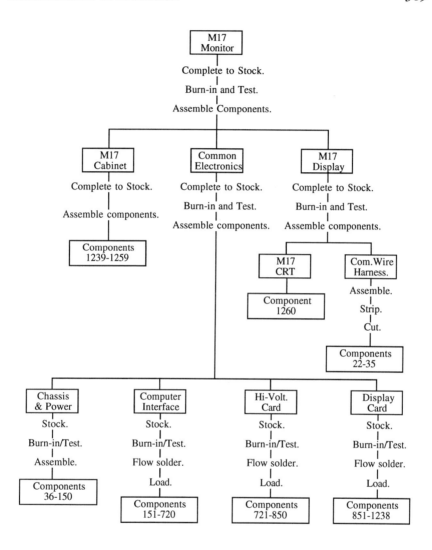

Diagram 2 Model 17 Product Structure

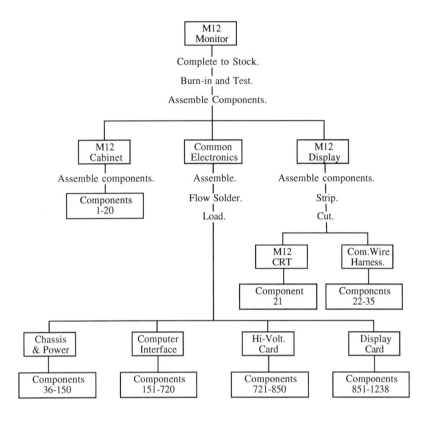

Diagram 3 Model 12 Product Structure

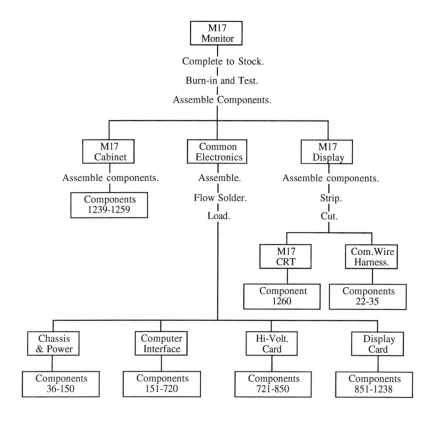

Diagram 4 Model 17 Product Structure

GLOSSARY

Audit The objective assessment of the intent, implementation and effectiveness of a specified process or group of processes.

Business objectives The quantitative, complementary expectations of the business which, if achieved, will result in Circle-4 Quality. Also referred to as Business Unit Objectives.

Circle-4 customer The four major groups which will influence the success of the business; the Shareholder, the End-user, the Employee, and the Supplier.

Circle-4 quality 1. The commitment to work in cooperation with the Circle-4 Customer in the pursuit of a profitable business. 2. The consideration of the needs of the Circle-4 Customer in all business activities and decisions. 3. The result of satisfying the prioritized requirements of the Circle-4 Customer.

Company, The The management team responsible for the results of a business or business unit; including the general manager, or business head, and those directly reporting managers.

Constraint The identified factor (or factors) which limits the performance of a specified process or system.

Constraint analysis The process of evaluating a process or system, identifying the limiting factors, or constraints, assigning responsibility for those constraints, thus allowing expected process results to be quantitatively stated in terms of the identified constraints.

Continuous improvement The regular and proactive actions taken to relieve constraints, leading to improved process performance and results.

Cost of ownership The total costs an End-user may incur to purchase, operate, support and repair a given product.

Culture An integrated pattern of human behavior and interaction.

Customer *See* Circle-4 Customer.

Customer satisfaction The TQM principle that advocates 100% satisfaction of customer needs and requirements as the primary means of business success.

Defect prevention The proactive pursuit of improved process and product performance, in response to given objectives. The logical continuation of continuous improvement following the elimination of obvious constraints and inefficiencies.

Employee The Circle-4 Customer influence group consisting of all personnel employed by the business or business unit.

Empowerment The acceptance of conferred responsibility, authority and accountability as a consequence of proactive self-management.

End-user The Circle-4 Customer influence group consisting of the individuals or organizations which purchase the products or services of a business or business unit.

External audit A special audit wherein senior management periodically visits, by invitation, End-users and Suppliers in order to fully understand their business and requirements.

Goal The defined, quantitative, desired outcome for any specific action.

Integrated business system The interactive group of business processes and subsystems which are defined to create, produce, sell, deliver and support specific products and services.

Internal audit The regular examination of the intent, implementation and effectiveness of a process or group of processes within the Quality System.

ISO-9000 Established as an international standard, ISO-9000 is the quality cornerstone of the European Economic Community, and is validated by recognized, third party audits. Certification to this standard must be renewed every three years and carries with it recognition that the certified business operates in a consistent manner, utilizing a business framework which supports continuous improvement, customer satisfaction and product quality. ISO-9000 does not certify the quality of the product, but the capability and consistency of the business.

JIT (Just-In-Time). A business philosophy, primarily used in manufacturing, that seeks to minimize inventory investment by reducing all leadtimes, thereby allowing customer demand to pull inventory into the factory from suppliers and through the production processes.

MRPII (Manufacturing Resources Planning). A formal system which involves the complete organization in the planning, execution and control of product manufacturing.

Material flow The physical movement of raw material, semi-finished, and finished products through the Quality Delivery System, characterized by amount of movement and time within the system.

MRP (Material Requirements Planning). A software tool for regenerating net production material requirements and for recommending new orders or order revisions to purchasing and the shop floor.

Motivation The drive or incentive required to precipitate action.

Objective Objectives are short term, quantitative customer requirements and business results which provide the motivation for measuring the performance of the Quality System. Objectives are based on the prioritized requirements of the Circle-4 Customer, and each must state the required measurable level of performance for a particular requirement over a specified period of time.

Operational network The formal structure of horizontal communication within the Quality Organization, consisting of cross-functional teams who seek to improve their performance to communicated objectives.

Policies Business documents which communicate the long term goals, establish the operational framework, and clarify functional responsibilities for the business unit. Policies can be either governing or operational, and all are part of quality documentation.

Proactive The initiative to sustain win/win relationships through responsible behavior which arises from value-based decision making.

Process A specific sequence of actions which must be repeated on a regular and consistent basis within the business operation in order to achieve a defined outcome.

Product The unique offering to a defined market which serves as a basis for the business or business unit, and which is intended to satisfy a need or requirement of the identified End-user.

Product definition Based on the Product Specification, the description and estimation of the processes and costs necessary to create, produce, sell, deliver and support a new product.

Product documentation The complete and controlled set of all documents necessary to, and resulting from, the creation, production, sales, delivery and support of a specific product.

Product quality 100% compliance with the requirements of Product Documentation in the execution of all Quality Delivery System processes. Product Quality can be no better than the completeness and accuracy of the Product Specification.

Product specification The thorough and complete description of a new product, driven by the Circle-4 Customer. The basis for product quality.

Quality The sum total of features, options, and characteristics of a product or service that bear on its ability to satisfy a given need.

Quality culture The behavior and interaction of the business operation in pursuit of sustained Customer satisfaction.

Quality delivery system A major element of the Quality System, consisting of the integrated group of processes defined to create, produce, sell, deliver and support the products and services of the business.

Quality documentation The defined set of business documentation, records, data, and information which must be accurate and controlled in order to enable consistent Customer satisfaction.

Quality information system A major element of the Quality System defined to ensure accurate, timely flow of information within the business and with the Circle-4 Customer, consisting of information pathways for Communicating Objectives, Performance Feedback, Recognition and Simulation, and Customer Feedback.

Quality organization A major element of the Quality System required to establish the basic system framework and comprised of functional responsibilities, macro definition of business processes, an operational network, and control of quality documentation.

Quality system The total business operation, consisting of the Circle-4 Customer, the Quality Organization, the Quality Information System and the Quality Delivery System. The vehicle which enables Circle-4 Quality and sustains Customer satisfaction.

Resource management The directed delivery system improvement activity of maximizing the production capacity of all available resources; time, labor, material, facilities, tools and machines.

Requirements The necessary conditions for reaching a defined goal.

Schedule, The The active interface between the Quality Information System and the Quality Delivery System, comprised of all the interrelated plans and schedules required to meet the business unit objectives.

Shareholder A Circle-4 Customer influence group comprised of the ownership of the business or business unit.

Supplier A Circle-4 Customer influence group comprised of all sources of supplies, raw materials and components required by the Quality Delivery System.

Supplier partnership A win/win relationship created between the purchasing and key Suppliers.

TQM Total Quality Management; the management philosophy which promotes total customer satisfaction through continuous improvement of products and processes, enabled by employee empowerment.

Win/win A relationship based on the mutual satisfaction of the involved parties.

Zero defects Consistently reproducing the product, through defined requirements, with 100% accuracy.

INDEX